Race Appeal

Charlton D. McIlwain
Stephen M. Caliendo

Race Appeal

*How Candidates Invoke Race
in U.S. Political Campaigns*

TEMPLE UNIVERSITY PRESS
Philadelphia

TEMPLE UNIVERSITY PRESS
Philadelphia, Pennsylvania 19122
www.temple.edu/tempress

Library of Congress Cataloging-in-Publication Data

McIlwain, Charlton D., 1971–
    Race appeal : how candidates invoke race in U.S. political campaigns /
Charlton D. McIlwain and Stephen M. Caliendo.
        p.   cm.
    Includes bibliographical references and index.
    ISBN 978-1-4399-0275-2 (cloth : alk. paper)
    ISBN 978-1-4399-0276-9 (pbk. : alk. paper)
    ISBN 978-1-4399-0277-6 (e-book)
    1. Political campaigns—United States.   2. Elections—United States.
3. United States—Politics and government—2001–2009.   4. United States—
Race relations—Political aspects.   I. Caliendo, Stephen M., 1971–   II. Title.

JK2281.M372 2011
324.708900973—dc22   2010028444

♾ The paper used in this publication meets the requirements of the American National
Standard for Information Sciences—Permanence of Paper for Printed Library Materials,
ANSI Z39.48-1992

Printed in the United States of America

2 4 6 8 9 7 5 3 1

For Amelia Caliendo
—Stephen M. Caliendo

For Marcus Adam McIlwain
—Charlton D. McIlwain

Contents

Acknowledgments

WE MET IN PRINCETON, New Jersey, in the summer of 2000 while teaching at Princeton University as part of the Junior State of America summer-school program. We had just begun our scholarly careers—Charlton was finishing his doctorate at the University of Oklahoma, and Stephen was heading into the final year of a three-year visiting assistant professorship at the University of Missouri, St. Louis. It was a transitional period for both of us, as Charlton was preparing to begin his appointment at New York University, and Stephen was getting used to being a father. Little did we know, however, that our professional lives would change dramatically as a result of that first meeting.

When we met again the next summer, we started to talk about how our disciplines—communication and political science—had been struggling to address the complex ways that language, images, and race interact in the public sphere. One evening, over a "beer summit" that, it appears, foreshadowed a much more famous and public one nearly a decade later, we decided to launch the Project on Race in Political Communication (then called the Project on Race in Political Advertising). This book is the product of the next eight years' worth of work, to which each of us equally contributed.

An endeavor of this magnitude rarely leads to a product that solely belongs to the folks whose names appear on the front of the book. We owe so many people a debt of gratitude for their support, encouragement, and helpful criticism. We have presented parts of this book at a dozen conferences, which means that scores of respondents, co-panelists, and audience members have offered their input, much of which has resulted in improvements to the manuscript. The anonymous reviewers of our proposal and of drafts were immensely helpful as we worked to refine our analysis, language, and organization. Our editor, Janet Francendese, and the rest of the staff at Temple University Press were supportive from the outset and have been patient and encouraging every step of the way. We owe a tremendous debt to our mentors—Rosalee Clawson, Mark Gibney, and Eric Kramer—who helped us develop as researchers, and to our peers, who have provided guidance and support for more than a decade. In particular, we thank Robin Means Coleman, Sharon Jarvis, Bob Jensen, Michele Ramsey, Denise Scannell, David Worth, and Kevan Yenerall, who invited us to their campuses to speak about various aspects of the Project on Race in the early years. Michele Claibourn, Courtney Cullison, Phillip Dalton, Lonnie Johnson, Aleisha Karjala, Weslynn Reed, Juliann Scholl, Craig Stapley, and Josh Stockley helped us recruit participants for pilot studies of some of the experiments. Rachel Cannon Humiston produced the ads we used as stimuli in Chapters 2 and 3; Jeremiah Wilson and Darrell Carter acted in the spots.

We thank Diana Mutz, Andrew Davis, Jeremy Freese, and Penny Visser, current and former principal investigators at Time-Sharing Experiments for the Social Sciences, which funded the experiments; their feedback and support—as well as that from their anonymous reviewers—greatly strengthened Chapters 2 and 3. Various funding sources at New York University, Avila University, and North Central College awarded grants that helped in a number of ways, as well.

We are indebted to Lewis Mazanti and the staff at the Julian P. Kanter Political Communication Archive at the University of Oklahoma; we spent many long hours in the viewing room coding spots, and Lewis was always helpful when we needed additional assistance. Tali Mendelberg provided excellent feedback and advice early in the process. A number of our colleagues—whether they knew it or not—provided formal and informal assistance, advice, feedback, and moral support that helped us in our thinking about and drafting of the manuscript. Many thanks go to Rodney Benson, Brett Gary, Radha Hegde, Ted Magder, Lisa Stuhlberg, Monique Turner, and Siva Vaidhyanathan.

We also need to take a little bit of space to thank, by name, the dozens of graduate and undergraduate research assistants from New York University; the University of Missouri, St. Louis; Avila University; and North Central College who have given tireless effort to different parts of this project over the past nine years (usually with no pay). Some of them have gone on to graduate school or successful careers, and others we have lost track of. We hope that we did not forget anyone: Gwen Bowman, Amanda Boyer, Jillian Maynard Caliendo, Lauren Condolucci, Liz Cotter, Michelle Eisenberg, John Fanning, Michelle Fernandez, Ann Fisher, Andrew Fu, Jacklyn Giron, Alyson Grant, Amy Griggs, Jennifer Gutierrez, Tiffany Hamilton, Chris Haroff, Jillian

Hentschel, Mark Jenkins, Terry Katz, Eric Koslowski, Nishi Kothari, Linda Lee, Jane Mabe, Simran Makur, Melisa Mason, Gwenn Florence Morreale, Michelle Novak, Jessica O'Brien, Mark Otto, Devang Panchal, Paula Pantogenis, Brandon Ramos, Benjamin Sacks, Kelley Spencer, Ariel Solaski, Jaclyn Sprawka, Jacqueline Stewart, Priscilla Dhas Vijilaselvi, Jillian Ann Walsh-Mattesino, and Julia Zangwill.

Finally, our families provide a continuous base of support for our professional and personal endeavors. Raechel, Marcus, Jillian, and Amelia—we love you all very much and appreciate all that you do for us. We are also grateful to our extended families—our parents, brothers, aunts, uncles, and cousins—all of whom have contributed meaningfully to our development as people and as scholars.

The Political Landscape of Race-Based Appeals

WILLIE HORTON'S racialized, criminalized, and vilified mug shot became the centerpiece of presidential hopeful George H. W. Bush's (and allied political interest groups') 1988 strategy to mar Michael Dukakis's image. First showcased in a set of now infamous political ads, Horton became the subject of headlines in national newspapers and led television newscasts across the country. Deploying the ads drew controversy and sparked debates pitting Blacks against Whites, Northerners against Southerners, and conservative ideologues against their liberal counterparts on issues of racial stereotyping, crime policy, and political campaign ethics. More than two decades later, Horton's image is an enduring icon; it represents persuasive political-campaign communication at its worst—insidious in its intents and contemptible in its targeting of White fear of Black aggression and savagery. The ad's potential was, perhaps, the greatest cause for alarm for those interested in fundamental fairness and racial equality.

This political powder keg spurred new scholarly interest in the intersections of race and political communication by researchers seeking to better understand racialized images and racially coded language and their influence on public opinion. Preceded by and predicated on a number of more limited studies in these areas, the political scientist Tali Mendelberg (2001) described the prevailing findings of the field at that time in her groundbreaking *The Race Card*, which advanced a theory of implicit communication that has driven much of the research in this area for close to a decade.

Mendelberg argued that the post-Reconstruction era in American politics and the post–Civil Rights age in which we now live are distinguished by a distinct cultural shift away from a norm of racial inequality to one in which egalitarian ideals are pervasive and, in principle, generally adhered to by the majority of the population (members of White society in particular). In the former era, explicit race-based appeals were tolerated and even expected by the primarily White electorate. In the present age, however, Mendelberg claims, such appeals violate an existing norm of racial equality and are tolerated only by the most overt bigots.[1] However, Mendelberg argues that political candidates in this post–Civil Rights period still have the possibility to gain (and interest in gaining) a competitive edge among White voters, whose latent racial prejudices, fears, and resentments may be activated to influence political decisions, whether it be their choice of candidates or their opinions on particular public policy issues.

This cultural shift, along with the politically advantageous possibilities of appealing to race, Mendelberg argued, produced a new, dominating mode for constructing and deploying race-based appeals—one marked by its subtlety and enhanced through its dissemination in visual imagery and racially coded language. Mendelberg's original empirical studies testing these claims led her to conclude that race-based appeals can and do have substantive effects on White voters in ways that disadvantage Black and minority policy interests. Further, she maintains that race-based persuasive appeals are most effective when they are constructed implicitly and when the underlying racial message remains hidden from public view.

In this book, we proceed from the premise that our current situation—twenty years after Willie Horton and approaching a decade since Mendelberg's book was published—demands a renewed look at the political landscape of race-based appeals in American electoral discourse. We argue that while Mendelberg (and many other scholars who have contributed to the varied literatures about race in political communication over the years) have succeeded in telling important aspects of the story about the nature and influence of race-based appeals, the story remains incomplete. This is largely the result of an evolving electorate and political culture that has promulgated new entanglements with race and politics that were nonexistent or not apparent even a decade ago.

However, our understanding of race-based appeals is also incomplete because research to date has primarily focused on a limited number of related, but narrow, issues regarding race and political communication. First, previous research has overwhelmingly dealt with what many see as the most morally, ethically, or ideologically objectionable form of race-based appeals: those that—like the Willie Horton ad—emanate from White candidates or political interests; appeal to negative racial stereotypes, fears, and resentments of African Americans; and target White voters as the principal subject for influence.

Second, the extant literature focuses on narrowly defined outcomes in that researchers primarily measure the effect of race-based appeals by focusing almost exclusively on their propensity to diminish public support for policy issues viewed as favorable to African Americans and other people of color. A third limitation is that research measuring the effects of race-based appeals has rarely juxtaposed candidates' race-based appeals with how the media frames election contests involving minority candidates, thereby shaping the influence that such race-based appeals might have. That is, the effects of race-based appeals have been considered in isolation rather than within a broader context of factors that might mediate their influence.

The arguments and research we present in this book rest on a set of overarching political realities that move beyond some of the limitations detailed above. First, White candidates do not hold a monopoly on race-based appeals, even as they continue to rely strategically on or benefit from them. Candidates of color increasingly appeal to race to serve their own strategic interests in gaining electoral support, though such appeals are constructed differently and used toward different strategic ends. Second, the success or failure of such appeals is integrally related not only to White voters' prejudicial and stereotypical attitudes about people of color, but also to Black and minority voters' attitudes about Whites, about their own perceptions of racial group identification, the degree to which they generally espouse identity politics as a preferred political strategy, and their perception of candidates' positions with respect to their own racial belief systems and ideology. Third, the news media are influential arbiters of race-based appeals, especially in campaigns involving minority candidates, where they become a powerful mediator between candidates and the voting public either by unwittingly supporting the racial message agenda of candidates or by confronting or refusing to communicate a racial frame of reference for a given contest.

Thus, while we, too, rely on certain premises and methods of previous research to address these matters, and although we would not be so arrogant as to claim to tell the "whole" story about the nature and influence of race-based appeals, we set out to add significantly to that story, using previous research as a basis for and means to explore the depths of racialized communication and the role it plays in contemporary American electoral politics. We do so by pursuing three primary objectives. First, we seek to understand how both White and Black candidates use language and visual imagery to construct race-based persuasive appeals. Second, we aim to shed light on the way that race-based appeals from White and Black candidates affect both White and Black voters. Finally, we explore more completely the way that news media cover campaigns involving candidates of color, including the array of both negative and positive consequences such coverage may have on the voting public and election hopes of minority candidates.

THE RACIAL TERRAIN OF CONTEMPORARY ELECTORAL POLITICS

Race, racism, and race-based political appeals are alive and well in America; they play a central role in the political discourses of candidates, affect how race is covered in national and local media of all kinds, shape public opinion and the voting decisions of Americans, and influence how we think and talk about race and race relations. One must only look as far back as the historic 2008 presidential and 2006 congressional elections for evidence. Throughout his historic election, President Barack Obama appealed to Americans across the racial divide. In a few short months his candidacy stirred debate about White Americans' willingness to vote for a Black president, stimulated questions about African Americans' readiness to close ranks and grant him unquestioned support, raised criticism about his leadership and experience, and invited a number of racial attacks from public figures across the ideological spectrum.[2]

During the 2006 elections we watched unfettered images of brown-skinned, Mexican "illegal aliens," undocumented workers, drug traffickers, and welfare recipients in countless television ads—images central to the political advertising and rhetorical appeals of candidates across the country hoping to capitalize on anti-immigrant, anti-Latino, anti-Mexican sentiment to gain political support for their candidacies. Black Republican organizations (such as America's PAC) also threw a barrage of racial messages targeting African Americans across the country with race-based appeals demonizing the Democratic Party as the party of enslavement and championing the Republican Party as the "party of Lincoln."[3]

Incidentally, during the same year, the Republican Party castigated Harold Ford Jr., a Black candidate for the U.S. Senate, for being a slick playboy who promiscuously cavorted with White women.[4] Pundits, politicians, and the press talked about why the Senate candidates Michael Steele, a Democrat from Maryland, and Lynn Swann, a Republican from Pennsylvania, as well as the gubernatorial candidate Ken Blackwell of Ohio, were not "Black enough" to win over Black voters.[5] This particular debate echoed the voices of the congressional foes Earl Hilliard and Artur Davis in Alabama, the mayoral contenders Cory Booker and Sharpe James in New Jersey, and the congressional opponents Denise Majette and Cynthia McKinney in Georgia—all during the 2002 election cycle. In each of those contests, the candidate's discourse addressed the influence of White (and "Jewish") money as the topic of Black authenticity persistently framed their campaigns.[6] Massachusetts elected its first African American governor in 2006, while Henry Bonilla and Ciro Rodriguez fought for the prize of being seen as the most authentic Latino candidate among voters in a majority-Latino congressional district in southern

Texas. In addition, the African American newcomer Keith Ellison became the first Muslim elected to Congress, overcoming obstacles set by those spewing anti-Black and anti-Muslim sentiments.

In the midst of all of this, the 2006 election cycle was fraught with debate surrounding what types of candidates can and should represent minority constituents. During the months leading up to the primary election in the Eleventh Congressional District in New York City (Brooklyn), prominent civil-rights activists—from Jesse Jackson to Al Sharpton—made vociferous objections to David Yassky's candidacy. Yassky, a White city councilman who moved into the district to challenge the crowded field of Black candidates, ultimately lost the seat held by retiring Congressman Major Owens and previously held by Shirley Chisholm. It was the first congressional district designed to fulfill the mandates of civil-rights legislation that ensured equal representation of Black citizens by Black elected representatives.[7]

Today, we find ourselves at an opportune moment in American history. The scholarly community, the media, and, increasingly, citizens at large are more keenly aware of, interested in, and concerned about the nature and effects of racialized communication in electoral politics and racial discourse in the broader sphere of American culture. As shown by the anecdotal references above, the racial terrain of American politics is quite different today and promises to become progressively more complex. Racial diversity proliferates in the electoral field among candidates and voters. African American candidates increasingly run in competitive contests against other African Americans, and more Black candidates are running for seats in the U.S. Senate (not just the House) and for governorships. More often than in earlier decades, they are running competitively in majority-White and non-majority-Black congressional districts (or states). They run more frequently under the banner of the Republican Party than they used to, and they increasingly pursue policy agendas that move beyond Civil Rights–era elected officials' traditional racial group interest politics.[8]

Latino Americans' increased role in American politics is also more solidified than it was a short time ago. In just a decade, Latino elected officials have gone from being virtually nonexistent in the U.S. Senate to having three prominent Latino senators, one of whom—Republican Senator Mel Martinez of Florida—served for a time as general chairman of the Republican National Committee before deciding not to seek re-election. In 1996, there were only seventeen Latino members of the U.S. House of Representatives. No Latinos occupied the governor's mansion in any state. Six Latinos were elected to statewide office, and state legislatures across the U.S. contained only 156 Latino elected officials. Yet in all elected offices, the number of Latino officials has now grown from 3,743 in 1996 to 5,041 in 2005—a 75 percent increase in less than a decade.[9]

This ever expanding diversity of candidates has, and is likely to continue to be, motivated to use—in old and more nuanced ways—various forms of race-based appeals in contemporary political life. Both Black and Latino voters have slowly but steadily withdrawn identification with the Democratic Party and express a greater range of public policy issues they say most concern them—issues that have no explicitly racial component. These and many other realities constitute our contemporary situation regarding race and electoral politics. Yet to date, the extant research in communication and political science generally, and in more specialized fields such as political communication, political psychology, and public opinion, has not fully addressed the complexities of our present circumstances regarding race-based appeals among the American electorate.

RACIAL DISCOURSE AND POLITICAL CAMPAIGNS: NEW QUESTIONS, NEW EVIDENCE

The first four chapters make up the first of this book's two sections. The chapters in Part I present new empirical evidence pertaining to some old, but mostly new, questions we explore about the scope and influence of race-based appeals. What constitutes a race-based appeal, and how are race-based appeals produced? Why do political candidates of all racial backgrounds rely on them? What potential influence might they have on Black and White voters alike? And how does the news media mitigate the influence such appeals might have on minority candidates' electoral success? These are the primary questions we ask in the first four chapters, and we offer empirical evidence that addresses each of them in significant ways. These questions are not completely new; they are questions inspired but largely unaddressed by a relatively limited array of scholarship in political psychology, political behavior, journalism, and media studies. These diverse areas represented in the scholarship share some basic theoretical approaches to the subject of racial discourse in electoral politics. This primarily includes theories about media effects (implicit communication, cognitive priming, framing and public opinion); theories about racial group psychology and behavior (theories of Black identity, Black ideological development, and symbolic and other variable forms of "new" racism); and theories related to visuality and visual culture, as well as rhetorical theory.

In Chapter 1, we explore how stereotypes about people of color find their way into White candidates' political ads and how this feature of White candidates' appeals influences how candidates of color construct and deploy race-based appeals. To do this, we analyze evidence from our content analysis study of some 800 advertising spots used in campaign contests (for federal office) that featured at least one minority candidate. Ultimately, we demonstrate how political ads get imbued with racist potential, how candidates of color respond accordingly, and how we can sidestep the issue of an individual candidate's intent to focus more effectively on how race-based appeals influence the electoral campaign landscape.

In Chapters 2 and 3, we move away from looking at the racialized content of political ads exclusively and turn our eyes to the range of potential effects such race-based appeals have on potential voters. Given some of the limitations identified above, we have two overarching goals: to demonstrate how both White and Black participants respond to certain race-based appeals, and to determine how race-based appeals affect minority candidates' electoral success. That is, our commitment to the normative ideal of equal representation drives our primary interest in how race-based appeals influence participants' assessment of and propensity to vote for (or not vote for) Black candidates.

In Chapter 4, the final chapter in Part I, we investigate how print journalists cover election contests involving candidates of color. Here, we are primarily interested in whether, to what degree, and how the news media racially frame candidates of color and the potential effect such framing might have on minority candidates' electoral success or failure. Here we present the results of a content analysis of some 2,500 news stories—print coverage of election contests between 1992 and 2006 that featured at least one racial minority.

The evidence and conclusions we present in the four chapters of Part I target three relatively distinct areas. We look at the characteristics of political ads, test the effects of such ads in experiments where participants view only political ads, and consider the racial elements replete within news stories of minority candidates. But this, of course, is not how political communication and voter behavior operate in the "real world." In the remaining three chapters, which make up Part II, we seek to add to our understanding of how racial discourse may work in political campaigns by looking at the empirical questions and evidence from Part I in broader contexts, through three different case studies. In Chapter 5, we use a different lens to demonstrate how race-based appeals get constructed. Here we look at issue-based campaign ads focused on the subject of immigration. In Chapter 6, we detail the racial dynamics (among candidates, the media, and the voting public) of three very different campaigns: an Alabama primary election between Earl Hilliard and Artur Davis for the U.S. House in 2002; the U.S. Senate contest between Mel Martinez and Betty Castor in Florida in 2004, and the U.S. Senate race between Harold Ford and Bob Corker in Tennessee in 2006. Finally, in Chapter 7, we revisit the racial circumstances of the 2008 Democratic Party presidential primary and general elections that produced Barack Obama's historic presidential victory. This chapter serves as an illustrative summary of the conclusions and arguments we make throughout the book.

How do candidates manipulate the visual, verbal, and acoustical content of political advertising messages to construct various forms of race-based appeals consistent with their underlying strategic goals? What are the varied effects that such appeals have on a variety of voters, their perceptions of minority candidates, and their likelihood to vote for candidates of color? How do the media set a racial agenda in contests featuring minority candidates, and what linguistic and other content attributes are present in media coverage that might prime negative or positive racial sentiment among voters? These are the central questions we seek to answer in the following pages. It represents our attempt to add depth and breadth to the ways we conceptualize, theorize, and understand the relationship between racial discourse and the public sphere of U.S. political campaigns.

Part I

The Empirical Evidence on Race Appeals

1

Producing Race Appeal

The Political Ads of White and Minority Candidates

ILLIE HORTON'S IMAGE achieved iconic status during the 1988 presidential campaign. His darkened, menacing Black visage came to represent an amalgam of visceral associations: Black brutality and unbridled sexual appetite; White innocence and vulnerability; and "liberal" crime policy run amok. The Democratic presidential candidate, Michael Dukakis, became entangled in the conglomeration of associated fears produced by the political ads, by news media ad watches, and by social commentary and political speeches that invoked Horton's name or likeness.

The fierce debate that followed over the nature of the race appeal involving Horton was largely motivated by widespread public recognition that something was questionable—if not wrong—with this form of political rhetoric. It made some political stomachs churn because, though the racial component appeared to many to be subtly deployed, this race appeal summoned the basest form of White voters' racial prejudices, stereotypes, and fears about African Americans (particularly Black men). Initial scholarly attempts to understand race-based appeals were motivated by this uneasiness, not only with negative advertising trends in general (Copeland and Johnson-Cartee 1991; Garramone, Atkin, Pinkleton, and Cole 1990; Jamieson 1992; Kaid and Johnston 1991; Merritt 1984), but with racialized political communication more specifically. It represented an attempt by researchers to understand the negative ramifications such appeals might have on the American democratic system, not to mention what it might reveal about the state of American race relations and social life more generally.

This concern notwithstanding, we argue that Willie Horton's race appeal—in both campaign politics and political scholarship—is but one of many forms of race-based persuasive messages political candidates have employed and continue to employ. This is to say that the Horton appeal represents but one of many particular types of race-based appeals that are tailored to a specific set of electoral circumstances, motivations of candidates, political strategies, and both anticipated and unforeseen consequences. The potential offensiveness of such appeals—firmly rooted in America's embarrassing, brutal, and oppressive racist history—led scholars to focus on this single form of racialized communication. This myopic focus, however, blinded us to the myriad other forms of race-based appeals that played out in American political campaigns, before and after we were introduced to Willie Horton. If we are to fully understand how race has served, and continues to serve, as a persuasive platform on which to mount strategic communication campaigns, we must look more broadly at this wider variety of race-based appeals.

Yet when we start down the path to investigate the broad landscape of racialized communication by political candidates, we immediately hit a roadblock. That is, we are forced to ask: What is a race-based appeal? Despite more than twenty years of scholarship about the racial discourse candidates employ in U.S. political campaigns, scholars and lay people alike approach discussions about race-based appeals using the same I-know-it-when-I-see-it logic that Supreme Court Justice Potter Stewart used in a 1964 case involving pornography. As with obscenity, however, the problem is that we all "see" different things in political advertisements, because we bring multiple cultural perspectives to our interpretations.

Despite the scholarly rush and empirical attempts to determine what effect race-based appeals might have on the electorate, scholars never have seemed to be very concerned with answering the most fundamental question: What exactly is a race-based appeal? That is, there is little empirical evidence enabling a viewer to make specific, reasonable determinations about whether a given message constitutes some form of a race-based appeal. Tali Mendelberg (2001) offers the broad distinction that implicit race-based appeals—those with which scholars generally concern themselves—are constructed through oblique, racially coded language, images, or (more effectively) some combination of the two. But deciphering code is tricky—racial codes, in particular. We have few guideposts for interpreting certain messages other than our own personal and private points of view.

We might consider some recent examples. In television ads and Internet messages used during the 2006 U.S. Senate campaign in Tennessee, the Republican National Committee (RNC) persisted in attaching the label "slick" to the African American Democratic Party candidate Harold Ford Jr. The RNC used the term to refer to everything from Ford's speech to his choice of clothing, his choice in women (usually White), and his explanations of policy positions. They added to this a televised ad featuring a White woman sensually whispering, "Harold, call me," as she simultaneously held her hand to her ear in a phone gesture, ostensibly suggesting a clandestine sexual liaison.

When the Black upstart Cory Booker challenged Sharpe James, the Black incumbent mayor of Newark, New Jersey, in 2002, James castigated Booker for being a "carpetbagger," saying he was "not one of us." He charged that most of Booker's financial support was coming from the White community, particularly from Jews. At one point, James was overheard calling Booker a "faggot White Boy," and he claimed that Booker had received campaign contributions from the Ku Klux Klan.

During the 2008 presidential race, Barack Obama incited controversy when he attempted to predict his Republican opponent's tactics, telling audiences, "They're going to try to scare you." Later in the same speech he added a separate and, for some, equally controversial statement: "Nobody thinks that [George] Bush and [John] McCain have a real answer to the challenges we face. So what they're going to try to do is make you scared of me. You know, he's not patriotic enough, he's got a funny name, you know, he doesn't look like all those other presidents on the dollar bills."[1]

Is each of these recent campaign communications an example of a race based appeal? Are any of them? Is one of them more racialized than another? How do we know either way? The fact that reasonable people—scholars included answer these questions differently speaks to the reality that we have no common understanding of race-based appeals' appearance and distinctive markers. That difference also attests to the lack of evidence-based markers for what constitutes a race-based appeal. The extant literature shows us how race-based appeals are operationalized when scholars test their effects on potential voters in laboratory experiments.

Nicholas Valentino, Vincent Hutchings, and Ismail White (2002) make the important point, for instance, that the mere presence of images of Blacks in ads is not sufficient to launch effective racial cues. They argue that the pairing of racial images with particular racial narratives is what makes cues powerful enough to prime negative racial predispositions, prejudices, and fears. Drawing on the longstanding connection between the "undeserving poor" and African Americans documented in the work of Martin Gilens (1996, 1998, 1999, 2000) and others, Valentino and his colleagues constructed a set of appeals by pairing various images of Blacks with distinct narratives about the undeserving poor.

They are not alone in conceiving race-based appeals in this way. Mendelberg (2001), Gregory Huber and John Lapinski (2006), and Ismail White (2007) also used the race and welfare connection as the basis of the race-based cues they tested.[2] Mark Peffley and Jon Hurwitz (2002) and Peffley, Hurwitz, and Paul Sniderman (1997) operationalize their racialized content in cues related to crime policy. Each of these studies uniquely suggests that, because of the strong relationship between welfare policy and crime, certain welfare- and crime-related language and images may stand in or become code for race. But is there more? Do political candidates mobilize race alongside these two issues alone, or are there other such connections? Do candidates and advertising producers construct race-based appeals beyond the realm of public policy rhetoric? Can we identify content within candidates' messages as being race-based, irrespective of whether the specific message has been or can be shown to prime or otherwise affect certain racial attitudes? The answer, quite simply, is "yes."

POLITICAL ADS:
PACKAGING CANDIDATES' RACE APPEAL

In many of the studies cited above, scholars use the term racial "cue" to identify the kind of racialized communication with which they are principally concerned. A cue provides a form of cognitive direction—a mental roadmap in the sense that they provide an idea about what we should think about when exposed to a certain form of communication, as well as how we should interpret it. Saying that "welfare" is a racial cue, for instance, means that hearing or seeing the term may cause us to think "African American, lazy, etc." as a result of longstanding and deeply held, usually latent, subconscious stereotypes that are reflected in multiple media forms, such as newsmagazines and textbooks (Clawson 2002; Clawson and Trice 2000). In some cases, it also means that when we hear or see the term, we should assume that the author of the communication is not just saying something about welfare or welfare policy, but that he or she is also making a statement about Black people more generally. This assumes that racial cues have the potential to communicate more to a viewer than the overt language in an advertising narrative. We incorporate these ideas about racial cues into our conception and treatment of the kinds of race-based political appeals we identify in the remaining pages of this chapter and book.

However, we consciously titled this book—and this chapter in particular—*Race Appeal* to signify additional characteristics that frame the way in which we both conceptualize (in this chapter) and operationalize (in the next two chapters) racialized political campaign communication. Scholarly work that tests the influence of racial cues focuses on the way that communication about public policy urges individuals to interpret ostensibly nonracial issues within a racial framework. That is, the term "racial cue" is aptly used when referring to a policy-oriented view about racialized communications, where the cue signals how to evaluate the policy (something we consider in Chapter 5).

We use the term "race appeal," however, to signal what we view as a candidate-centered orientation toward conceptualizing and analyzing racialized communication. What we mean by the terminology is certainly not wholly distinct from the existing construct, particularly as it relates to the cognitive processes that characterize the resultant attitudes and behaviors. However, the candidate-centered orientation embedded in our concept of race appeal more accurately reflects our primary interest in how candidates deploy race-based appeals and the fact that these appeals—like candidates' other messages—are presumably designed for the principal purpose of framing the sponsoring candidate as positively as possible (irrespective of any policy issues that might be mentioned) or one's opponent as negatively as possible. Our concept is also consistent with the medium in which we find the most sophisticated and, perhaps, most effective race-based appeals: televised political advertising.

Political communication scholars generally agree that candidates' images dominate political rhetoric in contemporary campaigns, where the thirty-second political advertising spot is now the normative means of communication (Kern 1989). Thus, when we speak of "race appeal," we speak to the sense that the primary import of racialized campaign messages is that that they build up or diminish a candidate's most significant electoral commodity: the image he or she portrays to voters. Given the political volatility of deploying race-based appeals, we recognize, as have other scholars, that the visual characteristic that dominates television advertising is best suited for packaging such appeals in ways that maximize their benefit and minimize the possible risk to the candidate on whose behalf the appeal is made (see Brians and Wattenberg 1996; Gordon and Miller 2005). Thus, we seek to discern how candidates construct and deploy race-based appeals by looking at the content of political advertising spots.

SPOTTING RACE

The Julian P. Kanter Political Commercial Archives, housed at the University of Oklahoma, contain the most comprehensive collection of political advertising spots in the country. This is where our search for race-based appeals in televised political advertising began. Three criteria determined the ads we analyzed: The ad's sponsor either had to have been a member of a racial minority group or had to have run in a general election contest against a racial minority; the contest had to have been for either the U.S. House of Representatives or the U.S. Senate; and the ad must have existed in the archive.[3] Ultimately, we coded a total of 765 distinct advertising spots.

In these spots produced for U.S. Senate and House contests between 1970 and 2006, Democratic and Republican party candidates are equally represented. Spots from contests that took place in the U.S. South made up almost half of those we analyzed, while 23 percent of the spots were from contests on the West Coast; 16 percent were from the Midwest; and 12 percent were from the Northeast. The majority of ads were from contests pitting Black candidates against White candidates (61%), followed by Latino versus White candidates (21%). Biracial contests including Asian American candidates versus a White candidate account for only 5 percent of the spots, while same-race contests that included Black candidates made up 3 percent, and same-race contests that included Latino candidates made up 2 percent. The overwhelming majority of the contests included male candidates (85%), and the vast majority of spots (94%) ran for thirty seconds.

Each spot was coded along fifty-six separate variables. They included demographic characteristics of the spot and contest for which it was produced, such as sponsor/opponent, year, party, racial makeup of the district/ state; variables that identified potential race-related content, such as the racial composition of people in the ad, whether explicit racial identifiers were used, and whether any of a number of character traits were mentioned; and variables related to general political characteristics of the spots (such as whether they were attack, contrast, or advocacy ads; whether issue content was included; whether fear appeals were used).[4] Before proceeding, we want to be more specific about the objectives of our analysis and articulate some important assumptions we rely on both here and in the chapters that follow.

Racist versus Racial Appeals

First, consistent with our conception of race appeal, we recognize that candidates of all racial backgrounds have strategic interests in deploying race-based appeals, despite the fact that racialized messages from White candidates dominate the literature on race-based appeals. The racial inclusiveness of candidates who rely on race-based appeals notwithstanding, our data reveal quite clearly that candidates' interest in deploying race-based appeals are categorically diverse. To deal with one stark difference between them, from this point on we distinguish between what we call "racist" and "racial" appeals.

The extant literature uses the term "racial appeal" or "racial cue" to refer to appeals by Whites that draw on anti-Black sentiment and are primarily targeted to White voters. We use the term "racist" to refer to this the type of appeal, one that advantages Whites as a result of systemic racist predispositions about people of color. We use the term "racial" to denote appeals by candidates that are racial in nature but do not target anti-minority sentiment for their efficacy. All racist appeals are racial, but not all racial appeals are racist (McIlwain and Caliendo 2009). Accordingly, we use the term "race-based" appeal, simply "appeal," or "racialized communication/message" to refer to any racial appeal, irrespective of the likely target or potential effect.

Given this distinction, we have two primary objectives in the remainder of this chapter. First, we aim to rescue determinations about what constitutes a racist appeal from the "he said, she said" kind of subjective arbitrariness that dominates both lay and scholarly debates about race-based appeals (colloquially referred to as "playing the race card").[5] We accomplish this not by providing a definitive distinction between racist and non-racist appeals (i.e., we do not propose that we should be the final arbiters). Rather, we develop an interpretive range by which scholars and others might convincingly argue that a particular advertising message does or does not, more or less, express a racist appeal. To escape the propensity to make categorical, binary distinctions between racist and non-racist appeals, we rely on the term "racist potential" to indicate the various gradations of possibly racial content found in political ads.

Our second primary objective is to examine and determine the strategic interests candidates have for deploying *racial* appeals in particular. That is, we presume that the vast majority of racist appeals originate from White candidates, while racial appeals are the form of racialized communication we most often see from candidates of color. Put simply, we see very little evidence to suggest that minority candidates have any interest in appealing to negative stereotypes, resentments, and prejudices associated with the racial group to which they belong. This does not mean, however, that they have no interest in appealing to race at all. So in addition to determining what constitutes the range for defining racist appeals, we also want to identify the various forms of racial appeals that racial minority candidates primarily use and the strategic interests they have for doing so.

Beyond defining the range of racist appeals, describing the strategic interests of minority candidates' uses of racial appeals, and demonstrating how each of these forms of race-based appeals are variably constructed, we have a fourth primary objective. Building on our conceptualizations of racist and racial appeals, we want to determine some of the broader contexts in which these appeals have been, and continue to be, deployed in campaigns over the past four decades (at least). We examine the prevalence of race-based appeals in the United States and some of the trends associated with their use to understand more fully what racialized political campaign communication might tell us about the broader circumstances of racial discourse in American political life.

Race-Based Appeals and Candidates' Intent

When it comes to political ads sponsored by candidates, we take the view that intention is not a necessary condition for producing a race-based appeal. This is to say, unconscious biases may very well influence the production of language and images that may be interpreted as a race-based appeal, despite a producer's intentions. Thus, when we later provide a rubric for what constitutes racist appeals in particular, we provide a range of evidence for what American voters might interpret to be a race-based appeal; we do not necessarily view a message as an intentionally communicated racist appeal. In other words, what matters is the potential effect, not intent.[6] That said, we generally take the position that the strategic nature of advertising—political advertising in particular—makes it difficult for us to categorically accept that race-based appeals are largely accidental. That is, we tend to view such appeals as a strategic component of a candidate's overall communication and message strategy.

THE ANATOMY OF RACIST APPEALS

Before we offer our determination of what constitutes a racist appeal, we will describe the elements that we hypothesize contribute to that decision. There is no litmus test that determines the presence of a racist appeal in a particular political ad. In the clearest examples, a combination of elements work together to lead one to interpret a message as having some form of racist appeal. So what categories of ad content might we look for to ultimately make our determination? What components of political ads might lead us to determine that an ad appeals to race in a way that draws on the kinds of racial prejudices, stereotypes, and sentiments that underlie racist appeals? There are five primary categories of race-related content, various combinations of which, we argue later, produce differing degrees of racist appeals: racial stereotypes, racial imagery, racially coded language, race-based public policies, and audience demographics.

Racial Stereotypes

Communicating some form of negative racial stereotype about the racial group of one's opponent is a critical component underlying racist appeals. The scholarly literature in social psychology, media studies, linguistics, history, and political science are replete with stereotypes historically associated with members of one or more non-White racial groups—African Americans and Latinos in particular.[7] Generally, most stereotypes associated with Blacks and Latinos throughout American history (Latinos more recently than Blacks) point to what most people regard as negative character traits prevalent among the group and that therefore are assumed to be reflected in any single member of the group.

In the ads we analyzed, we looked to determine whether common racial stereotypes were communicated in some form—that is, whether ads stated or implied that the opposing minority candidate was lazy, uncaring, irresponsible, untrustworthy, or criminal; took advantage (as we explain further later), or was unqualified. These stereotypes might be affirmatively expressed in directly stereotypical form (in a statement about a Black opponent such as "Internal Revenue Service *criminal* investigation") or conjured by appealing to the counter-stereotypical forms—that is, associating oneself with the opposing (positive) characteristic of the negative stereotype (such as when a candidate describes himself or herself as "hardworking," the flip side of the "lazy" stereotype). The presumption is that candidates are sometimes forthright about their criticism of their opponents, while at other times they highlight their opponents' shortcomings by emphasizing their own character strengths. Read comparatively against one's opponent (which is what all political ads inherently encourage), this suggests that the positive affirmation of one's own character strengths reveals something lacking in the character of one's opponent. One can already see why the presence of a racist appeal cannot be determined by the presence of a single factor. A candidate who points out that he or she "works hard" might be suggesting that his or her opponent is lazy, but maybe not. Determining which is the case depends on whether certain other content affirms or denies such an interpretation.

The term "lazy" is rarely, if ever, used to convey the stereotype. More often than not, laziness is communicated through phrases such as "falling down on the job" or "didn't do the work." In one notable example in Oklahoma, a White candidate (David Perryman, a Democrat) said about his Black opponent (J. C. Watts, a Republican), "He's paid $52,000 a year and admits to working only twelve hours a week."

The stereotype about being "uncaring" has its roots in in-group and out-group conceptions and how candidates identify which kinds of people get included in each. When a candidate says his or her opponent "doesn't care about the problems we face," the subtext is that the person does not care because he or she is not "one of us," not part of the community, district, state, or other collective identified by the candidate (or inferred by the audience). A candidate who says that his or her opponent "doesn't care" is not claiming that the opponent does not care about the candidate; the candidate means that his or her opponent does not care about the people who live in the district or state, the people he or she will represent, if elected. In this way, "he doesn't care" is read as "he doesn't care about *us*," in such a way that makes defining "us" interpretively important.

Three of the stereotypes are closely related but merit their own distinction in our data: irresponsibility, untrustworthiness, and criminality. Candidates' statements about irresponsibility faintly suggest some kind of wrongdoing by their opponent. Claims about irresponsible behavior, which typically arise when talking about financial matters, come by way of suggesting that a candidate has mismanaged (typically taxpayer) funds but stop short of more directly claiming the opponent cannot be trusted or, worse, that he or she has engaged in outright criminal behavior. The stereotype of being "untrust-worthy" is generally communicated directly. "You just can't trust him to . . ." "She says one thing and does another . . ." "Can you really believe it when he says . . . ?" Each of these examples commonly expresses the stereotype about untrustworthiness. Following the same path, some candidates make the more damaging claim that their opponents are criminals—or, at least, that they have engaged in real or potential criminal acts (i.e., they have, allegedly or in fact, broken the law). Like the untrustworthiness stereotype, allegations of criminality tend to be forthright and direct, using terms such as "criminal" and "lawbreaking," statements about someone "taking money from X and putting it into his or her own pocket," or stating, "If we all have to abide by the law, she should, too."

Two of the final three stereotypes are also related (to each other, as well as to the stereotype about laziness). The stereotype about "taking advantage" is linked to issues about undeserving populations, welfare, and the like. It expresses the sentiment that whenever possible, members of certain minority groups are looking for a handout, looking to capitalize on something for which they did not work or take what rightfully belongs to another. This final point is related to the last stereotype for which we coded: being "unqualified." This term is related more to the issue of the labor force and, specifically, affir-mative action policy. Candidates who suggest that their opponents "made government work for them" or "used their position to hire members of their family" and the like are expressing the idea of taking advantage, while the use of the specific term "unqualified" in ads suggests that someone is not fit for the office sought (or held).

There are three things to keep in mind about the role stereotypes play in constructing potentially racist appeals. First, as mentioned, these stereotypes might be directly articulated in their negative form or alluded to by candi-dates using the counter-stereotype, associating themselves with the positive character trait related to the negative stereotype. Second, stereotypes are often deployed in an indirect, associative manner. That is, a candidate might not directly state that his or her opponent is a criminal, yet mere allusions to criminality can associate that stereotype with the opponent in some way. A candidate who speaks about crime and his opponent within the same thirty-second span of time (even if the candidate does not say the opponent is the actual criminal), for instance, can link the two together without having to directly charge that his or her opponent is a lawbreaker (see Gibbons 1993).

The third and most crucial thing to remember about stereotypes is their historical group association. Some are likely to say (and often do), "White candidates running against other White candidates often attack their oppo-nents for being untrustworthy (or any of these negative character traits)."

TABLE 1.1 Stereotypes deployed in political ads of White candidates

Stereotype	Frequency (%) of use of stereotype				
	All ads (N = 355)	White vs. Black	White vs. Latino	White vs. Asian	p-value
Trustworthy	11	11	9	17	.49
Untrustworthy	20	25	14	9	.02*
Lazy	4	6	0	4	.04*
Hardworking	13	12	15	17	.60
Plays by rules	0	0	0	0	—
Criminal	13	14	11	4	.36
Liberal	12	20	2	0	.00**
Taking advantage	7	11	3	4	.04*
Self-reliant	1	1	0	9	.00**
Inexperienced	4	4	5	0	.47
Uncaring	3	4	1	0	.21
Responsible	0	0	1	0	.35
Irresponsible	1	1	2	0	.81
Qualified	1	1	2	0	.69
Unqualified	0	0	0	0	—

Note: Data are cross-tabulations comparing the percent occurrence each stereotype in White vs. Black contests, with the racial composition of the contest in each subsequent column. The first column includes the percent use of stereotype found in all ads by White sponsors, irrespective of the racial makeup of the contest.

** $p < .01$; * $p < .05$

This is, of course, quite correct. The question to ask, however, is whether there is a longstanding association between Whites as a racial *group* and the negative character trait invoked. For some, a negative character attack is just a singular negative character attack. For others, the same character attack is a stereotype—a trait historically and commonly imputed not just to a specific individual, but categorically to most members of one's racial group that, in turn, becomes ascribed to all members of that group.[8]

The data in Table 1.1 provide a glimpse at how frequently these stereotypes are found in the political ads we analyzed and against whom they were most often deployed. Considered in their stereotype–counter-stereotype pairings, when appropriate, the second column lists the frequency with which White candidates invoked these stereotypes. References to untrustworthiness, laziness, and criminality dominate the field of stereotypes used. The remaining columns in Table 1.1 express the racial group of the candidate against whom these stereotypes were most frequently deployed. It is interesting to note that White candidates expressed stereotypes about untrustworthiness and criminality at a similar rate against both Black and Latino opponents. However, laziness and taking advantage seemed to target almost exclusively Black candidates. This is an important observation, because it demonstrates the fact that all stereotypes are not categorically relevant for all people of color or for particular racial groups. Stereotypes about groups of people are historically formed. Thus, because different racial groups—Blacks and Latinos, for instance—have different histories with and within the United States, certain stereotypes have developed about one group that are not particularly applicable to the other (Henderson and Olasiji 1995; Larson 2005). Here, too, when we looked at the political ads, we found that certain stereotypes seemed to make sense when associated with candidates of particular racial groups, though clearly some were used across the board.

Racial Imagery

While the presence of one or more racial stereotypes is a critical marker of a racist appeal, it is not the only one, and the fact that it alone appears in a political ad does not constitute sufficient evidence to make an overwhelming case that the ad does communicate a racist appeal. A second category of content provides additional grounds for judging the potential for political ads to convey a racist appeal. If researchers agree on anything regarding racist appeals, it is that racial imagery is central to communicating racist appeals, particularly those that are implicit in nature. Many forms of racial images can be found in political ads. We looked for two in particular. The first was whether a still or moving image of the White candidate, the candidate of color, or both candidates appeared in the ad. Images of candidates are one way that race is made apparent to viewers. Given the cultural ubiquity of Whiteness in the United States (Bonilla-Silva 2006), we suggest that images of minority candidates—darker-skinned ones even more so (see Caruso, Mead, and Balcetis 2009; Terkildsen 1993)—are more likely to call attention to race (though a White candidate's image certainly invites a modicum of racial identification from White voters). The propensity to highlight race in the eyes of the viewer is also likely when both candidates appear in the ad, providing the contrast between the light and dark skin color.

Minority candidates appear in one-third of their White opponents' ads; the majority of the time, they are depicted in still, rather than moving, images (25% and 6%, respectively). White candidates, however, most often appear in moving images in their own ads. White sponsors and minority opponents appear together in only about 10 percent of White candidates' ads, either in moving images or in still images.

The racial makeup of people who are not candidates and who appear in political ads is a second visual medium used potentially to signal race. Racial images serve a representative function. People who are shown with or in place of the candidates in political ads represent "us," or those whom the candidate portends to represent. Thus, when a White candidate walks down the middle of Main Street, U.S.A., flanked by people who look like him or her, it represents—accurately or not—the composition and complexion of the district. In 65 percent of ads sponsored by white candidates, the majority of non-candidates who appear are other Whites; in one-third of them, Whites are the *only* people who appear. Again, such images do not definitively communicate some form of racial exclusion, but they certainly might. Whether they do or do not depends on the presence or absence of other content.

Racially Coded Language

After close consideration of a representative sample of ads, we determined that, although a variety of racially coded language exists in contemporary American life, little is likely to find its way into political ads, primarily because it is not particularly germane to the electoral arena. Thus, we looked for two forms of potential racially coded language—code words, if you will. In keeping with the idea of racial inclusion and exclusion as an underlying ground for racist appeals, we are interested in the degree to which candidates use first-person and third-person (plural) language in their ads. That is, to what degree do candidates refer to some general form of in-group or out-group collective? As it turns out, White candidates made in-group references frequently ("us," "we," "our") in more than one-third of ads they sponsored, while they almost never made specific out-group references, such as to "they" or "them." Again, it is important to remember that the presence of in-group and out-group language is only one piece of the puzzle in determining the degree to which an ad might express a racist appeal.

Second, we looked for White candidates' use of the ideological label "liberal." This term is a racial code word because, beyond deploying the label to castigate left-leaning Democrats generally, it especially has been applied to Blacks, in many ways as a proxy for "radical," "extremist," and the like. Frequently, in ads against Black opponents in particular (see Table 1.1), the "liberal" label was preceded by a negative adjective such as "*too* liberal," "*extremely* liberal," "*dangerously* liberal," or "*destructively* liberal" in ways that made the ideological marker a convenient vehicle for other, more typical Black stereotypes. In a political sphere in which both White and Black candidates get labeled "liberal" in a pejorative way (i.e., having little respect for the traditions and values that have characterized the American experience), the label carries with it an additive component of being racialized, extending further to the political left—more extreme, to the point of being potentially "dangerous," when applied to Black candidates in particular.

Race-Based Public Policy

We also surmised from the outset that references to certain public policy issues that have a clear racial dimension might be a vehicle for candidates to signal race in political ads. While we coded for a large number of policy issues, we looked at a handful in particular—crime, affirmative action, immigration, deadbeat dads, drugs, welfare, and capital punishment. These issues, because of their racialized background in public discourse, may have the ability to trigger racial thinking.

Audience Demographics

When studying candidate communications and racist appeals, audience matters. That is, knowing the racial makeup of the electorate is necessary, though like all others, it is not a definitive clue to whether one can make a strong case that a racist appeal has been made. Consider, for example, an ad that is sponsored by a White candidate in which he or she appears with several other people, all of whom are also White. The candidate uses the words "us" and "we." This ad's message would be interpreted quite differently if we knew that 90 percent of the candidate's district was White as opposed to 40 percent non-White. For each of the contests in our data, we have included the racial makeup of the district so we can accurately contextualize any and all appeals to race.

Given the many forms of content candidates have at their disposal to construct ads that may intentionally or unintentionally express racist appeals, what we want to find out is which of these forms of content typically gets used to do so. All may possibly communicate a racist message, but which is the most common?

MEASURING RACIST POTENTIAL

In 1981, Gerald Carlson, a White Republican from Michigan, ran for Congress. In one of his advertisements, he appeared standing in front of a camera in a sparsely furnished, lowly lit office, where he made the following pitch (maintaining an intensely heated tone and stern countenance throughout):

> Are you a member of the middle-class White majority? Are you now being discriminated against? Whatever happened to *our* civil rights? Chrysler went bankrupt because of drinking, drugs, gambling, and prostitution by Negroes on the job. And Benton Harbor is bankrupt because Negroes cannot run cities built by White people. Federally court-ordered cross-district bussing into Benton Harlem [*sic*] goes into effect this September. How much more of this are we going to take? My name is Carlson. Vote for me, and I'll speak for you.[9]

The racist nature of this ad is unquestionable. The racial language is explicit; the stereotypes replete throughout and the sentiment behind them is evident in the anger visible in Carlson's face as he delivers his political rant. So apparent is the ad's racist foundation that the television station on which it aired felt compelled to include a disclaimer at the end, stating that it did not necessarily share the candidate's views and pointing out the requirement that the station air any ad by a legally qualified candidate. Contemporary common sense tell us that few, if any, candidates today would be likely to put forth such an overtly bigoted message. Indeed, of the almost 800 ads we reviewed, only 4 percent included an explicitly race-based appeal (and many of those were from the same few candidates).

A Sharper Tool

Of course, the bulk of race-based appeals we consider are implicit in nature and, by definition, are inherently more nuanced than explicit ones. Accordingly, we should measure implicit messages with a sharper tool. Thus, we constructed an index that captures an ad's potential to communicate a racist appeal. The index is calculated for each ad in which there is some appeal to stereotypes about Blacks or Latinos or in which the majority of people in the ad (besides the candidates) are White when the district is less than 80 percent White. We allocate "points" for language that refers to an opponent of color in ways that are consistent with one of the negative stereotypes of Blacks and Latinos discussed earlier (in stereotypical or counter-stereotypical form).

The measure adds one point for each stereotype (ten points are possible) and one-half point for each counter-stereotype (seven points are possible).[10] Additional points are added if either the sponsor (.5) or the opponent (1) appears in the ad (signaling the race of either or both). To reflect the degree of racial diversity in a district or state, the higher the percentage of White voters, the more points are included in the scale for the ad (0–4). Of the total number of spots coded (765), 617 were indexed, with scores ranging from 1 to 9.5. The mean score was 4.4; the median was 4.5; and the standard deviation was 1.6.

The 8.5-point range between the lowest and highest points on the scale is the foundation for what we subsequently refer to as the Index of Racist Potential (IRP). We developed the IRP by dividing the range of aggregate scores into five distinct points. Each point represents subsequent standard deviations from the mean beyond the first possible point. The IRP provides an interpretive range, assessing the degree to which a particular ad may communicate a racist appeal. Points at the lowest end of the scale represent ads that have little potential for doing so, while points at the highest end of the scale represent ads that have the greatest potential to communicate a racist appeal. In other words, while there is some evidence to support viewing each of the ads scoring at least 1 on the scale as racist, the higher an ad's score, the more evidence there is suggesting that the underlying message draws on some form of anti-minority prejudice, stereotype, or negative racial sentiment for its persuasive efficacy.

Core Elements: Racial Mistrust

The previous section described each of the content areas that we theorize make up a racist appeal. That is, we advance the notion that racist appeals consist of at least one anti-minority stereotype and one or more forms of imagery, language, or policy issue that not only have some potential to cue race in general, but that are likely to make the underlying stereotype within the appeal more salient. Having factored each of these dimensions into the formula that produced the IRP, our first objective is to understand which of these elements in particular are most associated with various points on the index. This is to say that, while each of these components may construct a particular racist appeal, we aim to discover which types of content seem to be most essential to constituting a racist appeal. We do so by correlating each specific content component with the IRP and using the strength of this association to determine which specific content most acutely applies to racist appeals.

As previously mentioned, the presence of at least one racial stereotype—expressed in either positive or negative form—is a primary criterion for assessing racist appeals. But are there particular stereotypes among the fourteen that are strongly related to ads with the greatest potential to express racist appeals? The first section of Table 1.2 addresses this question. From the outset, we see that only two of the nine stereotypes significantly and positively associated with the IRP were expressed in the form of a counter-stereotype. This tells us that, more often than not, candidates invoking any form of racial stereotype tend to do so more or less directly. That is, even in their subtlety, candidates tend to refer to the negative aspect of a particular stereotype rather than associate themselves with the positive and implicitly implicate their opponents in a failure to meet a certain character standard.

More important, the four stereotypes most strongly associated with the IRP form an interesting constellation of negative sentiments that pervade racist appeals. Each of these distinct stereotypes speaks to an underlying theme of mistrust. One can never trust a lazy person; he or she will always be looking to take advantage of some person or situation that yields more than he or she deserves; and criminal conduct is the ultimate manifestation of this underlying desire to "get over" on others.

But this specific group of stereotypes is even more revealing. It perfectly reflects that fine line of racial culpability and intentionality inherent in racist appeals, the outcome of which is potential reward or electoral risk, depending

TABLE 1.2 Ad content associated with Index of Racist Potential (IRP)

Item	Correlation	Mean IRP	N
Stereotype			
Untrustworthy	.404**	5.6	142
Criminal	.335**	6.0	60
Takes advantage	.307**	6.4	33
Lazy	.220**	6.6	15
Responsible	.141**	5.7	18
Uncaring	.138**	5.2	47
Irresponsible	.119**	5.9	9
Inexperienced	.110**	5.2	27
Plays by rules	.099*	5.3	19
Self-reliant	.027	4.6	46
Unqualified	.011	4.7	3
Trustworthy	0	4.4	96
Qualified	−.009	4.3	19
Hardworking	−.057	4.3	177
Racial images			
Minority opponent appears	.447**	5.4	200
Only whites appear	.271**	5.1	156
White sponsor appears	−.149**	4.3	489
Mostly Whites appear	−.091**	4.2	156
Racial issues			
Welfare	.103*	7.3	2
Affirmative action	.076	6.5	2
Crime	.054	4.9	19
Immigration	.049	5.8	2
Division/polarization	−.166**	2.0	7
Drugs	−.016	4.2	6
Deadbeat dad	—	—	—
Capital punishment	—	—	—
Race-coded language			
They/them	.152**	6.6	7
Liberal	.117**	5.0	52
Us/we/our	.023	4.5	238
State/district demographics			
Percent White	.736**		

Note: Data are bivariate Pearson's correlation coefficients.

** $p < .01$; * $p < .05$

on whether viewers recognize a racial connection and whether they interpret their own recognition as extending to the sponsoring candidate's communicative intentions. Each of these four stereotypes has significant race appeal because, as political attacks go, they are quite ubiquitous. Americans in general do not trust politicians (Heatherington 2006). In any given campaign, the charge that one's opponent has breached the public trust in some way conveniently comes with the territory. Put simply, attacking someone's trustworthiness—by pointing out his or her perhaps less malicious opportunism, on one hand, or his or her outright criminal deeds, on the other— is relatively safe terrain, the kind of attractive attack that may provide cover for the candidate who intentionally hopes to cash in on the rewards that racist appeals may generate among those in the electorate whose negative racial predispositions are firmly intact. That is, they create an alibi of sorts. Those who are questioning a candidate's intention can point to some other (nonracist) motivation for the ad's content. Looking back at the example of Willie Horton, when the Bush team was questioned about the potential racist basis of the ad, they simply replied that the ad had everything to do with crime policy, not race.

However, the candidate deploying a message based on one of these four stereotypes engenders some risk and demonstrates why intention matters little when it comes to racist appeals. While these charges may be lodged at political opponents irrespective of race, the fact that each of them has a strong historical connection to Blacks and Latinos in particular opens the possibility that an ad making such charges against a racial minority will be viewed as racist. "But I didn't intend to attack my opponent's race," a sponsoring candidate of such an ad may claim. "You're telling me just because the guy is Black, if I point out that he's been using taxpayers' money for his own gain, all of sudden I'm being racist?"

In an episode of the 1970s sitcom *All in the Family,* Archie Bunker's son-in-law, Michael, is talking to a Black friend who, he discovers, is competing for the same prestigious teaching job. Michael admits that he has stiff competition. "I mean, you're qualified, and personable, and bright, and uh . . . ," Michael says. "And Black," his friend says, ending the sentence, "and you think that they may pick me over you because of my color?" Michael gives a brief explanation about affirmative action policy and university hiring. "So in this situation, your color isn't going to exactly hurt you," he says. "Ain't that a switch," the Black friend sarcastically exclaims.

The same could be said here. For most of America's history, Whites gained significant advantages over Blacks and other people of color by holding and calling attention to a range of negative stereotypes. Now, when Whites are in competition with candidates of color, they are alarmed that they find themselves potentially disadvantaged when they simply carry on electoral business as usual. But fortunately or unfortunately for political candidates, race matters.[11]

Attacking a Black or Latino candidate's trustworthiness; charging him or her with criminal conduct; chastising him or her for taking advantage of American citizens or of his or her own position or the U.S. government; and lambasting him or her for lying down on the job is dangerous stuff. In the world of racial stereotypes, advertising messages conveying these stereotypes especially have the potential to constitute and convey racist appeals, especially given the fact that ads that refer to these stereotypes in particular fall into the highest range of IRP scores. That is, when candidates refer to these stereotypes against opponents of color, the ads tend to present a wealth of supplementary content that adds to their racist potential. We should point out, however, that even though the remaining four stereotypes with positive IRP associations are comparatively weak, they also find themselves among other content that provide ads with some racist potential.

Critical Images, Critical Language, and Not-So-Critical Issues

As we continue down the list in Table 1.2, another critical constellation unfolds. As other researchers have shown and we theorize here, political advertising images are a critical component of potential racist appeals. Ads featuring one's minority opponent are strongly associated with ads' racist potential, as are those ads where all non-candidates who appear are White. We originally surmised that images of both candidate and sponsor might more powerfully trigger racial thinking by providing a stark racial contrast in an ad. As it turns out, it is when a minority candidate's image alone appears alongside one or more all-White, non-candidate images that provides this critical contrast.

"Liberal" functions as both a code word and a stereotype. As mentioned earlier, it is generally used to label Black candidates, branding them not only as Democrats but also as morally permissive, out of touch with the mainstream, politically extreme and dangerous. It, too, has fairly strong associations with midpoints on the IRP, as does its linguistic counterpart, the third-person plural "they" and "them." While third-person references are strongly and positively associated with the IRP, the actual references appear infrequently. As we will see later, however, an implied us–them, in-group–out-group dynamic seems to permeate many ads with moderate to strong racist potential, the implication often made through the arrangement of images and language on the screen.

It appears that talk of using racialized issues as a vehicle for conveying racist appeals has no real import. Welfare is the only race-related issue that has any association with the IRP, and it is quite weak. Not even in the broader list of policy issues present in these political ads (29 in total) is there any one issue positively associated with the IRP. Much of the explanation for this can be found in the fact that the presence or absence of substantive policy issues in political ads in general seem to have no bearing at all on ads' racist potential. That is, ads that do convey potential racist appeals do so irrespective of whether they do or do not refer to issues (as opposed to candidates' personal character). This conclusion is borne out in the additional finding that there is no substantive difference between "issue" and "image" ads when it comes to the potential for communicating potentially racist appeals.

Audience Matters

By far, the strongest factor associated with ads' racist potential is the percentage of Whites in the electorate. This may not be surprising, but it is instructive in that it provides us with a critical clue about where and when potentially racist appeals are deployed by candidates. Within the results we have presented thus far, a clear picture begins to emerge, a critical constellation of racial content with specific racist potential: (1) The ad refers to the untrustworthy, criminal, lazy, or takes advantage stereotype or uses the "liberal" label; (2) the ad features a minority opponent's image; (3) the ad uses non-candidate images that are all White; and (4) the ad appears in election contests where the proportion of Whites in the district (or state) is greater than 60 percent. One hundred seventy-three ads fit these criteria—nearly one-third of all of the ads that had some racist potential and one-quarter of the total ads.

VIEWING ADS WITH RACIST POTENTIAL

Thus far, we have talked about the core components of political ads that contribute to their racist potential. A few examples of actual political ads will help us to think about each of these components in a more holistic way and to further explore how we conceptualize the various dimensions of racist appeals. We begin by looking at an ad that represents the core constellation of racial content mentioned above. The ad depicted in Figure 1.1 was sponsored by Peter Fitzgerald, a White candidate for the U.S. Senate in Illinois, opposing the incumbent Black Senator Carol Moseley Braun in 1998.[12] The ad features each of the primary components of what we refer to as an ad with typical racist potential.

The untrustworthiness stereotype is insinuated from the beginning, first appearing with the statement that Moseley Braun "distorts" and subsequently communicated again in the phrase, "unwillingness to shoot straight." The stereotype is clearly mentioned in the quoted phrase pictured in the final frame and verbally repeated by the narrator. The charge is also made through the newspaper headline depicted in the frame in the third row of the first

Dropping in the polls and already desperate, Carol Moseley Braun and her allies are distorting Peter Fitzgerald's record on gun control.

The truth is, Fitzgerald has a centrist position on gun control. Fitzgerald supports the Brady Bill, the ban on assault weapons,

and he supports family safety measures like trigger locks.

So the next time you see Moseley Braun's distorted attack ads,

remember her unwillingness to shoot straight, and the doubts about her truthfulness.

FIGURE 1.1 Ad by Peter Fitzgerald vs. Carol Moseley Braun, U.S. Senate, 1998, Illinois *("Twisted," sponsored by Fitzgerald for Senate, PFFS-TV-38, 30 seconds, September 19, 1998, produced by Stevens Reed Curcio and Company)*

column, which highlights Braun's "ethics" charges. Moseley Braun appears and her lips are moving, but Fitzgerald (by way of the narrator) does all the talking. When it is Fitzgerald's turn to represent himself, he refers to his centrist positions in both words and images. He talks to "us"—those with whom Moseley Braun is incapable of "shooting straight." The families and family protectors are all White in a state that, at the time, was 78 percent White. Each component of the ad—the repeated stereotype of untrustworthiness that runs throughout, the contrast between Moseley Braun's Blackness and the mainstream, the Illinois community's Whiteness—in a state where most people look like Fitzgerald rather than like Moseley Braun—calls attention to race; magnifies the negative association between Moseley Braun, Blacks, and the untrustworthy stereotype; and accentuates Moseley Braun's implied racial otherness. These characteristics are emphasized, but relative to what? If this ad is typical for its racist potential, what kinds of ads lie on either side of it, having less or more potential?

Ads at the lowest extreme of the IRP have some, but almost no, racist potential. Table 1.3 demonstrates what an ad at the low end of the IRP looks like. The ad was sponsored by the White Republican candidate John Mitnick, who ran against the Black Democratic candidate Cynthia McKinney for Georgia's Fourth District congressional seat in 1996. The district had been redrawn and was no longer the majority-Black district in which McKinney had previously run. The ad's source of racist potential comes with Mitnick's two references to crime and violent criminals. Yet when we look at the imagery in the ad, we see first that McKinney does not appear. All of the images in the ad feature Whites, with the exception of a Black woman who appears in the opening frame. Despite this, and despite the annexation of DeKalb County (to which Mitnick refers) to the new district, Mitnick refrains from using first-person plural language, choosing instead to specify at the close that he will represent "all the people in DeKalb and Gwinnett counties." As previously mentioned, references to crime and criminality within the context of Mitnick's Black opponent gives the ad some racist potential. However, there is little additional visual and linguistic content—even given the possibility that Mitnick's mentioning the two counties might be a veiled attempt to signal race.

At the opposite end of the scale are ads whose racist potential is extremely significant. They are not explicit, but they include multiple layers of content that provides overwhelming evidence about its racist potential. An ad sponsored by Toby Moffett, a White candidate and Democrat vying for a U.S. Senate seat in Connecticut in 1990, against Black former Congressman Gary Franks—a Republican—illustrates the kind of ad with the strongest racist potential.[13] Seen in Figure 1.2, the ad's opening statement begins to signal Franks's untrustworthiness, insinuating that he is hiding something from the public.

**TABLE 1.3   Ad by John Mitnick vs. Cynthia McKinney,
U.S. House of Representatives, 1996**

Ad image	Ad narration
Live footage of one Black woman and one White woman seated, facing each other on a park bench	*Unidentified female voice:* "I'm worried about my family's future."
Live footage of two White girls playing in park filled with fallen leaves. Fade to image of two White boys playing in same park. Text "Cynthia McKinney voted against portability of health-care coverage" appears on screen.	*Narrator:* Cynthia McKinney voted against portability of health-care coverage.
Live footage of one White girl playing in same park, fade to image of all children holding hands in a circle in the same park. Text "Cynthia McKinney voted against violent criminals to serve at least 85% of their sentences" appears on screen.	*Narrator:* Cynthia McKinney voted against violent criminals to serve at least 85% of their sentences.
Live footage of John Mitnick seated on the front porch of a house	*Mitnick:* I'm John Mitnick. As your congressman, I will oppose higher taxes, vote to shut the revolving door on violent criminals, and work to improve health-care coverage. I'll be a voice of reason for all the people of DeKalb and Gwinnett counties.

The second frame and corresponding statement brings the additional stereotype of Franks's irresponsibility and allusions to laziness—his failure to show up and do the job he was paid to do; his unwillingness (or inability) to fulfill his responsibilities to the taxpayers. All the while, Franks's image remains on the screen.

Subsequent frames repeat the untrustworthiness stereotype, and the fourth introduces us to yet another: Franks the lawbreaker, violator, criminal (white collar as it may be). The ad's final statement repeats the untrustworthy stereotype yet again, this time using direct language, repeating twice its appeal to "us," which is verbally emphasized each time it is spoken by the narrator as the spot concludes. Finally, the ad was run in a state where 93 percent of the citizens are White. So we see here at the extreme end of the scale that there is nothing much different in terms of the distinct content components included; it is more about repetition and greater numbers of specific content—specifically, several distinct stereotypes mentioned and repeated first-person and third-person references. Each of these additional layers of content do not signal distinct constructs; they simply amplify key messages, which significantly increases the ad's racist potential.

What do we really know about
politician Gary Franks?

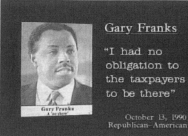

We know Alderman Gary Franks was
thrown off an important committee
by his fellow Republicans for
failing to show up.

We also know Gary Franks is a
millionaire real-estate speculator
who's hiding the truth by refusing
to disclose his tax returns.

And now we know that landlord
Gary Franks has been repeatedly cited
for health and safety violations at
properties he rents to families.

And Gary Franks is asking us to trust him to fight for us in Congress.

FIGURE 1.2 Ad by Toby Moffett vs. Gary Franks, U.S. Senate, 1990, Connecticut
("Rent," sponsored by Toby Moffett, TM-TV-08, 30 seconds, October 24, 1990, produced by Joe Slade White Communications)

POLITICAL STRATEGY, RACIAL APPEALS, AND CANDIDATES OF COLOR

Racist appeals dominate the scholarship and lay discussion surrounding race-based appeals. The social science community has spent little time examining the ways that candidates of color mobilize race to their strategic advantage in political campaigns running either against Whites or other candidates of color. For most of the time that race-based appeals have been the subject of debate within the public sphere, these types of appeals—racial appeals—have not been approached with the same air of controversy that usually surrounds racist appeals. This is because unlike racist appeals, racial appeals—at least when we have taken time to consider them—are not broadly viewed as negative with respect to their intent or their potential effect. While some racial appeals rely on racial stereotypes, candidates do not invoke them in the same manner that they do in racist appeals. Other racial appeals dispense with stereotypes altogether while maintaining their core racial basis.[14]

The ways that candidates of color mobilize race is just as important to the story as racist appeals are when trying to understand the complicated and multilayered racial dynamics at work during American-style political campaigns, and with respect to American race relations more generally. Racial appeals are distinctive; while they do not rely on the kinds of negative racial prejudices, stereotypes, and resentments that make up racist appeals, they nevertheless indirectly implicate negative White racial attitudes and sentiments in their messages and, more important, in their strategic import. With racist appeals, we were most interested in how they are constructed and how best to identify and interpret the racial cues that their content provides. Our understanding of the racial dynamics of race-infused electoral contests is enhanced by addressing racial appeals, drawing not so much from how they are constructed as from why.

Three strategic interests underlie the racial appeals candidates of color mobilize in their political advertisements. Before we talk about each of them directly, we will point out some of the general characteristics they have in common. First, racial appeals are overwhelmingly sponsor-focused, advocacy appeals (75% of the time). However, of the 25 percent that are non-advocacy ads, a slight but significant majority are attack ads rather than contrast ads. Overall, the racial appeals made by candidates of color spend more time focused on themselves than on their opponents. Thus, it is to be expected that critical racial content featured in such ads (such as references to stereotypes) also focus on the ads' sponsors rather than on their opponents. Second, racial appeals are similarly overwhelming in emphasizing the sponsoring candidates' image rather than issues. That is, 69 percent of ads with racial appeals feature no issue content. Thus, before we get into the specific reasons that candidates of color use racial appeals, we know that they use them generally to make a statement about themselves and their own candidacies—unlike sponsors of racist appeals, who use such appeals as kind of an electoral weapon to attack and diminish the personal and political appeal of their opponents.

Racial Inoculation

Alan Wheat was first elected to Congress in 1982. He had the distinction of being the first African American in the United States elected to represent a majority-White district since Reconstruction—Missouri's fifth, which he represented for a decade. When he decided to run for the U.S. Senate seat vacated by John Danforth in 1994, Wheat was convinced of his ability to appeal to White voters. He apparently was also keenly aware that his decade-long service to his predominately White constituents could not whitewash his Black image in 88 percent of the state's White minds. Figure 1.3 typifies the string of ads Wheat sponsored in 1994, when he squared off against his White opponent, John Ashcroft.[15] Further, it represents the quintessential racial inoculation ad, used in more than 70 percent of ads with racial appeals.

The distinctive features of the racial inoculation strategy underlying many racial appeals are seen throughout Wheat's ad. First, Wheat repeatedly makes counter-stereotype references. "Working hard" and "playing by the rules" are, as previously discussed, counter-stereotype references for Blacks who have long been represented in media and popular attitudes as lazy, shiftless, untrustworthy, and criminal. These counter-stereotype references are the most distinctive feature of minority candidates' strategy to separate themselves— individual candidates of color—from the longstanding stereotypes commonly held about the racial group that their skin color reflects.

The narrator in more than one of the ads for Gary Franks, a Black candidate for the U.S. Senate, put it this way: "The great-grandson of a slave, the son of a mill worker, Gary Franks *worked hard,* graduated from Yale." In his campaign for the U.S. Senate from Tennessee in 2006, African American Harold Ford Jr. said: "Whenever I talk with kids, I tell them three things: *work hard,* play by the rules, and keep God first. . . . It's about responsibility." The Latina Linda Sanchez said she would stand up "for *working* families. . . . The daughter of immigrant parents, she *put herself through* . . . Law School." And the African American candidate Artur Davis phrased it this way: "One powerful set of values . . . no matter where you start in life, that you have the opportunity to go as far as your talent and your dreams will take you." The narrator in his ad ended the statement with, "Artur Davis, *working* for us."

Besides counter-stereotype references, other distinctive features of racial inoculation appeals are exemplified in Wheat's ad. Wheat appears in his ad, as the candidates in 95 percent of all inoculation ads do. What stands out in

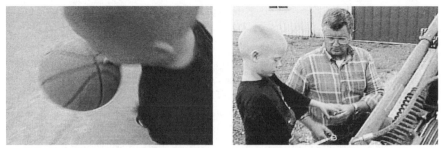

The American dream, to me it's always meant that if you work hard enough,
you could find opportunity and become anything you wanted to be.
That's the dream we should pass along to our children.

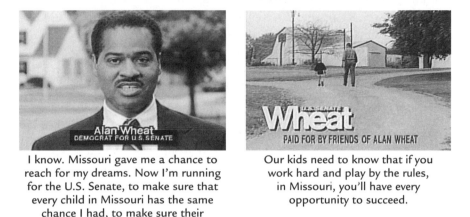

I know. Missouri gave me a chance to
reach for my dreams. Now I'm running
for the U.S. Senate, to make sure that
every child in Missouri has the same
chance I had, to make sure their
dreams come true.

Our kids need to know that if you
work hard and play by the rules,
in Missouri, you'll have every
opportunity to succeed.

FIGURE 1.3   Ad by Alan Wheat vs. John Ashcroft, U.S. Senate, 1994, Missouri
*("Dream," sponsored by Alan Wheat for Senate, no. 106, 30 seconds, 1994, produced by Trippi, McMahon,
and Squire)*

Wheat's ad in particular, however, are the subjects represented in the remaining images: If the viewer did not know who Wheat was or what he looked like, the dominant portion of the ad, focusing on images of White father-and-son rural farmers and lacking a detectable and familiar Black vernacular in the candidate's voice, would lead him or her to believe that Wheat was (or, at least, could be) White. It is not until the very end of the ad that the viewer sees that the candidate is Black. As the ad continues, Wheat makes frequent collective references (often, but not overwhelmingly, found in inoculation ads) to "our children," "we," "our kids." In this case, the collective is defined by who is represented in the dominant images of the ad. Wheat's message is not so much that he wants potential voters to view him as White. On the contrary, he wants them to see him as *not Black,* not the Black stereotype(s), but as someone who values the same things Whites do. It is a message of non-distinction. That is, "Just because I'm Black, don't see me as any different than the folks in my ad—folks like you."

This message lies at the heart of the racial inoculation strategy. The strategy recognizes that the salience of racial stereotypes coincides with the very fact that the candidate is non-White. That is, whether truth or fiction (who could ever know?), candidates of color mobilize such appeals assuming that the reality of their always already racialized image fundamentally accords with a series of stereotypes. Thus, the racial inoculation strategy seeks to allay Whites' negative prejudices, predispositions and fears from the beginning, with the hope that the stereotype will not remain White voters' dominant perception of the minority candidate.

In a memorable moment in Spike Lee's film *Do the Right Thing*, Mookie, a Black character played by Lee, tells the Italian American Pino that all of Pino's heroes are Black. Pino admits that his favorite movie star is Eddie Murphy and favorite basketball player is Magic Johnson. Eager not to confirm Mookie's argument, however, Pino claims that these people—"Magic, Eddie, Prince, they're different. They're not niggas, I mean, they're not Black, I mean. . . . Let me explain myself. They're not really Black. I mean, they're Black, but they're not really Black. They're more than Black, it's different." Pino's confused and convoluted attempt to clarify his view of certain Blacks expresses the kind of pained position candidates of color find themselves in when having to appeal to White voters.

Given the long history of ingrained prejudices that candidates of color believe Whites still harbor about members of their racial group, candidates of color find it necessary to inoculate themselves from Whites' potential stereotypical judgment. To do so they have to walk a fine line, claiming to be beyond the stereotype (a special, not typical, kind of Black or Latino) while not inadvertently distancing themselves from other members of their racial group (who are also represented in the electorate) or coming off as disingenuous among Whites. Candidates of color cannot stop White voters from acknowledging the color of their skin, yet they find it strategically necessary to carve out some kind of identity position that is neither White—which they cannot become (even if they wish to)—nor stereotypically Black. They have to be super-Black or super-Latino or vice versa—exceptional.

At first glance, the inoculation strategy evident in racial appeals seems to resemble what has long been referred to as Black candidates' "de-racialization" strategy, a theory used to explain Black candidates' potential to succeed in majority-White electoral contests (Gillespie 2009; McCormick and Jones 1993). However, taken from the perspective of candidates' political ads, there is an important distinction. The focus of the de-racialization strategy is to minimize racial discourse in political campaigns, to reduce the potential that White voters will take race into account when making their voting decisions. But the

TABLE 1.4 Counter-stereotype references in racist inoculation ads

Counter-stereotype	Correlation	% used (N = 164)	% used by White sponsors (N = 356)
Self-reliant	.470**	23	1
Plays by the rules	.331**	7	0
Responsible	.293**	4	0
Hardworking	.267**	60	16
Qualified	.244**	8	2
Trustworthy	.064	20	11

** $p < .01$

overwhelming message from the kind of racial inoculation strategies candidates of color express in their political ads suggests that candidates of color approach their electoral circumstances with the guiding assumption that minimizing White voters' racial thinking is either not possible or not enough to persuade them to vote for them.

Rather, the inoculation strategy presumes that candidates of color must proactively and affirmatively offer White voters a clear argument for why they should think about the candidate of color differently from the prevailing stereotypes. Preferably—in the mindset of candidates of color—their counter-stereotype arguments will be framed in such a way as to comport with the dominant racial characteristics normatively associated with the American (White) ideal. We see this in Table 1.4, which shows that five of the six counter-stereotype references are strongly associated with this kind of inoculation appeal used by candidates of color. Three such counter-stereotype references are most often featured: hardworking, self-reliant, and trustworthy. Beyond this, we see that White candidates running in contests against candidates of color do not exercise the same compulsion to emphasize any of these character traits that, for Black and Latino candidates, are counter-stereotypes. It is as if candidates of color are running against a kind of invisible but very real ghost. That is, candidates of color oppose White candidates whose character seems fundamentally taken for granted, while they must fight tooth and nail (almost half of inoculation ads include two or more counter-stereotype references) to convince White voters that their true character belies the color of their skin.

Racial Authenticity

While most of the racial appeals in our data—in ads sponsored by candidates of color—reflect the dominant form of election contest (biracial contests), another notable and primary form of racial appeal is often found in election contests pitting two candidates of the same racial group against each other.

Of the twenty-three ads from contests involving either two Black candidates running against each other or two Latino candidates doing so, twenty-two of them fit the general qualities of what we refer to as appeals to racial authenticity. Such appeals are distinguished and delineated by four primary characteristics: the absence of references to a racial stereotype or counter-stereotype; the inclusion of two candidates from the same racial group; a majority of voters belonging to the same racial group as the candidates; and the inclusion of first-person-plural references.

The Black or Latino community is the primary frame of reference in political ads with authenticity appeals; thus, racial group uplift, rather than denigration, provides a communicative public sphere relatively free of anti-minority stereotypes. First-person references to "us" and "we" define and qualify the relationship between candidates and voters as one predicated on racial group identity and the pursuit of racial group interests. That is, political advertising messages appealing to racial authenticity frame political interests as racial group interests. We deal with the subject of racial authenticity and authenticity appeals in more theoretical and empirical detail in the following chapters. Here, we simply define the primary persuasive message of authenticity as one in which candidates ask voters to vote for them because they are "more" authentically Latino or Black and assert that their fidelity to *the* Black or Latino community best qualifies them to pursue and protect Blacks' or Latinos' interests. As in the other forms of appeals, the relative absence of substantive policy issues potentially heightens the racial salience of appeals to authenticity. (The vast majority of authenticity appeals feature no substantive issue.)

Racial Defense

Racial defense is a final strategy underlying the racial appeals candidates of color use in political campaigns. It proved difficult in our data to delineate a discrete category of ads using this strategy; thus, it is difficult for us to deal with it in the same systematic way we have discussed other forms of appeals. However, we will briefly point out this form of appeal because it contributes to our understanding of the kinds of appeals candidates of color have used in the past. More important perhaps, it speaks to what may become an increasingly common feature of candidates' appeals. Candidates of color sometimes invoke racial references because they want to defend themselves against what they see as a racist attack lodged against them. An ad sponsored by the Black candidate Harvey Gantt in his U.S. Senate race against North Carolina Senator Jesse Helms in 1990 serves as a prime example. A preceding ad by Helms had this message: "How did Harvey Gantt become a millionaire? He used his position as mayor and his minority status to get himself and his friends a free

TV station license from the government. Only weeks later, they sold out—to a white-owned corporation for $3.5 million. The black community felt betrayed, but the deal made the mayor a millionaire. Harvey Gantt made government work for Harvey Gantt." Gantt responded to the ad directly, using the same kind of explicit racial language Helms had used. Looking directly at the camera in his response ad, Gantt said:

> Jesse Helms is running another smear campaign, charging me with using my race for financial advantage, charging me with wanting to require gay teachers in schools. They're lies, and Jesse Helms knows it. For eighteen years, he's been playing on people's fears and killing this state's hopes in the process. Don't be taken in by the smears.

While the racial statements here are clear, it is interesting to parse the language Gantt uses to reply to Helms's charges. Specifically, by using the term "advantage," instead of "gain," Gantt identifies not the ethical and political charge that he used his minority status for financial gain but, rather, the element of racial resentment communicated in the term "advantage." That is, Gantt recognized Helms's attempt to link, or the resulting likelihood of linking, Gantt's Blackness to statements about financial profit.

RACE-BASED APPEALS AND THE AMERICAN ELECTORATE

In *The Race Card,* Mendelberg argues that the shift toward a norm of racial equality in the United States did not erase White candidates' electoral interest in mobilizing White voters' prejudices, fears, and resentments against Blacks to get elected (hence, the inception of implicit communication). Mendelberg based this realization on the demographic and psychological makeup of the White electorate, large portions of which retain—consciously or unconsciously— these stereotypes, resentments, and fears. It was also based on anecdotal evidence at the time—the Willie Horton case primarily—that candidates' political communication could draw out Whites' negative racial attitudes.

When we systematically examine large numbers of actual political advertisements, we find not only that tapping into White voters' negative racial attitudes is an electoral possibility that may further their strategic interests, but also that White candidates appear to have continued to embrace the electoral potential that racist appeals in particular have to contribute to their electoral success (see Table 1.5). White candidates' propensity to construct and deploy racist appeals is perhaps best seen in light of the fact they construct and deploy these appeals when the racial group prejudices and stereotypes their ads target are reflected in their opposing candidates' racial appearance. It is one thing to deploy race-based appeals when one's opponent is also White—when a racist appeal is coupled with either a White candidate and/or a policy issue. It is quite another to do so when one's opponent is Black or Latino. More than one-third of all ads that were run in contests where White candidates opposed Black or Latino candidates contained some

TABLE 1.5 General trends of racist appeals

Comparators	Mean IRP	N	% potential racist appeals
Racial composition of contest			
White sponsor–Black opponent	5.0	172	82
White sponsor–Latino opponent	4.7	88	79
Decade			
1970s	5.3	9	60
1980s	3.1***	40	80
1990s	4.7***	416	84
2000s	3.9***	152	76
Office			
U.S. Senate	4.5	300	78
U.S. House	4.3	317	83
Region			
Northeast	5.9	66	73
South	4.0***	302	81
West	4.4***	143	80
Midwest	4.6***	105	84
Type of ad			
Advocacy	3.9	352	77
Contrast	4.8***	82	77
Attack	5.3***	183	92
Focus of ad			
Issue	4.4	248	74
Image	4.4	369	86
Dominant speaker in ad			
Candidate	4.0	154	74
Narrator	4.7***	357	83

Note: Each row includes paired means tests comparing the top row of each section with each subsequent row in the section. The final column includes the percentage of the total number of ads that have some racist potential.

*** $p < .001$

racist potential; the vast majority of these included significant potential, scoring an average of five points on the IRP (a score above the mean IRP score for all ads).

Irrespective of whether they vie for seats in the U.S. House or Senate, White candidates increasingly and consistently have deployed potentially racist ads over the past four decades. Ads with significant racist potential proliferated in the 1990s, signaling an increased mobilization from that of the 1980s. This trend coincides with the increasing number of biracial election contests in which Black and Latino candidates ran against White opponents in the 1990s. The increasing trends of both the numbers of biracial election contests and the proportion of White candidates' potentially racist appeals maintained course at the turn of the twenty-first century. The relative frequency with which potentially racist appeals appear in the political campaign landscape will likely hold steady throughout the current decade, if ads from the 2008 and 2010 elections reflect the same character as those from the first four election cycles of the decade.

Ads with some modicum of racist appeal also consistently appear in White candidates' political advertising throughout the United States. While popular opinion may lead us to believe that racial prejudice—especially against politicians of color—is a mainstay of Southern politics exclusively, the data show that White candidates construct and deploy ads with racist potential with equal frequency regardless of the region in which the contests are conducted. This notwithstanding, evidence suggests (perhaps surprisingly) that ads originating from White candidates in the Northeast have a higher average of racist potential than in any other region of the United States.

Black and Latino candidates attempt to use race to their strategic advantage, as well, as it is a necessary and important component of the racial landscape of American-style political campaigns. The divergent ways that we see White candidates constructing potentially racist appeals and Black and Latino candidates deploying racial appeals presents an interesting picture of how race operates both within the electoral sphere and beyond. In one respect, White candidates mobilize race in vastly different ways from Black and Latino candidates. Consistent with White candidates' references to negative racial stereotypes, White candidates' ads with potential racist appeal almost always attack their opponents of color (92 percent of ads with some racist potential are attacks ads).[16] While negativity has become a hallmark of contemporary political advertising, when coupled with racial stereotypes and the fact that one's opponent is a racial minority, the potential negativity of such attacks is exacerbated. That is, attack-oriented ads enhance—symbolically and empirically—any racist appeal the ad might have. To the degree that political candidates risk potential backlash by deploying attack ads (Basil, Schooler and Reeves 1991; Garramone 1985; Roddy and Garramone 1988), the risk may be compounded if potential voters interpret the negative attack as a racist attack (something we explore in detail in the next chapter).

Candidates of color, especially those running in biracial contests against White candidates, seem to take the view, however, that White candidates risk little when making racist appeals, especially when such appeals are made primarily to audiences of White potential voters. While White candidates are frequently on the attack against their opponents of color, candidates of color almost always advocate. Seventy-four percent of all ads from biracial contests are advocacy ads. They do not advocate the candidate's position on health care or interests in economic reform. They do not even spend their time pursuing policy causes such as affirmative action, school desegregation, and racial profiling. They expend much of their political advertising time and content advocating for themselves, building up their own images and characters not just as candidates, but as candidates of color. It is popular to hear many candidates today say they put faith in White voters' ability to look beyond race and not allow racial prejudice to influence their political decisions. When he ran for governor of Alabama in 2010, for instance, Artur Davis stated early in his campaign that he was following Barack Obama's example from the 2008 presidential race. "Barack Obama trusted the country," Davis said, referring to criticisms about whether White Alabamans would vote for a Black candidate. But if the content and tenor of the political ads we analyzed is any indication, such public expressions of faith in White voters by candidates of color are quite disingenuous.

Indeed, White racial prejudice is so enduring and runs so deep that most candidates of color anticipate and fear the negative effects of White candidates' racist appeals before they even make them (or even if they ultimately do not). Most of the advertising messages candidates of color construct demonstrate that they are keenly aware of the reality that Whites still view Blacks and Latinos in stereotypical ways. For candidates of color, the reality is that the die has already been cast. Candidates of color surely assume that White voters' prejudices about them will enter the electoral sphere as soon as their candidacy and their racial background are known—which is why the first question on political analysts' minds when candidates of color run in contests with White voting majorities is: "Will White voters vote for the candidate of color?" In this position, candidates of color find themselves spending much of their time and energy not ignoring or downplaying race but building up the character traits they possess, despite their race. They continually focus on communicating to White voters that they share their values—hard work, personal responsibility, honesty, and the like—traits not generally imputed to other members of the racial group to which they belong.

When we consider the racial content of political ads alone, we are dealing with candidates' communications strategies, potential, expectations, and prob-

abilities. Here, our primary focus is on the underlying forms of racial thinking, motivation, or communicative potential that intentionally or unintentionally find expression in candidates' (and their advertising consultants')
political ads. Will racist appeals live up to their potential to disadvantage candidates of color among the White electorate? Will they backfire if and when
White or non-White voters recognize a White candidate's racist appeal? Can
candidates of color successfully inoculate themselves from White voters'
racial prejudices or appeal to racial group interests to gain electoral support?
The answer to each of these questions is purely speculative in the intervening
moment between when an ad is produced and when it hits the public airwaves. We now turn our attention to that moment, when the private production of race-based appeals meets the public perceptions of potential voters.

2

The Advantages and Disadvantages of Deploying Racist Appeals among Black and White Voters

COMMUNICATIVE PROCESSES are interdependent, making it necessary for media effects studies to address the interplay between the sender and receiver and the message itself. Now that we have a solid understanding of the types of messages that are employed in electoral contests in which racial minority candidates are involved, we need to explore what, if any, effects can result when those messages are received by (potential) voters. The next two chapters are dedicated to answering those questions. We are principally concerned with two types of race-based messages: racist appeals and racial appeals. As we described in the previous chapter, racist appeals rely on preexisting negative stereotypes about people of color for their effect, whereas racial appeals invoke race but do not rest on racist predispositions. In this chapter, we focus on racist appeals. Chapter 3 is devoted to an examination of one specific category of racial appeals (the appeal to racial authenticity). We are ultimately interested in the general question of whether racist appeals affect potential voters, and if they do, how and why.

RACIAL PREDISPOSITIONS AND CANDIDATE EVALUATIONS

Many scholars in psychology, sociology, critical race studies, political science, anthropology, and communication studies have examined the broad notion of White racial predispositions and resentment (see, e.g., Feldman and Huddy 2005; Frederickson 1971; Jordan 1974; Kinder and Sanders 1996; Kinder and

Sears 1981); conceptualizations of racism (Henry and Sears 2002; McConahay 1986); and the psychological basis of stereotyping, prejudice, and discrimination (Allport 1979; Fiske 1998; Zuckerman 1990). An increasing amount of work in social psychology seeks to tap into subconscious predispositions about race (Banaji, Hardin, and Rothman 1993; Baron and Banaji 2006). Still other researchers have drawn on findings in the area of mediated representations that depict minority images as largely negative and stereotypical to demonstrate that Whites' perceptions of Black candidates mirror many of those stereotypes played out the broader forms of media, such as television and film (Coleman 2000; Cottle 2000; Drago 1992; Entman and Rojecki 2001; Gibbons 1993; Hall 1997; Kamalipour and Carilli 1998; Larson 2005).

Research on the intersection of race, political communication, and voting behavior has focused largely on two distinct, yet related, sets of questions. First, what perceptions do White voters have about minorities in general, and about minority candidates specifically? And second, how might those attitudes influence voting choices in election contests in which either a minority candidate or a White candidate championing minority interests is involved (Sigelman, Sigelman, Walkosz, and Nitz 1995; Terkildsen 1993; Williams 1990)?

While much scholarship regarding the election of minorities to political office has focused on discussions about the efficacy of redistricting policies for descriptive and substantive representation, comparatively few studies have focused directly on individual-level attitudes toward Black candidates and officeholders and how they are evaluated by voters in terms of their fitness for office. Conclusions from this body of literature assert that, by and large, White voters tend to hold negative perceptions of Black candidates and evaluate them more negatively than their White counterparts.

Williams (1990), for example, found in a national survey that when Whites were asked to evaluate Black and White candidates, they more often than not attributed positive characteristics such as "intelligent," "hardworking," and "trustworthy" to White candidates more than Black candidates. Terkildsen (1993) reported similar conclusions, adding to the mix the fact that Black candidates' skin color and tone significantly affected Whites' negative evaluations of them. Terkildsen concluded that while Black candidates as a whole were evaluated more negatively than White candidates, dark-skinned Blacks were evaluated most harshly. More recently, Caruso, Mead, and Balcetis (2009) found that respondents tended to view biracial individuals (Barack Obama and a fictitious candidate for public office) with whom they shared party identification as having lighter skin, choosing a lightened version of a photograph over the actual picture as being most representative of the person in question. Conversely, participants tended to choose darkened images as accurate representations of those with whom they disagreed politically.

These studies cite race and skin color as primary determinants of Whites' negative evaluations of Black candidates. However, Sigelman, Sigelman, Walkosz, and Nitz (1995) suggest that, despite the correlation between espoused stereotypes and perception or evaluation of candidates, a minority candidate's race is not necessarily the most salient predictor of his or her negative evaluations. They conclude that an individual's previously held ideologies and political expectations of minority candidates are more significant factors. Howell and McLean (2001) determined that, for minority holders of political office, performance rather than race was a more significant predictor of Whites' evaluations.

The majority of the research to date shows, however, that race is at least one factor among others. Thus, it is important to explore the type and degree of effect race has on voting decisions. As some scholars point out, it is difficult to dissociate race and ideology because they have been integrally connected for so long (Kinder and Winter 2001). These points notwithstanding, the extant literature fails to address adequately whether mediated messages may in part be responsible for the negative attitudes voters—particularly White voters—hold with respect to Black candidates. Parallel studies about racial attitudes and evaluations, however, add to this area of research by focusing more on the cognitive priming processes that make such attitudes accessible and, more specifically, the use of mediated racial messages in the context of political campaigns to do so.

RACIST PRIMING AND IMPLICIT APPEALS

A second broad area of research on race, political communication, and political decision making focuses on the forms of race-based messages used in political campaigns and their propensity to prime White racial attitudes (primarily related to specific public policy issues) that may function as the basis for White voters' political decisions. (For general treatment of the topic, see Perry 1996; Persons 1993.) Although conclusions regarding the direct link between Whites' existing prejudicial attitudes and voting choices are mixed, research thus far supports the notion that racial cues are effective in priming such attitudes and, in doing so, affecting Whites' voting decisions.

Mendelberg's (2001) work, which convincingly argues that implicit racial appeals by White candidates significantly prime negative racial attitudes among White voters, is supported in subsequent studies. Valentino, Hutchings, and White (2002) not only demonstrated support for Mendelberg's conclusions but isolated more precisely the kinds of messages that have greater priming effects. They found that messages using imagery in political ads linking Blacks to comments about undeserving groups had the most significant priming effect. In addition, their results show that race-based priming is mediated by the accessibility of race in memory rather than self-reported levels of the importance of group representation. They also found that expectancy-violating, negative racial cues regarding Blacks suppressed race-based priming, while the violation of positive stereotypes of Whites had a positive priming effect. In a related study, Valentino, Traugott, and Hutchings (2002) found that ads containing racial cues significantly strengthened the effect of ideological self-placement in evaluating candidates. This was especially so in cases where ads portrayed some advantage of Whites over Blacks. Conclusions from this study suggest that group cues (especially group cues related to race) are powerful in priming political ideology.

However, portions of Mendelberg's initial model have come under attack by Huber and Lapinski (2006), who argue that in some populations implicit racial messages are no more effective than explicit racial messages in priming racial resentment underlying participants' policy opinions. The scholars exchanged arguments in the March 2008 issue of *Perspectives on Politics* (Huber and Lapinski 2008; Mendelberg 2008a, 2008b), debating the veracity of Mendelberg's implicit communication model, with Mendelberg citing the preponderance of evidence from other studies that support her conclusions. Huber and Lapinski cite flaws in the design of the experiments in Mendelberg's study and in others' studies that support her theory while drawing attention to the expansiveness of their experimental design, which, they claim, was better for testing potential priming effects.

The purpose of our work here is not to engage in this particular debate, except inasmuch as we accept the conclusions found in most studies that demonstrate the potential priming effects of implicit communication. We sidestep this debate not simply because it is expedient, but also because we have fundamentally different interests. Whereas most—if not all—previous studies in this area have been concerned with priming effects on policy opinion formation, we are singularly interested in whether implicit race-based appeals, formed by candidates for the express purposes of drawing support for their candidacy, as opposed to a specific policy issue, affect potential voters' perceptions of and likelihood to vote for a specific candidate. More specifically, we are interested in whether race-based appeals disadvantage Black candidates by influencing White voters' to act on the basis of negative racial predispositions they have about African Americans. While work on the infamous Willie Horton ad from the 1988 presidential election has helped us to understand the effect of racial messages in general (see Jamieson 1992, 16–42; Kinder and Sanders 1996, chap. 9; Mendelberg 1999; Reeves 1997), it cannot account for the effect of racial messages on voters' perceptions of a racial minority candidate.

Because we are fundamentally interested in this chapter with the ways that implicit racist appeals ultimately shape the election hopes of Blacks (and by extension other candidates of color) and influence the degree of descriptive representation in government, we also seek to address what we see as another major limitation in the extant literature about race-based appeals. This limitation was first articulated by Valentino, Hutchings, and White (2002, 78), who reflect on their own study, saying:

> In keeping with this practice, we too focus on nonblacks, though we do so reluctantly. We believe that the theory of implicit communication applies to blacks as well as whites, though individual differences will certainly moderate the size of the effect. . . . Ultimately, however, the theory of racial priming must be extended to include and understand the reactions of *all* audience members.

Thus, based on the preponderance of previous findings about racist priming and implicit communication and our critical interest in how it may influence the balance of racial equity in federal government bodies in particular, we pursue the following question in the remainder of this chapter: How do racist appeals deployed in political advertising affect both White and Black voters' evaluation of and likelihood to vote for Black and White candidates?

This question—and the broader question about how racial cues might affect evaluation of racial minorities more broadly—is increasingly pertinent given the dramatic increase of the minority population in the U.S. (especially Latino: see Hero and Tolbert 1995) and the increase in minorities elected to local and state offices (Bositis 2002a; Joint Center for Political and Economic Studies 2009), which suggests that federal election contests in certain areas will increasingly involve minority candidates competing with Whites. Further, continued reliance on redistricting has increased the number of majority-minority congressional districts throughout the United States.[1]

THE EXPERIMENTS

We begin with the following question: Do racial cues by a White candidate differentially and generally affect Black and White voters' candidate evaluation and vote choice? Our expectations are informed by the aforementioned empirical studies of race-based messages and theoretically rooted in the group identity literature, which suggests that in the American context, racial identity is often a powerful predictor of social and political attitudes and behavior (Herring, Jankowski, and Brown 1999; Schmermund, Sellers, Mueller, and Crosby 2001).[2]

We address these nagging questions about the effect of racist messages on candidates of color by focusing on the attitudinal and (simulated) behavioral effects of participants viewing ads communicating racist messages and subsequently evaluating the candidates. We conducted two separate 1 × 2 (type of contest [biracial] × type of message [no racist appeal versus racist appeal]) post-test only experiments—one with White participants and one with Black participants.[3] Pretest measures were not taken to avoid potential priming prior to the introduction of stimuli.

Stimuli and Experimental Procedures

The stimuli for each experiment were two thirty-second television advertisements from a fictitious election for the U.S. House of Representatives: David Jackson, a Black man, is running against Jim Herbert, who is White.[4] Both candidates appear to be approximately the same age. The ads were contrast ads (see Jamieson, Waldmann, and Sherr 2000), wherein each candidate pointed out the advantages of his own position while criticizing that of his opponent. Neither candidate's party identification was mentioned at any time, though the substance of their message, by necessity, was varied to simulate a policy disagreement between them.

The content of the ads we produced for the experiment was informed by our study of actual television ads for candidates in biracial elections (see Chapter 1, as well as an experiment with undergraduate college students using ads from the 1990 Jesse Helms–Harvey Gantt race for U.S. Senate in North Carolina as stimuli [Caliendo, McIlwain, and Karjala 2003]). In the Helms–Gantt study, we found that the ads generated responses from participants consistent with Mendelberg's (2001) conclusions about the efficacy of implicit racial ads over explicit messages or no messages at all.

Rather than rely on existing advertisements, we commissioned three unique spots to be produced for the fictitious contest so we had complete control over the manipulation of messages in each condition.[5] We used the same substantive policy issue (education) in both candidates' ads to maximize control over as much content as possible so that we could isolate the cause of any variance. The key content featured in each of the three ads used is shown in Table 2.1. The first row includes the key policy-related language, phrases, and visuals included in David Jackson's ad, which was used in both the control group and the test group; thus, the message did not change. In the ad, Jackson evokes the language of "choice" and proceeds to contrast his position on education (supports school choice and tough standards) with that of his opponent, Jim Herbert, who, Jackson says, is against these two education principles. Jackson describes his own candidacy as a crucial choice between himself, who is on the right side of the education issue, and his opponent, who ostensibly is on the wrong side. No race-related visuals are included (other than, of course, the fact that Jackson is Black and Herbert is White, both of which are clearly visible in the images that appear).

TABLE 2.1 Key ad content for each experiment condition

Experiment group ad	Policy-related language	Election statement	Race-neutral visuals	Racially coded visuals
Jackson control and test group	"crucial choice," "school choice," "tough standards," "right choice"	"You have a crucial choice in this election. I'm David Jackson, and I want to be your choice, because I'm the right choice."	Jackson, live footage and color still image; Herbert, black-and-white still image	None
Herbert control group	"differences between my opponent and me," "interests of the citizens of the First District," "grew up here," "grew up outside the district," "went to school here," "schools outside the district," "supports vouchers," "supports public schools"	"Who is really equipped to fight for this district in Washington: someone who's been outside it all his life, or someone who has been part of it for all of his?"	Herbert, live footage in park; Jackson, black-and-white still image	None
Herbert (White candidate) test group	Same as control group	Same as control group	Same as control group	One color image of suburban school playground with nice equipment; one black-and-white image of playground with dilapidated equipment and Black kids playing basketball

Note: In this experiment, Jackson is the Black candidate, while Herbert is the White candidate.

Herbert's message is the only one that changes from one condition to the next. In the control group ad, described in Table 2.1, row 2, Herbert begins by citing the differences between him and his opponent. Herbert cites the fact that he grew up and went to school in the district and supports public schools in principle as the biggest difference between him and Jackson, who grew up and went to school "outside the district." Herbert's final conclusion is that being an insider makes him better suited to represent the district. Again, other than the images of the two candidates, no visuals appear.

Finally, the Herbert test-group ad shown in Table 2.1, row 3, includes the exact same policy-related language, election statement, and visuals of the candidate. What changes in the ad is that when Herbert states he grew up and went to school "here" and supports public schools, color images of new, suburban playgrounds and a school appear alongside. When he mentions that Jackson grew up and went to school outside the district, the associated images depict a dilapidated school with Black kids playing basketball. The implicit racist appeal is constructed here by connecting Herbert's in-group–out-group language with racially encoded visuals: the color, new, "good" images associated with Herbert, the White candidate, and the black-and-white, dilapidated, "poor" images associated with Jackson, the Black candidate.

Participants were drawn from a nationally representative, probability-based panel of adults recruited by Knowledge Networks through its cooperation with the Time-sharing Experiments for the Social Sciences (TESS) program and were randomly assigned to one of two groups.[6] Those in the control group viewed David Jackson's ad and Jim Herbert's control group ad. Participants in the test group viewed David Jackson's ad and Jim Herbert's implicit racist appeal ad. The order in which participants viewed each ad was randomly alternated to control for any potential order effects. After viewing their ads, participants in each group immediately completed a post-test.

Variables

Two primary dependent variables—candidate evaluation and vote choice—measure participants' responses to the stimuli. The first variable is measured by a question asking participants to indicate which candidate they would be most likely to vote for if given the opportunity. The second variable is measured by the respondents' ratings of both candidates on a feeling thermometer ranging from 0 to 100. This construct is designed to tap a more affective or visceral component of preference. Each participant was instructed to assign a number from 0 to 100 to reflect his or her feelings about each candidate independently, where "51 degrees to 100 degrees" indicated that he or she felt "favorably or warm" toward the candidate; 0–49 indicated that he or she did not feel favorable; and 50 meant that the participant did not "feel particularly warm or cold toward him." To deal with the fact that these dimensions might vary from one respondent to another, we computed a new variable by subtracting one candidate's score from that of the other and used the differential score as the indicator of candidate evaluation for each respondent (see Kahn and Kenney 1999; Smith, Brown, Bruce, and Overby 1999). The resulting measure runs from −100 (very warm feelings for Jackson with very cold feelings for Herbert) to 100 (very warm feelings for Herbert with very cold feelings for Jackson). Finally, we also asked participants to indicate their perception of which candidate, if either, was making an appeal to race and whether the participant would go to the polls to vote for the candidate of his or her choice.

We used a number of independent variables as predictors or controls. Besides demographic information (sex, age, race), participants were asked to indicate their political ideology on a seven-point Likert scale ranging from "extremely liberal" to "extremely conservative" and to report the degree to which they "follow what's going on in government and public affairs." For White participants, scores from the Henry and Sears (2002) Symbolic Racism 2000 Scale were included as a potential covariate.[7] For African American participants, we asked questions designed to tap linked fate and immersion in Black information networks, as well as views about what kinds of candidates (i.e., Black or White) were best able to represent the Black community.[8]

WHITE PARTICIPANTS' REACTIONS TO RACIST APPEALS

This experiment—White participants viewing ads in a biracial election contest—included 123 adults (see Table 2.2 for a description of the sample).[9]

The existing literature leads us to expect that Whites who view ads containing implicitly racist messages from a White candidate running against a Black opponent will evaluate the White candidate more favorably than the Black candidate than will Whites who do not view such messages. That is, because Herbert, the White candidate, is the one whose message changes—from having no racist appeal in one condition to including a racist appeal in another—we are primarily interested in whether participants evaluate Herbert more negatively or positively when they view his ad that includes a racist appeal. We expect this to be the case, and we further expect that doing so will be somewhat dependent on the respondent's degree of symbolic racism. Peffley, Hurwitz, and Sniderman (1997), for instance, found that Whites who held negative racial predispositions were likely to evaluate Blacks more harshly on the racially charged issues of crime and welfare policy than were Whites with less negative predispositions.

Contrary to historical trends, however, the participants in this study preferred David Jackson, the Black candidate, over the White candidate, Jim Her-

TABLE 2.2   Profile of participants

Black participants (N = 125)		White participants (N = 123)	
Gender		Gender	
Female	44.8%	Female	49.6%
Male	55.2%	Male	50.4%
Age		Age	
18–24	5.6%	18–24	17.1%
25–34	14.4%	25–34	12.2%
35–44	21.6%	35–44	11.4%
45–54	24.0%	45–54	17.9%
55–64	22.4%	55–64	21.1%
65–74	6.4%	65–74	10.6%
75+	5.6%	75+	9.8%
Education		Education	
Less than high school	9.6%	Less than high school	4.9%
High school	25.6%	High school	27.6%
Some college	32.8%	Some college	31.7%
Bachelor's degree or higher	32.0%	Bachelor's degree or higher	35.8%
Geographic region (based on state of residence)		Geographic region (based on state of residence)	
Northeast	17.6%	Northeast	22.8%
Midwest	14.4%	Midwest	26.8%
South	55.2%	South	28.5%
West	12.8%	West	22.0%
Home ownership status		Home ownership status	
Own	60.8%	Own	86.2%
Rent	38.4%	Rent	13.0%
Occupied (no rent)	0.8%	Occupied (no rent)	0.8%
Household income		Household income	
Median range (annual)	$40,000–$49,999	Median range (annual)	$60,000–$74,999

Note: Some totals may not equal 100% due to rounding.

bert, by a sizable margin. Fifty-nine percent of the participants who chose a candidate indicated that Jackson would be their choice, compared with 41 percent who preferred Herbert. Table 2.3 shows that this finding was not affected by the experimental group: Herbert fared marginally better when he invoked an implicitly racist message against Jackson, but the difference was negligible (less than one-half of one percentage point).

TABLE 2.3   Cross-tabulation of vote choice and experiment group

	Vote for Herbert	Vote for Jackson
White participants (N = 121)		
Herbert's racist message	1.5% (27)	58.5% (38)
No racist message (control)	41.1% (23)	58.9% (33)
$\chi^2 = 0.003$, p = .959 (two-sided)		
Black participants (N = 123)		
Herbert's racist message	35.0% (21)	65.0% (39)
No racist message (control)	38.0% (24)	62.0% (39)
$\chi^2 = 0.127$, p = .852 (two-sided)		

To determine whether any other factors contributed to candidate prefer-ence, we examine a number of models that include theoretically relevant vari-ables (Table 2.4). Again, it is clear that exposure to the implicitly racist mes-sage from Herbert is not a significant predictor of voting choice. After controlling for media attentiveness, ideology, age, gender, education, income, geographic location, and level of symbolic racism, the messages that partici-pants viewed did not have a statistically significant effect on voting choice. Further, interaction between experimental condition and theoretically power-ful predictors such as symbolic racism, ideology, and media attentiveness similarly were not good indications of support for either candidate. Rather, the strongest predictor of support for Herbert was the participants' percep-tion that David Jackson had invoked race in his message. The strongest pre-dictor of support for Jackson was participants' perception that Herbert had invoked race in his message.

Of course, the ad for David Jackson was not designed to invoke race either textually or through images. It appears that his very presence—that is, being Black in a race against a White opponent—was enough to invoke race in a way that resulted in support for his opponent among the participants (41%) who believed that he was or might be making an appeal to race. In contrast, 59% of the participants believed that Herbert did invoke or may have invoked race. Fifty-one percent of those in the control group thought that Herbert might be appealing to race, while 66 percent of participants in the test group thought that this was possible. Thirty-four percent of those who believed that Herbert might have appealed to race indicated that they would vote for him anyway. Nearly half (47%) of the participants who believed that Jackson might have invoked race indicated that they would vote for him.[10]

The picture that emerges is that Jackson was the stronger candidate in the eyes of the White participants who evaluated the two in the spring of 2010. Only the belief that Jackson had appealed to race was able to attract voters to

TABLE 2.4 White participants and vote choice

Predictors	Model 1	Model 2	Model 3	Model 4
Implicit racist message condition	0.155	0.433	0.407	0.312
	(0.398)	(0.435)	(0.437)	(1.807)
Perception of Jackson's use of race		1.454**	1.402**	1.380**
		(0.503)	(0.508)	(0.509)
Perception of Herbert's use of race		−1.563**	−1.502**	−1.528**
		(0.511)	(0.519)	(0.533)
Symbolic Racism Scale (SR2K)			0.040	−0.011
			(0.049)	(0.072)
Ideology	−0.086	−0.105	−0.157	−0.033
	(0.129)	(0.137)	(0.152)	(0.240)
Media attentiveness	0.150	0.112	0.119	−0.080
	(0.251)	(0.271)	(0.273)	(0.372)
Condition × ideology				−0.207
				(0.318)
Condition × SR2K				0.093
				(0.097)
Condition × media attentiveness				0.296
				(0.475)
Constant	−0.572	0.203	0.197	0.051
	(1.451)	(1.587)	(1.592)	(1.887)
N	115	115	115	115
χ^2	4.270	14.806**	0.689	1.193
−2 log likelihood	152.632	137.826	137.136	135.943
Nagelkerke R^2	.049	.205	.212	.224

Note: Coefficients are generated by binary logistic regression (standard errors appear in parentheses). The dependent variable is a dichotomous indicator of electoral preference in which 0 = Jackson and 1 = Herbert, the White candidate who invokes the racist message in the test condition. Implicit message condition is a dummy variable that represents inclusion in the test condition (as opposed to the control). Perception of candidates' use of race is a dichotomous measure in which 0 = belief that the candidate was "definitely not" making a racial appeal and 1 = belief that he "definitely" did, "maybe" did, or "don't know" if he did. Symbolic racism is borrowed from Henry and Sears 2000; higher values represent greater levels of symbolic racism. Ideology is measured using a seven-point Likert scale in which higher values indicate a greater degree of conservatism. Media attentiveness is measured using a four-point Likert scale that has been coded so that higher values represent greater levels of self-reported attentiveness. The following variables were included as controls in all models: participant's age, gender, education, income, and geographic region of residence.

** $p < .01$

TABLE 2.5   White participants and perceptions of candidate

Predictors	Model 1	Model 2	Model 3	Model 4
Implicit racist message condition	−4.277 (6.862)	−1.270 (6.284)	0.589 (6.340)	3.328 (27.699)
Perception of Jackson's use of race		29.653*** (6.772)	29.219*** (6.896)	28.226*** (7.149)
Perception of Herbert's use of race		−25.202*** (6.746)	−24.657** (6.924)	−24.226** (7.149)
Symbolic Racism Scale (SR2K)			0.269 (0.703)	−0.509 (1.070)
Ideology	−2.308 (2.201)	−2.814 (1.994)	−3.137 (2.173)	−0.326 (3.511)
Media attentiveness	−0.535 (4.409)	−0.751 (4.036)	−0.760 (4.053)	−4.042 (5.743)
Condition × ideology				−4.361 (4.507)
Condition × SR2K				1.282 (1.389)
Condition × media attentiveness				4.738 (7.220)
Constant	−35.322 (25.379)	−26.631 (23.936)	−26.750 (24.042)	−31.883 (28.256)
N	111	111	111	111
F		1.424	3.524***	3.236***	2.681**
Nagelkerke R^2	.037	.214	.208	.195

Note: Coefficients are generated by ordinary least squares regression (standard errors appear in parentheses), processed in four blocks. The dependent variable is a construction of separate feeling-thermometer scores for each candidate (Herbert–Jackson), so that positive values indicate support for Herbert, the White candidate who invokes the racist message in the test condition. Implicit message condition is a dummy variable that represents inclusion in the test condition (as opposed to the control). Perception of candidates' use of race is a dichotomous measure in which 0 = belief that the candidate was "definitely not" making a racial appeal and 1 = belief that he "definitely" did, "maybe" did, or "don't know" if he did. Symbolic racism is borrowed from Henry and Sears 2000; higher values represent greater levels of symbolic racism. Ideology is measured using a seven-point Likert scale, where higher values indicate a greater degree of conservatism. Media attentiveness is measured using a four-point Likert scale that has been coded so that higher values represent greater levels of self-reported attentiveness. The following variables were included as controls in all models: participant's age, gender, education, income, and geographic region of residence.

*** $p < .001$; ** $p < .01$

Herbert. At least in this experiment, neither candidate had to do anything to convince some White participants that Jackson did, in fact, invoke race. There is no statistically significant relationship between experimental condition and perception of either candidate invoking race, which suggests that their presence and, perhaps, the substance of their messages, is at least as important as, if not more than, the imagery used in generating perceptions of race being used in a biracial election, at least among White participants.

With respect to feeling-thermometer measures, the mean net difference for participants who thought that Herbert might have invoked race was 14 points in Jackson's favor (compared with only 1 point for those who said that Herbert definitely did not make a race-based appeal). Similarly, the net difference for participants who believed that Jackson might have made an appeal to race was 5 points in Herbert's favor (compared with a 17-point advantage for Jackson among those who believed that Jackson did not appeal to race). Table 2.5 contains the results of models designed to determine variance in the net feeling-thermometer calculation. Consistent with the results for voting choice, it was participants' perception that Jackson appealed to race that resulted in the greatest net gains for Herbert, and it was participants' perception that Herbert invoked race that resulted in the greatest net gains for Jackson. No other theoretically grounded predictors, including interactions between variables, reached conventional levels of statistical significance in any of the models.[11]

We are also interested in the degree to which voters might be mobilized to go to the polls to support the candidate of their choice. A number of the predictor and control variables are significantly correlated with anticipated mobilization. Education and living in the Northeast are positively correlated with willingness to vote ($p < .05$). Vote choice for neither candidate is correlated with mobilization, but Jackson's feeling-thermometer score was correlated with mobilization ($r = .39$; $p < .01$) (Herbert's feeling-thermometer score is not correlated with mobilization). Perhaps not surprisingly, the feeling that either candidate did or might have invoked race was negatively correlated with anticipated turnout, which means that such a belief is associated with less willingness to go to the polls.[12]

BLACK PARTICIPANTS' REACTIONS TO RACIST APPEALS

The existing theoretical and empirical literature is not particularly helpful as we try to develop formal expectations about how Black participants might respond to a racist message by a White candidate in a biracial election. As we previously mentioned, existing research about race-based appeals focus primarily on their effect on policy opinion rather than on candidates and certainly do not target minority candidates in biracial or any other kind of

TABLE 2.6   Black participants and vote choice

Predictors	Model 1	Model 2	Model 3	Model 4
Implicit racist message condition	−0.170	−0.193	−0.285	−1.557
	(0.418)	(0.458)	(0.482)	(3.949)
Perception of Jackson's use of race		0.396	0.573	0.481
		(0.522)	(0.552)	(0.567)
Perception of Herbert's use of race		−1.977***	−2.005***	−2.097***
		(0.532)	(0.566)	(0.582)
Linked fate			0.068	0.187
			(0.324)	(0.478)
Vote for Black candidates			−1.120*	−1.145
			(0.526)	(0.700)
Whites represent Blacks' interests			0.119	0.081
			(0.366)	(0.660)
Exposure to Black media			−0.204	−1.145
			(0.167)	(0.700)
Ideology	−0.073	−0.137	−0.297	−0.601†
	(0.193)	(0.211)	(0.232)	(0.365)
Media attentiveness	−0.082	0.396	−0.080	−0.095
	(0.255)	(0.522)	(0.292)	(0.313)

(continued on next page)

election scenarios as a principal area of concern. Similarly, with the exception of White's (2007) study on news priming, we know of no other studies on race-based appeals that assess their influence on non-White voters.

These imitations notwithstanding, common sense would have us predict that messages that play on preexisting racist stereotypes will be counterproductive to securing support from racial minorities—particularly members of racial minority groups that are targets of the attacks. Accordingly, we expected that Black respondents who viewed ads containing implicitly racist messages from a White candidate running against a Black opponent would evaluate the White candidate less favorably than the Black candidate. An additional consideration was the degree to which Black participants were more likely to differentiate between the types of appeals used by Jim Herbert. That is, we expected that more African Americans would perceive Herbert as appealing to race than Whites did. The participants for this part of the study included 125 African American adults from a random national sample. More information about the participants can be found in Table 2.1.

Consistent with group identity theory (discussed in detail in Chapter 3) and the findings among White participants, Black participants preferred David Jackson to Jim Herbert by a sizable margin (63%–37%) when asked which can-

TABLE 2.6 (*continued*)

Predictors	Model 1	Model 2	Model 3	Model 4
Condition × ideology				0.518
				(0.485)
Condition × linked fate				−0.170
				(0.648)
Condition × vote for Black candidates				0.022
				(1.034)
Condition × White officials represent				−0.143
				(0.332)
Condition × exposure to Black media				−0.589
				(4.177)
Constant	−3.528*	−4.524	−1.816	−0.589
	(2.278)	(2.468)	(3.254)	(4.177)
N	111	111	111	111
χ^2	5.545	16.812***	7.098	1.598
−2 log likelihood	141.700	124.887	117.789	116.191
Nagelkerke R^2	.066	0.248	.317	.244

Note: Coefficients are generated by binary logistic regression (standard errors appear in parentheses). The dependent variable is a dichotomous indicator of electoral preference in which 0 = Jackson and 1 = Herbert, the White candidate who invokes the racist message in the test condition. Implicit message condition is a dummy variable that represents inclusion in the test condition (as opposed to the control). Perception of candidates' use of race is a dichotomous measure in which 0 = belief that the candidate was "definitely not" making a racial appeal and 1 = belief that he "definitely" did or "maybe" did. The three "linked fate" variables are borrowed from Dawson 2001; higher values indicate higher levels of linked fate. Exposure to Black media is an additive index in which higher values indicated greater levels of self-reported exposure to Black media. Ideology is measured using a seven-point Likert scale, where higher values indicate a greater degree of conservatism. Media attentiveness is measured using a four-point Likert scale that has been coded so that higher values represent greater levels of self-reported attentiveness. The following variables were included as controls in all models: participant's age, gender, education, income, and geographic region of residence.
*** $p < .001$; ** $p < .01$; † $p < .10$

didate they would vote for if given the opportunity. As can be gleaned from the data in Table 2.6, the margin of "victory" was slightly greater (30%) among participants in the test condition than in the control group (24%). The models for understanding determinants of voting choice are also similar to those generated from the White participants, with one notable difference: It was the perception that Herbert, not Jackson, had invoked race that most strongly predicted voting choice. Specifically, as we expected, Black participants who believed that Herbert had invoked race were more likely to vote for Jackson, even controlling for demographic and other attitudinal factors.

Similarly, Jackson's net feeling-thermometer advantage greatly increased when participants perceived Herbert's message as racist in nature (Table 2.7).

TABLE 2.7   Black participants and perceptions of candidate

Predictors	Model 1	Model 2	Model 3	Model 4
Implicit racist message condition	4.390	4.137	1.398	−27.176
	(6.673)	(6.101)	(5.991)	(48.029)
Perception of Jackson's use of race		10.919	13.862*	12.205†
		(6.973)	(6.839)	(7.054)
Perception of Herbert's use of race		−32.433**	−30.671***	−31.826***
		(6.5558)	(6.402)	(6.491)
Linked fate			−2.672	1.263
			(3.807)	(5.824)
Vote for Black candidates			−14.799*	−16.400*
			(6.014)	(8.262)
Whites represent Blacks' interests			−4.704	−6.646
			(4.261)	(8.199)
Exposure to Black media			−2.344	−3.919
			(1.749)	(2.421)
Ideology	7.813*	7.104*	4.948†	0.190
	(3.057)	(2.814)	(2.871)	(4.665)
Media attentiveness	2.052	0.271	0.893	0.490
	(3.959)	(3.601)	(3.575)	(3.784)

(continued on next page)

On the whole, the mean feeling-thermometer scores did not differ much from those of the White participants: Jackson's mean was 58.96 (SD = 22.425), while Herbert's mean was 49.63 (SD = 23.047). There was no significant difference in these averages between experimental groups. It is interesting to note, as well, that the measure of perceived importance of voting for Black candidates was statistically significant in predicting an advantage for Jackson on the net feeling-thermometer measure, even though it was not significant in the voting choice model in Table 2.6.

We expected the African American participants to be more likely than the White participants to recognize Herbert's implicit appeal to race, and that was confirmed by the data, though not to the degree that one might anticipate. More than half (52.5%) of the African American participants thought that Herbert was making a race-based appeal, compared with 45 percent of White participants who had thought so in the previous experiment. While only 12 percent of Whites believed that Jackson had invoked race, 39 percent of Black respondents indicated that he did. Unlike the White participants, though, the Black participants did not perceive Jackson's invoking of race negatively, as 72 percent of those who believed that he had done so also indicated that they would vote for him. Of the participants who believed that Herbert had invoked

TABLE 2.7   *(continued)*

Predictors	Model 1	Model 2	Model 3	Model 4
Condition × ideology				7.942
				(6.070)
Condition × linked fate				−7.054
				(7.684)
Condition × vote for Black candidates				5.565
				(12.642)
Condition × White officials represent				3.320
				(9.721)
Condition × exposure to Black media				3.301
				(3.308)
Constant	−63.461†	−67.694*	1.744	27.962
	(36.259)	(32.877)	(39.302)	(53.162)
N	111	111	111	111
F	0.920	2.986**	3.063***	2.492**
Nagelkerke R^2	−.007	.177	.229	.220

Note: Coefficients are generated by ordinary least squares regression (standard errors appear in parentheses), processed in four blocks. The dependent variable is a construction of separate feeling-thermometer scores for each candidate (Herbert–Jackson), so that positive values indicate support for Herbert, the White candidate who invokes the racist message in the test condition. Implicit message condition is a dummy variable that represents inclusion in the test condition (as opposed to the control). Perception of candidates' use of race is a dichotomous measure in which 0 = belief that the candidate was "definitely not" making a racial appeal and 1 = belief that he "definitely" did or "maybe" did. The three "linked fate" variables are borrowed from Dawson 2001; higher values indicate higher levels of linked fate. Exposure to Black media is an additive index where higher values indicated greater levels of self-reported exposure to Black media. Ideology is measured using a seven-point Likert scale, where higher values indicate a greater degree of conservatism. Media attentiveness is measured using a four-point Likert scale that has been coded so that higher values represent greater levels of self-reported attentiveness. The following variables were included as controls in all models: participant's age, gender, education, income, and geographic region of residence.
*** $p < .001$; ** $p < .01$; * $p < .05$; † $p < .10$

race, only 21 percent indicated that they would vote for him. Finally (and also similar to the White participants), perception of the use of race was not significantly related to experimental condition, which means that the participants were not moved by the implicit racist appeal within the advertisement.

These variables perform similarly when regressed on the measure of whether a participant predicts that he or she would be likely to go to the polls to vote for the candidate of his or her choice. In these models (not reported), political attentiveness was a strong predictor of voter mobilization, and the "linked fate" measure was statistically significant and negative, indicating that those with greater levels of linked fate are more likely to predict participants' decision to go to the polls to vote for their preferred candidate.

RACIST APPEALS IN BLACK AND WHITE

It is not particularly surprising that the models designed to predict voting choice and candidate support have less than clear results. While there are theoretically grounded reasons to anticipate how racist messages might affect voters, much of this ground has yet to be tilled. A few conclusions are evident, however.

First, as we suspected, Black folks and White folks respond to implicitly racist messages in very different ways. While both preferred the Black candidate to the White candidate in the electoral scenario we presented to them, they appear to have done so for different reasons. For some Black participants, a predisposition toward David Jackson existed that might be due, at least in part, to the fact that he was Black. Although only 3 percent of the Black participants indicated a belief that Black voters should choose Black candidates when they run, responses to that question were significantly related statistically to support for Jackson. Much more important than skin color for Black participants, however, was the perception that Herbert had "played the race card," though exactly as many participants (52.5%) who saw his advertisement that invoked racial imagery believed that was the case as those who were in the control condition where there was no intent to invoke race. That is, Black voters choosing between a Black candidate and a White candidate may exercise heightened racial awareness and may even perceive that a racial appeal is being made by a White candidate even when no racist appeal is invoked (intentionally or otherwise). The a priori preference for the Black candidate is heightened when Black voters perceive that the White candidate is making an appeal based on negative predispositions about Blacks.

Conversely, for White participants, the most powerful predictor of support for Herbert was the belief that Jackson had "played the race card," an interpretation that cannot be reasonably inferred from the substance of his message or the content of the imagery in his advertisement. Indeed, exposure to the implicitly racist message from Jim Herbert was not an important factor for either White or Black participants. Instead, the perception that race was invoked mattered more than anything else we measured. Either participants' racial schemata were not activated by the attack (perhaps because of the unnatural situation within which they were exposed to the stimuli), or the racist message was overshadowed by other factors, such as the candidates' race or substantive message. Whatever the reason, support for the candidates was not affected by the specific absence or presence of the White candidate's implicitly racist appeal.

Among Black participants, the racial identification literature would lead us to expect more support for the Black candidate, all other things being equal. It is counter-intuitive, however, that there would be disproportionate support for a minority candidate in a biracial contest among Whites. What could account for such support when historical trends would lead us to suspect the opposite? It is possible that Herbert's message was simply less attractive to all voters. Herbert advocated support for public schools while Jackson supported funding charter schools as a way to strengthen the educational system. However, polling on charter schools shows the electorate virtually split in their support for the issue in general.[13] It is also possible that the White participants were affected by the election of the first Black president in U.S. history and therefore were simply more open to—or even excited about— the opportunity to vote for a Black candidate who expressed a message that they embraced. That is, perhaps the racial context had shifted enough, at least in the short term, to set the stage for increased support for a Black candidate in a biracial election.

Finally, we should be clear that we do not have historical data to support the notion that Black candidates are selected less frequently than Whites in biracial contests. Certainly, there have been disproportionately fewer Black elected officials than White ones, but we do not know the success rate of Black or other minority candidates when they run against Whites in various contexts.

Given the empirical evidence discussed in Chapter 1 that Black and White candidates mobilize racial appeals in vastly different ways and for different reasons, this suggests the need to understand more fully the circumstances of the messages that Blacks consider to be "too racist." Further, we need to understand the circumstances within which White voters do or do not perceive candidates as "playing the race card," especially in biracial election contests in which a Black candidate claims that a White candidate has made a racist appeal. That is, the implicit associations literature explains, and previous empirical studies have shown, that implicit racist appeals work because White voters do not recognize the underlying racist appeal as being "about race." However, what would result if the Black candidate in that scenario criticized a White opponent for making a racist appeal (e.g., if Jackson had "called out" Herbert's racist appeal in a response advertisement)? Would White voters view the Black candidate's response as "playing the race card" and respond to the Black candidate less favorably?[14] But the question is even more complicated. If the dark complexion of a Black candidate already heightens White voters' propensity to suspect the candidate is appealing to race (as appears to be the case in these results), does that make it even more risky for Black candidates (and potentially Latino candidates, as well) to attempt to inoculate themselves against or respond to a White candidate's racist attack?

What all of this suggests is that the factor we may need to most consider more fully as we move forward in our attempts to understand the impact of racist appeals is voters' definition of the "race card" and the communicative circumstances in which they consider it to have been "played." Is there a single "race card," or are there many? Do they all offend equally, or are some more tolerable than others? Are there circumstances in which the use is acceptable or even expected? For White participants in this study, the answer is not clear. Perceptions that Jackson invoked race were related weakly related to less self-reported attention to news media ($r = -.226$; $p < .05$), as was perception that Herbert did so ($r = -.200$; $p < .05$). For Black participants, the belief that Jackson had used race was weakly related to ideology ($r = .181$; $p < .05$), so that conservatives were more likely to believe that he did so, and to household income ($r = -.226$), so that poorer participants were more likely to believe that he did so.

There is no statistically significant correlation between a belief that Herbert used race and any demographic marker. Researchers conducting future experiments to better understand this would do well to test electoral scenarios not only when one candidate in an election mobilizes race in some way, but when both do (which is actually more typical in real election campaigns). We need to understand whether voters consider and evaluate a *response* to racialized communication similarly to initial appeals to race, as well as the dynamic that exists in which the initial appeal may not be recognized until a response is made.

Finally, the results described in this chapter are relevant to the existing controversial debate regarding racial representation and issues of electoral redistricting policies. This debate hinges partly on whether voters rely on racial attitudes to make voting decisions (as suggested in Guinier 1995; Lai 1999; Lublin 1999) or whether voters are sophisticated enough to sublimate racial attitudes (as suggested in Abrajano, Nagler, and Alvarez 2003). In short, we need to understand whether it is substantively necessary for members of a social group to be represented by a member of that group. Can men appropriately represent the interests of women? Can Whites represent issues that are of particular concern to Blacks? The answers reside as much in the way that members of the groups perceive such representation as they do in the ways that members of privileged groups perceive their abilities, intentions, and effectiveness in representing the interests of historically oppressed groups.

We have much more to say about the similar and differential reactions Black and White participants have to racist appeals. Because we find many of the same similarities and distinctions made when Blacks and Whites view racial appeals, we refrain from pointing out some of the broader implications of these scenarios until we have had the opportunity in the next chapter to explore the specific ways that Blacks and Whites respond to one of the more common forms of racial appeals: appeals to racial (Black) authenticity.

3

Neither Black nor White

The Fruitless Appeal to Racial Authenticity

RACIST APPEALS have long since been shown to have more or less significant effects on potential voters' opinions about public policy. While their effect on perceptions of candidates and voting choice seems to reside with related perceptions about which candidate has appealed to race in his (or her) political advertising communication, it is apparent that viewing advertising appeals by a biracial pair of candidates influences that perception. The view that one candidate appealed to race has the potential to detrimentally affect participants' view of either Black or White candidates so that, for some, there is an influence on their decision about the candidate for whom they would be likely to vote. Given the fact that potential voters' beliefs about which candidate in a contest mobilized race affects their evaluation of, and likelihood to vote for, certain candidates, it is especially important that we now turn our attention from racist appeals (studies of which dominate the literature) toward the forms of appeals that candidates of color (Black in particular) are likely to make in certain election scenarios. That is, if attentiveness to "playing the race card" seems to warrant attention in today's electoral landscape, then we need to know whether particular forms of racial appeals might also incite participants to interpret such appeals as, indeed, appealing to race.

As we described in Chapter 1, there are a variety of racial appeals that candidates of color find especially beneficial. In this chapter, we focus on one of those: the appeal to racial (Black) authenticity. We are most likely to see such appeals in electoral contests that feature two Black candidates running against each other, which historically has occurred most often in districts where Blacks make up either the majority or a near-majority of the voting population. Such appeals are increasingly relevant in today's political land-scape in ways that we discuss below.

SHIFTING ELECTORAL REALITIES

Black candidates running for public office in Civil Rights–era America appealed to masses of Black voters by claiming to be able to best represent "Black interests." Despite this, a norm of racial solidarity within the African American community (and the fact that most Black elected officials repre-sented districts made up of primarily African American constituents) made the question of race a relatively moot point in Black candidates' political cam-paign strategies and communications. In the years since, several demographic and ideological shifts have taken place, as we outlined in Chapter 2. Further, the ideological diversity within African American communities has increased, as demonstrated by a number of factors: the nonracial types of policy issues that Blacks say concern them; the increasing number of Blacks who self-identify as either Independent or Republican; and African Americans' chang-ing view of what "Black leadership" means (Bositis 2002b).

Though as a whole, the vast majority of Black voters still identify as Dem-ocrats or vote for Democratic Party candidates,[1] this growing diversity has already changed—and is likely to continue to change—the degree of competi-tiveness among candidates vying for seats in majority-Black districts. Authors such as Gerber (1996) have recognized that there traditionally has been a lack of competition among minority candidates within majority-minority dis-tricts. As the degree of competitiveness increases, however, we can expect Blacks to be targeted with a wider range of candidate messages aimed at a greater diversity of attitudes and policy issues (see Gillespie 2009; Persons 2009). Consequently, Black voters will be faced with the necessity to make more discerning choices about the candidate for whom they vote.

For instance, in the first decade of the twenty-first century, a surprising number of Black candidates have sought statewide office, and a number of them have been Republican. Michael Steele, Alan Keyes, and Herman Cain sought U.S. Senate seats from Maryland, Illinois, and Georgia, respectively, in 2004. Lynn Swann and Ken Blackwell ran for governorships of Pennsylvania and Ohio, respectively, in 2006. While none of the Black Republicans were successful in those contests, Steele was elected chairman of the Republican National Committee in 2009, and there is every reason to suspect, given Barack Obama's election as president in 2008, that the Republican Party will continue to at least tacitly recruit, train, and support non-White candidates in their bids for high-profile office in the years to come.[2]

The bulk of all-Black electoral contests, however, have taken place in Democratic primaries in areas in which—for all intents and purposes because of the partisan makeup of the electorate—primaries serve as the general election, as well. As we noted in Chapter 1, it is in these races that we have observed a trend in the use and tone of racial messages by Black candidates targeted toward Black voters that can be characterized as appeals to "Black authenticity."

The use and character of such messages are perhaps most clearly illustrated in the 2002 Democratic primary campaign for Alabama's Seventh Congressional District, which featured two Black men (Earl Hilliard and Artur Davis) running for the party's nomination (and, because of the district's heavily Democratic composition, the seat). Press accounts of the contest pivoted on the race issue, particularly with respect to the interpretation that the incumbent, Hilliard, was claiming that "his lighter-skinned opponent [was] not really Black at all."[3] Such claims were made in a number of other high-profile races during and since that election cycle, such as in the U.S. House Democratic primary contest between Denise Majette and Cynthia McKinney in Georgia's Fourth District and the mayoral race in Newark, New Jersey, between the incumbent, Sharpe James, and Cory Booker, which is immortalized in Marshall Curry's film *Street Fight*.

The demographic and ideological shifts within the African American public and the lack of empirical understanding of Black candidates' communication and voting behavior necessitate the development of a theory to guide our understanding about the growing trend and potential effects of Black candidates' use of appeals to Black authenticity in political campaign strategy. In this chapter, we offer a theory of African Americans' authenticity appeals that focuses on the following dimensions and questions: (1) the necessary and sufficient conditions under which appeals to Black authenticity are used (When can we predict they will be employed by candidates?); (2) how such appeals are constituted in common forms of campaign communication (How do we know them when we seem them?); (3) the psychological attitudes that are primed to give such appeals their weight (What is it about Blacks' psychology that makes such an appeal potentially effective?); and (4) the factors that determine the effect of such appeals (Under what conditions will they succeed or fail?).

THE BLACK BODY POLITIC: AFRICAN AMERICAN VOTERS' PSYCHOLOGY AND BEHAVIOR

The scholarly literature to date does not provide a comprehensive theoretical framework for understanding the voting behavior of African Americans or the appeals commonly used by African American candidates who vie for their votes. In this chapter, we review the extant literature that informs our theory, beginning with the psychological aspects of voting choice by African Americans and the empirical findings related to their voting behavior, followed by a discussion of broader findings related to appeals to race, racism, and identity in political campaigns. Looking at past research in this area is instructive as we cobble together the dimensions of our theory of authenticity appeals.

Understanding the dynamics of voting behavior among Black candidates within majority-minority districts is an important, but neglected, aspect of political psychology and political communication.[4] Very little is known about how and why African Americans make voting decisions generally or how they respond to political advertising more specifically. Blacks have generally been seen as a monolithic voting bloc, but this is an outdated assumption (Morris, Roberts, and Baker 2001). Accordingly, two significant psychological factors may have a bearing on Blacks' voting decisions: racial group identification and political ideology (which also relates to views about appropriate methods of political strategy). Black candidates running in districts with large Black populations and against other Black candidates, we suspect, will increasingly express these factors in appeals to racial authenticity.

Such appeals are likely to be a principal form of persuasion because an appeal to authenticity can serve as a significant marker of distinction between candidates. That is, one candidate can claim that he or she is different from (and more desirable than) the other because he or she is more authentically Black. Candidates would find such an appeal strategically beneficial especially under the circumstance such as a party primary, where ideological and party distinctions are not likely to separate the candidates. The use of these appeals is rarely mentioned in the existing scholarly literature, but more general discussions about authenticity—and, more particularly, racial authenticity—help us to provide a solid characterization of the concept that we rely on later to operationalize Black authenticity into specific advertising messages so that their effects can be tested experimentally.

As Taylor (1994) and McLaren (1994) note, authenticity is premised on the idea of originality. The concept of authentic identities associated with the individual social or political self reflects the notion that there is only one way to be (as we use it here, only one way to be Black). To claim to be authentically Black inherently asserts (implicitly or explicitly) that there is only one way to be Black—to be an identifiable member of the racial group. Thus, the appeal to authenticity is in part an appeal to racial (Black) solidarity (McCormick and Franklin 2000; Sniderman and Piazza 2004). In political parlance, this has less to do with ignoring individual differences within the Black community than with sublimating those differences for the sake of solidarity as a necessary strategy to pursue and secure a racial group's political interests. This is an idea signaled, for example, in the former congressman and Congressional Black Caucus founder William Clay's (1993) characterization of Civil Rights–era politics as one of "just permanent interests." This phrase

expresses the prevailing notion at the time that there would always be interests that are primarily based in racial-group concerns.

But the concept and appeal to Black authenticity conceptually includes
more than this. It is an appeal to resist assimilation, an idea consistent with
the notion of autonomy as used by Dawson (2001), Sniderman and Piazza
(2004), Hajnal (2007), and others. It is a call to see the Black community as
being able to operate in some ways as separate from and independent of the
norms and interests of White society, maintaining distinctive cultures and
racial group interests. The appeal to authenticity suggests first and foremost
that Black voters think about their voting decisions primarily in racial terms.
That is, candidates making such appeals seek to racialize the nature of the
election contest and castigate the opposition for de-racializing it.[5] As Hajnal
(2007) notes, in such an arrangement the claim of de-racialization by the
opposition is interpreted as an interest in moving closer to White values and
interests (primarily to gain White support) and away from one's own racial
group interests. In sum, the claim to authenticity asserts, "I am one of us, and
my opponent is not." This is illuminated by Black conservatives' characterization about the Black political establishment, as expressed by Dawson (2001,
281):

> Similarly, [Black conservatives] bemoan what could be called the
> "authenticity game," through which they claim that black national-
> ists, "liberals," and feminists attack conservative positions specifically
> and moral stances more generally by claiming that either the espoused
> practice ("acting respectfully towards whites") or its advocates (black
> conservatives) are not part of black culture or the black community.
> Yet they use the "authenticity" derived from their own blackness to be
> particularly acute and visible critics of practices, values, ideologies,
> and leaders which they claim are damaging to the black community.

Each of these dimensions of Black authenticity is expressed in the appeals by
Black candidates toward Black voters that we test below.

The concept of authenticity is also strongly related to, and is in part a
manifestation of, the tensions between myriad ideological positions long
espoused by members of the Black community (Harris-Lacewell 2006). Dawson (2001) identifies six salient ideological positions, which he is careful to
distinguish from racial identity itself, as well as the identity concept of "linked
fate," in particular. Adherence to a strong sense of individual racial identity,
which encompasses seeing one's destiny as linked to that of other members of
the racial group, may exist independently of a particular belief in or position
on what one sees as the best political strategy for pursuing racial group interests. Given the possibility that strongly identified African Americans may

espouse a varying array of ideologies and the fact that, as Dawson (2001, 61) mentions, such ideological positions are "messy," there seems to be one primary point of distinction among five of these ideological positions (radical egalitarianism, disillusioned liberalism, Black Marxism, Black feminism, and Black nationalism) and the sixth, Black conservatism: the degree to which race is at the center of and makes up the principal framework for political action. That is, for each of these espoused ideologies—except for Black conservatism—race and racial group interests drive one's view of appropriate political interests and strategies.

Along these lines, Smith (1990) argued that Black politics are degenerating because of the decreasing fidelity to which Black politicians (and Blacks in general) have, in the absence of a highly racially charged atmosphere (as compared with the 1960s and 1970s), devoted themselves to race-based politics. Characterizing the results of such a trend, Smith (1990, 161) states, "Like the transformations of Black music, it will be a hollow victory if in order to achieve equitable descriptive-symbolic representation Blacks are required to sacrifice their substantive policy agendas." Such debates surrounding authenticity in terms of group identity, political ideology, and normative practices of racial politics have recently come into questions as a divide between elected officials of the Civil Rights generation and more recent waves of Black politicians elected to office throughout the country such as Mayor Cory Booker of Newark, Governor Deval Patrick of Massachusetts, and, of course, President Barack Obama, among others (see the essays in Gillespie 2009; Ifill 2009).

Such attitudes about Black identity, ideologies, and political action have arisen from the history of American culture that has necessitated: (1) the development of psychological beliefs about the self to combat double-consciousness (Akbar 1984; Hall, Cross, and Freedle 1972; White 1991); (2) Black political solidarity to gain power and legitimacy in fighting anti-Black sentiment and power (Clay 1993; Smith 1990); and consequently (3) the entanglement of race with specific political issues or ideologies (Glaser 1995). Thus, the literature firmly supports the breadth and depth with which ideas about individual identity generally, and about Black identity particularly, contribute to African Americans' cognitive processing of political information and decision making (Allen, Dawson and Brown 1989; Gandy 2001).

In summary, it is reasonable to expect that African Americans' voting decisions will be heavily influenced by the degree to which African Americans identify themselves individually with a racial group, the degree to which they identify with members of the larger racial group, and their espoused political ideology and strategies for realizing political goals, all of which also vary with other demographic factors, such as age, income, and residential setting (see Bledsoe, Welch, Sigelman, and Comb 1995; Cohen and Dawson 1993). As Morris, Roberts and Baker (2001) point out, however, these factors are largely out of one's control at the moment when one is making a voting decision. What can be controlled and varied significantly are the kinds of appeals candidates use to persuade voters. Given the cultural foundations that produce African Americans' individual attitudes and beliefs about normative political practice, the form of racial appeal used by candidates will seek to prime Black voters' sense of authenticity in relation to the attitudes and ideologies discussed above.

TOWARD A THEORY OF AFRICAN AMERICAN AUTHENTICITY APPEALS

Mendelberg (2001) established two sets of cultural norms that essentially provide the framework for how citizens view race generally and racial minorities and race-related political issues in particular. These two sets of norms coincide less with the division between the period of Reconstruction and the post–Reconstruction/Civil Rights era. The first norm she outlines—one of exclusion, racial prejudice, and inequality—gave way to a norm of inclusion, racial tolerance, and equality. These two sets of norms are directly linked to the presence and form of race-based appeals made in political contexts, particularly racist appeals. The first is linked to explicitly racist appeals, while the second is linked to implicit appeals. It is important to understand, however, that the explicit–implicit dynamic she and others have used is considerably less relevant in the context of racial messages made by Black candidates aimed primarily at Black voters in much the same way that we noted earlier. That is, the implicitness of the message, as Mendelberg argues about racist appeals, was both a necessary and perhaps unforeseen byproduct of the new norm of racial equality imposing a societal prohibition against making appeals based on negative racial prejudices, stereotypes, and resentments. Such a prohibition does not traditionally exist within the racial contexts in which authenticity appeals have been and are likely to be communicated. Thus, there is no driving necessity to disguise (if one purposefully chooses to make it) such an appeal, and, therefore, there are no historical trends that would have forced such prohibitions to be internalized in such a way that they might be unconsciously communicated by Black candidates seeking to persuade Black voters.

The Norm of Racial Solidarity

A theory of African American authenticity appeals, consequently, must first establish the dominant patterns of behaviors and attitudes about Blackness and the relationship among Black people. That is, the following questions must be addressed: (1) What are the norms of viewing race, Blackness, and the role of Blacks in American government? (2) How do such norms relate to the various forms of political communication by Black politicians? and (3) What normative shifts account for divergent kinds of messages?

The theory presented here is rooted in a norm of racial solidarity that emerged in direct response to the newly prevailing norm of racial equality in White America that gave Black Americans space to more fully explore and express their individual and collective identities. The Harlem Renaissance, for instance, gave rise to popular expression of the Black experience in a variety of forms. We can see evidence of this trend in the birth and development of Black art, music, theater, and literature, as well as Black (or Afro-American or African American) Studies departments at colleges and universities throughout the United States. All such cultural expression, study, and intellectual and artistic development is greatly understood, in part, through the Black psychology movement that emerged in the 1960s.

The Black psychology movement was a response to overwhelmingly White models of psychology that permeated academia and practice for nearly a century. The standard form of psychology, already preoccupied with notions of individual personality, was amended by Black psychologists who posited the need for the development of "authentic" Black identities to counteract Blacks' internalized hatred of themselves given White perceptions of them (Akbar 1984; Hall, Cross, and Freedle 1972; White 1991). Where the development of Black identity was the individual psychological response to the problem of racism, the notion of Black solidarity (group identity) around the same time became the group political response. It was suggested that, to gain the political agency necessary to redress problems associated with America's racist past, Blacks would need to band together under a common banner of identity and political strategy to achieve gains in the political and socioeconomic contexts of the day (Clay 1993; Smith 1990).

This norm of racial solidarity, motivated by the need to increase Blacks' political and social capital, was expressed in myriad ways throughout the 1960s and beyond. It was built into the structure of the American electoral and governing process with the institutionalization of racial gerrymandering. It was less formally, but still powerfully, institutionalized in the development and maintenance of political-party alliances between the African American community and the Democratic Party. African Americans have long been the most cohesive constituent of the Democratic Party (Stanley and Niemi 1995; Wielhouwer 2000), a relationship dually characterized by structural dependence and group (African American and Democratic Party) loyalty (Tate 1995). Beyond the political arena, other social expressions of Black solidarity emerged in the form of economic solidarity (McIlwain and Johnson 2003), where the increase in Black wealth began to be channeled back into the Black community with a "for us, by us" mentality, perhaps first championed by various members of Black nationalist movements in the 1960s and 1970s.

The norm of racial solidarity, simply put, is the long dominant position by Black Americans that a common agenda, ideology, goal, and political strategy is necessary to gain political and social power in a country where they have had relatively little.[6] Breaking ranks in any of these areas is seen as weakening both individual and group attempts to progress socially and politically in ways that would more positively affect the Black community. It is this norm (and the recent and steady departure from it) that gives rise to the possibility, probability, and potential of appeals to Black authenticity.

Necessary Conditions

It is important to identify the individual and collective racial and political conditions under which appeals to authenticity are likely to emerge and have strategic import. We theorize that these conditions, and the possibilities of influence that resultant appeals might have, are associated with three ways in which Black voters perceive themselves within the sociopolitical arena. They include the degree of Blacks' individual identity or self-concept, the ways Blacks perceive their relationship with other members of their racial group, and the ways these identities manifest themselves in voters' attitudes regarding substantive political and ideological issues.

Individual racial identification. The Black psychology movement promoted the notion that the success of Black individuals was highly dependent on the development of a "healthy" self-concept rooted in Black, rather than White, perceptions of members among the African American racial group. This position emphasized that one's identity was essentially racial but nevertheless based on a valuation of Blackness as equal to (or, in some cases, superior to) Whiteness. This concept of what would constitute a "healthy" sense of self for the Black individual has persisted to this day as a necessary condition for proper Black psychological functioning (Cross 1991; Grossman, Wirt, and Davids 1985; Phinney 1990; Shelby 2002; Thompson 1999, 2001).

Appeals to racial authenticity, consequently, are appeals to one's individual racial identity and, more particularly, to the maintenance of such an identity. In other words, for the individual who sees himself or herself, or defines himself or herself, primarily as "African American," the appeal to authenticity works to support this type of self-concept. Acceptance of such an appeal allows one to maintain this racial sense of self, while rejecting it works to de-center or devalue one's racially defined identity—in effect, to deny one's own "Blackness."

Collective racial identification. It is clear, both empirically and phenomenologically, that one's self-identification within a racial group does not preclude him or her from having a differing level of investment in or connection to his or her larger collective racial group. Thus, the emergence and potential success of appeals to authenticity cannot be explained solely on the degree to which any individual sees himself or herself in racial terms—as essentially a "Black" person by culture or definition. Questions about racial authenticity, perhaps more so than any other form of expression, have emerged within popular and academic discussion of rap music. Scholars such as Kapano (2002) and McLeod (1999), for example, view authenticity of expression as a way to oppose the threat of assimilation by maintaining a minority group's collective identity. According to each of them, appeals to authenticity emerge when such an assimilative threat is present within a given context and the appeal targets those who maintain a sense of racial group identification, inducing a greater sense of the need to maintain racial group solidarity.

We suggest that, as a whole, such identification exists within a majority-Black district, where two Black candidates compete with each other. In addition, we posit that an appeal to authenticity will be successful because such an appeal suggests that not voting for the "authentic" Black candidate may translate into a loss of social and political capital and thereby diminish the collective power of voters' racial group members. Perhaps most of all, we expect that such appeals will be successful because they implicate the voter in these possible detrimental effects (if he or she decides to vote against the "authentic" Black candidate).

Racial issues and ideology. The final pillar of our theory regarding the conditions surrounding, and the potential effectiveness of, authenticity appeals relates to the degree that one's individual and collective identity translates or diffuses into strongly held or predictable support for specific ideological or issue positions. This may take two forms: the degree to which Blacks cite "racial" issues as the most salient political issues of importance or concern to them, or their degree of support for the "acceptable" position on such issues. We would expect that Blacks who define themselves principally in racial terms and those who identify strongly with the collective would tend to have a heightened sense of racial awareness and that such awareness would manifest itself in citing race-based political issues as being most important to them. In addition, we would expect that such individuals would take positions on these issues in ways most traditionally held by the group. For example, Blacks heavily invested in "Blackness" both individually and collectively would most likely view issues such as affirmative action and racial profiling as some of their most important political concerns and would tend to take a position in support of affirmative action and against racial profiling policies.

This third necessary condition is central to our theory because, despite the expectations above, it is quite plausible that African Americans with strong individual and collective racial identities will act contrarily (i.e., not cite racial issues as their most salient of policy issues or take the traditional stance on these issues [Schmermund, Sellers, Mueller, and Crosby 2001]). Therefore, it is not enough simply to know the degree to which individuals identify themselves racially or in relationship to a larger racial group. How such identification translates into actual political concerns and policy positions is also necessary to understanding how authenticity appeals may affect Black voters in particular.

AUDIENCES FOR AUTHENTICITY APPEALS

Even in districts with Black majorities, given the recent demographic shifts we have previously mentioned and the changes that are likely to continue as we approach the 2010 census and resulting round of redistricting, non-Blacks make up a portion of the voting population. So while it is the case that a Black candidate may appeal to Black authenticity to court the support of the majority of a district's Black citizens, non-Blacks will also (over)hear such appeals and perhaps be influenced by them in different ways from their Black counterparts to whom the appeals to authenticity are targeted. Accordingly, we attempt to learn more about the effects of appeals to African American authenticity among both White and Black voters.

Black Voters

Appeals to authenticity should be most effective with Black voters who hold strong individual and group ties to their racial group—in Dawson's (2001) conception, those who show a strong sense of Black linked fate. We argue above that authenticity appeals are likely to be interpreted by individuals with these characteristics as a threat to their individual and collective identities and are likely to contribute to a sense of guilt in weakening the collective political and social power of the community. Appeals to authenticity also would have an effect on Black voters who do not identify strongly either individually or collectively with the racial group, or on those whose identity does not translate into salient concerns about racial issues or traditional stances on racial issues. However, in this context the appeal would serve not to heighten Black voters' threat level with regard to individual and collective identity or political power; rather, it would tend to heighten their attitudes of opposition—to amplify their frustration with what they are likely to see as claims of essentialism (Delgado and Stefancic 1999). They might see such ideas as having a negative effect on public perceptions of African Americans, and they might perceive that appeals to authenticity could consequently weaken their social and political power.

White Voters

We should expect appeals to authenticity made by Black candidates to have a detrimental effect among White voters. The precise effect is less determinable, primarily because of the differential relationship Whites may have with regard to the norm of racial solidarity that underscores African Americans' political ideology and behavior. While racist messages may have a disconcerting effect on some Whites when used by a White candidate in a biracial election, the extant literature suggests that the lack of identity investment by Whites in Blackness—or, we might say, Whites' minimal sense of linked fate with Blacks—is likely to result in few Whites even recognizing an appeal to Black authenticity as such and will have a minimal effect on White voters compared with Black voters. For instance, McIntosh (1992) suggests that few Whites acknowledge their position of privilege above Blacks and other minorities. Jackson and Heckman (2002) suggest as much by identifying White college students' lack of concern over a circulated racial "hate message" compared with the reaction of Black students. These and other studies suggest that because Blacks have more of a stake in the outcome, they, more than Whites, will be affected by an appeal to racial authenticity that is bounded within the confines of a primarily African American community (i.e., majority-minority districts, where such appeals are most likely to be used). This is to say that an appeal to racial authenticity might suggest to a White voter that the Black candidate who holds himself or herself out to be more authentic will favor "Black interests" over the White voters' interests. This may be the only likely perception Whites have if they even recognize an appeal to authenticity. However, a White voter who perceives that one Black candidate does not have his or her best interests in mind politically may be influenced to choose the Black candidate who does not appear to favor the racial interest of one group over another.

It follows, then, that the tenuous relationship with, or identity investment in, such outcomes will lead appeals to authenticity to have little effect at all on White voters' perception of a Black candidate making an appeal to Black authenticity. Further, it is possible that an implicit racial appeal may not even register with White voters, and even if it does, it may not prime any attitudes or behaviors on their part. Under these circumstances, the White voter would most likely default to other determinants of voting choice (party identification, issue compatibility, candidate character and likeability, etc.), where available.

TESTING THE THEORY

We test our theory of African American authenticity appeals in the same manner we tested the effects of racist appeals in the previous chapter. The primary question is whether and how an appeal to Black authenticity affects Black and

White participants' perceptions of and likelihood to vote for the Black candidate making such an appeal.

Study Design and Data

Consistent with our procedures for the studies in Chapter 2, we employ two separate 1 × 2 post-test only experiments to test the hypotheses related to these questions. Again, pretest measures were not taken to avoid priming prior to the introduction of the stimuli. The difference between the two iterations of this study is the racial makeup of the participants (all Black in one iteration and all White in the other). Each study includes a control group in which the participants were exposed to no race-based appeal and a group in which participants were exposed to an authenticity appeal by one of the Black candidates.

Stimuli

As with the studies in Chapter 2, we used television ads from a fictitious election contest between David Jackson and Jim Herbert. While the names of the candidates remained the same, Herbert (who was the White candidate in the Chapter 2 studies) was Black for these experiments and was similar in age to his Black opponent, David Jackson. Like the racist appeal in the previous studies, the primary difference in ad content resided only in the presence or absence of an appeal to Black authenticity. Ads with no authenticity appeal served as a control for each group of participants. Table 3.1 provides the key content elements of each of the ads used in each of the present studies.

The entire script for these ads was the same as those in the studies in Chapter 2. What changed in terms of key content was Jim Herbert's race. Jackson's ad used in all conditions remained the same, free of any racial appeal. The Herbert ad that made the appeal to authenticity did so by connecting the in-group–out-group language to himself. In this instance, the images used to denote the nice, suburban (White) playgrounds and schools, and the images showing him cavorting with White college students were associated with Jackson, who, as in the biracial experiments, Herbert claims grew up and went to school outside the district. The images of the inner-city school and playground with Black kids playing basketball were associated with Herbert, who grew up and went to school in the district. The authenticity appeal thus connected the in-group to images of Blackness, while the out-group images of Whiteness were associated with David Jackson.

Participants

As in Chapter 2, participants in this study were part of a nationally representative panel convened by Knowledge Networks.[7] The Black participants included 145 adults (75 in the control group and 70 in the group with an authenticity

TABLE 3.1 Key ad content for each experiment condition

Experiment group ad	Policy-related language	Election statement	Race-neutral visuals	Racially coded visuals
Jackson control and test group	"crucial choice," "school choice," "tough standards," "right choice"	"You have a crucial choice in this election. I'm David Jackson, and I want to be your choice, because I'm the right choice."	Jackson, live footage and color still image; Herbert, black-and-white still image	None
Herbert control group	"differences between my opponent and me," "interests of the citizens of the First District," "grew up here," "grew up outside the district," "went to school here," "schools outside the district," "supports vouchers," "supports public schools"	"Who is really equipped to fight for this district in Washington: Someone who's been outside it all his life, or someone who has been part of it for all of his?"	Herbert, live footage on a busy intersection in the district; Jackson, black-and-white still image	None
Herbert test group	Same as control group	Same as control group	Same as control group	One color image of suburban school playground with nice equipment; one black-and-white image of playground with dilapidated equipment and Black kids playing basketball; one color image of Jackson, at college talking to White friends and classmates

Note: In this experiment, both Jackson and Herbert are Black.

message by one of the Black candidates), and the White participants included 124 adults (60 in the test group and 64 in the control group). Demographic information about the participants appears in Table 3.2. Participants were randomly assigned to experiment groups and, like the participants in the experiments reported in the previous chapter, were shown the candidates' ads in random order.

TABLE 3.2 Profile of participants

Black participants (N = 145)		White participants (N = 124)	
Gender		Gender	
Female	57.9%	Female	47.6%
Male	42.1%	Male	52.4%
Age		Age	
18–24	6.9%	18–24	11.3%
25–34	13.8%	25–34	9.7%
35–44	20.7%	35–44	22.6%
45–54	19.3%	45–54	13.7%
55–64	22.1%	55–64	25.0%
65–74	11.0%	65–74	12.1%
75+	6.2%	75+	5.6%
Education		Education	
Less than high school	12.4%	Less than high school	6.5%
High school	31.0%	High school	25.0%
Some college	31.0%	Some college	30.6%
Bachelor's degree or higher	25.5%	Bachelor's degree or higher	37.9%
Geographic region (based on state of residence)		Geographic region (based on state of residence)	
Northeast	17.2%	Northeast	19.4%
Midwest	23.4%	Midwest	25.0%
South	48.3%	South	34.7%
West	11.0%	West	21.0%
Home ownership status		Home ownership status	
Own	62.8%	Own	83.9%
Rent	35.2%	Rent	13.7%
Occupied (no rent)	2.1%	Occupied (no rent)	2.4%
Household income		Household income	
Median range (annual)	$40,000–$49,999	Median range (annual)	$60,000–$74,999

Note: Some totals may not equal 100% due to rounding.

Variables

Two primary dependent variables measured participants' responses to the stimuli. We asked participants to indicate which candidate they would vote for if given the chance and to rate each candidate on a feeling thermometer (the results of which are presented by way of a subtractive index to account for variability amongst participants; see Kahn and Kenney 1999; Smith, Brown, Bruce, and Overby 1999). As we did for the experiments in Chapter 2, we asked a series of questions about participants' demographic information and general political attitudes. White participants answered questions from the Symbolic Racism 2000 Scale (Henry and Sears 2002), while Black participants indicated levels of linked fate (Dawson 2001) and exposure to Black information networks.

BLACK PARTICIPANTS AND AUTHENTICITY APPEALS

We expected Black participants to evaluate more favorably a candidate who appealed to racial authenticity than a candidate who did not appeal to racial authenticity; we also expected Black participants to be more likely to anticipate going to the polls to vote for that candidate when they were exposed to an appeal to racial authenticity than when they were not exposed to such an appeal by either of the candidates. We further hypothesized that those with higher reported levels of Black linked fate would be more likely to respond favorably to the candidate who made the authenticity appeal.

Among Black participants, Jim Herbert was the preferred candidate (54%), but, as seen in Table 3.3 and contrary to our expectations, his support diminished among participants who saw him making an appeal to authenticity (48%) compared with participants who saw him make no appeal to authentic-

TABLE 3.3   Cross-tabulation of vote choice and experiment group

	Vote for Herbert	Vote for Jackson
Black participants (N = 144)		
Herbert's authenticity appeal	47.8% (33)	52.2% (36)
No authenticity appeal (control)	58.7% (44)	41.3% (31)
χ^2 = 1.698, p = .193 (two-sided)		
White participants (N = 121)		
Herbert's authenticity appeal	52.5% (31)	47.5% (28)
No authenticity appeal (control)	51.6% (32)	48.4% (30)
χ^2 = 0.010, p = .919 (two-sided)		

ity (59%). Put another way, when Herbert appealed to authenticity, he lost the hypothetical race to David Jackson by more than 4 percentage points; when neither candidate appealed to authenticity, Herbert beat Jackson by more than 17 percentage points. Although a chi-square (χ^2) test of these relationships does not yield statistical significance, the results are substantively interesting enough to warrant further investigation.

A more rigorous examination of these trends appears in Table 3.4, which provides the results of regression models designed to test effects of a number of variables while holding other factors constant. While there is no direct effect of being exposed to the appeal to authenticity, a couple of notable trends emerge. First, the most powerful predictor of feelings toward the candidates is the belief that one of the candidates made a racial appeal. While neither of these variables had a statistically significant effect on voting choice (in fact, none of the included variables did), with respect to participants' feelings about the candidates, Jackson was helped by the perception that Herbert had made a racial appeal, and vice versa.

What appears to be relevant in this context, as it was in the biracial context reported in Chapter 2, is not necessarily whether a candidate invokes race (or intends to do so) but whether he or she is perceived to have done so. A closer examination of who perceived a racial appeal reveals that participants noticed that Herbert was invoking race when he made an implicit appeal, though not disproportionately so: Sixty-seven percent of participants believed that he did so in the test condition, as opposed to 56 percent of participants who believed that his message was racial in the control condition. However, a slim majority of participants also believed that Jackson invoked race: 56 percent in the test condition and 52 percent in the control group. It is clear that, while our careful construction of text and images had the overall effect we desired, a notable number of participants did not see race when the intent was to invoke it, and a notable number did see race when the intent was to avoid it. Seventy percent of participants thought that at least one of the candidates had invoked race. Further, when a participant believed that one candidate had invoked race, he or she tended to indicate that the other candidate had, as well (r = .487; p < .001). In the test condition (in which Herbert invoked an implicit appeal to Black authenticity), only 19 percent of participants expressed the belief that Herbert had "definitely" or "maybe" invoked race and that Jackson definitely had not (as would have been consistent with the intent of the design). Nearly half of the participants indicated that both candidates had used race in the test condition, while 26 percent indicated that neither had. Similar findings exist in the control group. Forty-one percent of participants believed that both candidates had invoked race, while an additional 33 percent believed that neither had. In other words, 26 percent of participants in this study indicated that they perceived that only one or the

TABLE 3.4   Black participants and vote choice

Predictors	Model 1	Model 2	Model 3	Model 4
Implicit racist message condition	−0.027	0.024	0.107	−6.286†
	(0.396)	(0.403)	(0.417)	(3.546)
Perception of Jackson's use of race		0.513	0.482	0.513
		(0.446)	(0.448)	(0.476)
Perception of Herbert's use of race		−0.450	−0.508	−0.574
		(0.456)	(0.470)	(0.493)
Linked fate			0.175	0.207
			(0.240)	(0.379)
Vote for Black candidates			−0.303	0.142
			(0.371)	(0.470)
Whites represent Blacks' interests			0.104	0.127
			(0.312)	(0.404)
Exposure to Black media			0.004	0.035
			(0.133)	(0.142)
Ideology	−0.079	−0.076	−0.095	−0.244
	(0.145)	(0.146)	(0.157)	(0.211)
Media attentiveness	−0.102	−0.072	−0.012	−0.029
	(0.254)	(0.257)	(0.266)	(0.276)

(continued on next page)

other candidate had invoked race in his advertisement.[8] Conservatives were slightly more likely to believe that Jackson had invoked race ($r = .169$; $p < .05$), but beyond that, no demographic or attitudinal covariates are related to this perception.

The perception that race had been invoked, however, did not have a bearing on hypothetical voting choice or net feeling-thermometer scores. Substituting a measure for whether the participant believed that either candidate had invoked race into the models in Tables 3.4 and 3.5 did not yield a statistically significant coefficient for that variable; nor did its presence alter the effect of any of the other predictors or covariates.

The last consideration should be the degree to which perception that race has been invoked interacts with any of the other variables, as might be suggested by the literature and the results we explored earlier. With the exception of ideology, which has a weak relationship to the perception that David Jackson had invoked race ($r = -.169$; $p < .05$) such that liberals were more likely to believe that he had done so, no other demographic or attitudinal measures had a statistically significant relationship with the perception that either candidate had appealed to race.

TABLE 3.4   (*continued*)

Predictors	Model 1	Model 2	Model 3	Model 4
Condition × ideology				0.448
				(0.333)
Condition × linked fate				−0.042
				(0.511)
Condition × vote for Black candidates				1.326†
				(0.785)
Condition × White officials represent				0.206
				(0.692)
Constant	1.534	1.333	0.251	−0.996
	(2.104)	(2.114)	(2.580)	(2.964)
N	133	133	133	133
χ^2	18.921*	1.616	1.057	6.403
−2 log likelihood	164.184	162.568	161.511	155.107
Nagelkerke R^2	.177	.191	.200	.254

Note: Coefficients are generated by binary logistic regression (standard errors appear in parentheses). The dependent variable is a dichotomous indicator of electoral preference in which 0 = Jackson and 1 = Herbert (both of whom are Black). Herbert is the candidate who invokes the authenticity message in the test condition. Implicit message condition is a dummy variable that represents inclusion in the test condition (as opposed to the control). Perception of candidates' use of race is a dichotomous measure in which 0 = belief that the candidate was "definitely not" making a racial appeal and 1 = belief that he "definitely" did or "maybe" did. The three "linked fate" variables are borrowed from Dawson 2001; higher values indicate higher levels of linked fate. Exposure to Black media is an additive index where higher values indicated greater levels of self-reported exposure to Black media. Ideology is measured using a seven-point Likert scale, where higher values indicate a greater degree of conservatism. Media attentiveness is measured using a four-point Likert scale that has been coded so that higher values represent greater levels of self-reported attentiveness. The following variables were included as controls in all models: participant's age, gender, education, income, and geographic region of residence.

* $p < .05$; † $p < .10$

WHITE PARTICIPANTS AND AUTHENTICITY APPEALS

It is still a rare electoral occurrence when White voters are presented with a choice between two Black candidates. Even in majority-minority districts, though, White votes matter to candidates as they attempt to assemble a plurality of votes. Further, with the demographic shifts and increasing success of minority candidates, it is likely that we will see this occurring more frequently in the coming years, especially as the number of Black conservatives running in competitive contests rises, as many of them may share more ideologically with many of the White citizens in the cities and states in which they run than with other Black voters.

TABLE 3.5   Black participants and perceptions of candidate

Predictors	Model 1	Model 2	Model 3	Model 4
Implicit racist message condition	0.597	2.495	2.742	−52.033
	(6.657)	(7.094)	(6.869)	(51.864)
Perception of Jackson's use of race		15.175*	15.248*	15.322*
		(7.088)	(7.211)	(7.353)
Perception of Herbert's use of race		−19.047*	−20.009**	−20.991**
		(7.252)	(7.533)	(7.658)
Linked fate			−1.004	0.876
			(3.908)	(6.151)
Vote for Black candidates			−0.569	2.601
			(5.951)	(7.527)
Whites represent Blacks' interests			1.028	2.020
			(5.039)	(6.615)
Exposure to Black media			−1.456	−1.276
			(2.193)	(2.229)
Ideology	0.726	0.545	0.045	−2.365
	(2.394)	(2.366)	(2.557)	(3.397)
Media attentiveness	−5.059	−3.533	−3.478	−3.294
	(4.230)	(4.166)	(4.342)	(4.423)

(continued on next page)

The White participants who were exposed to this experiment preferred Jim Herbert to David Jackson by a 4-point margin (51%–47%), and, as is evident in the data presented in Table 3.3, the gap was slightly greater among those in the test group (5%) than among those in the control group (3.2%). In other words, White participants responded slightly more favorably to Herbert when he employed an authenticity appeal. White participants clearly believed that Herbert might be making a racial appeal, even when he was not trying to do so. Sixty-six percent of those in the test condition believed so, as did 70 percent of those in the control group. That was not at all the case for David Jackson. While 58 percent in the test group (where Herbert attempted to appeal to race) thought that Jackson might be making a race-based appeal, only 48 percent of those in the control group believed that he was doing so. In essence, those who believed that one candidate was appealing to race tended to believe that they both were (χ^2 = 30.172; p < .001).

As with the African American participants, the perception of invoking race was the most important predictor of support for the candidates on the feeling thermometers. In addition, the perception that a candidate was appealing

TABLE 3.5 *(continued)*

Predictors	Model 1	Model 2	Model 3	Model 4
Condition × ideology				6.236
				(5.136)
Condition × linked fate				2.394
				(8.161)
Condition × vote for Black candidates				8.392
				(11.240)
Condition × exposure to Black media				0.375
				(10.795)
Constant	31.210	26.007	23.933	206.022
	(35.640)	(34.903)	(43.041)	(177.984)
N	132	132	132	132
F	0.848	1.415	1.069	0.998
Adjusted R^2	−.012	.036	.008	.000

Note: Coefficients are generated by ordinary least squares regression (standard errors appear in parentheses), processed in four blocks. The dependent variable is a construction of separate feeling thermometer scores for each candidate (Herbert–Jackson), so that positive values indicate support for Herbert, the Black candidate who invokes the authenticity message in the test condition. Implicit message condition is a dummy variable that represents inclusion in the test condition (as opposed to the control). Perception of candidates' use of race is a dichotomous measure in which 0 = belief that the candidate was "definitely not" making a racial appeal and 1 = belief that he "definitely" did or "maybe" did. The three "linked fate" variables are borrowed from Dawson 2001; higher values indicate higher levels of linked fate. Exposure to Black media is an additive index where higher values indicated greater levels of self-reported exposure to Black media. Ideology is measured using a seven-point Likert scale, where higher values indicate a greater degree of conservatism. Media attentiveness is measured using a four-point Likert scale that has been coded so that higher values represent greater levels of self-reported attentiveness. The following variables were included as controls in all models: participant's age, gender, education, income, and geographic region of residence.

** $p < .01$; * $p < .05$

to race significantly predicted voting choice among White participants (see Tables 3.6 and 3.7). White voters who perceived that Jackson had invoked race had a higher net feeling-thermometer rating and tendency to vote for Jim Herbert, and vice versa. Model 4 of Table 3.7 shows that those with lower levels of symbolic racism were also more supportive of Jim Herbert, although the relationship did not meet conventional levels of statistical significance.

A few factors are related to participants' perception that one of the candidates invoked race. Education was negatively correlated with the belief that Jackson might have invoked race ($r = -.303$; $p < .01$), which means that those with less formal education tended to feel as if he had done so. As suggested by the previous models, the belief that Jackson might have invoked race was

TABLE 3.6 White participants and vote choice

Predictors	Model 1	Model 2	Model 3	Model 4
Implicit racist message condition	0.166	0.044	0.012	1.759
	(0.423)	(0.441)	(0.449)	(2.012)
Perception of Jackson's use of race		1.197*	1.254*	1.458*
		(0.528)	(0.541)	(0.574)
Perception of Herbert's use of race		−1.404*	−1.460**	−1.635**
		(0.548)	(0.554)	(0.583)
Symbolic Racism Scale (SR2K)			−0.088†	0.076
			(0.049)	(0.070)
Ideology	−0.166	−0.133	−0.098	0.057
	(0.138)	(0.142)	(0.143)	(0.186)
Media attentiveness	0.256	0.373	0.359	0.323
	(0.264)	(0.280)	(0.281)	(0.381)
Condition × ideology				−0.446
				(0.332)
Condition × SR2K				0.017
				(0.113)
Condition × media attentiveness				0.031
				(0.535)
Constant	−0.906	−1.039	−1.529	−2.216
	(1.731)	(1.850)	(1.882)	(2.163)
N	113	113	113	113
χ^2	12.610	8.613*	3.356†	1.897
Log likelihood	143.324	134.711	131.355	129.458
Nagelkerke R^2	.141	.229	.261	.279

Note: Coefficients are generated by binary logistic regression (standard errors appear in parentheses). The dependent variable is a dichotomous indicator of electoral preference in which 0 = Jackson and 1 = Herbert (both of whom are Black. Herbert is the candidate who invokes the authenticity message in the test condition. Implicit message condition is a dummy variable that represents inclusion in the test condition (as opposed to the control). Perception of candidates' use of race is a dichotomous measure in which 0 = belief that the candidate was "definitely not" making a racial appeal and 1 = belief that he "definitely" did, "maybe" did, or "don't know" if he did. Symbolic racism is borrowed from Henry and Sears 2000; higher values represent greater levels of symbolic racism. Ideology is measured using a seven-point Likert scale, where higher values indicate a greater degree of conservatism. Media attentiveness is measured using a four-point Likert scale that has been coded so that higher values represent greater levels of self-reported attentiveness. The following variables were included as controls in all models: participant's age, gender, education, income, and geographic region of residence.

** $p < .01$; * $p < .05$; † $p < .10$

TABLE 3.7 White participants and perceptions of candidate

Predictors	Model 1	Model 2	Model 3	Model 4
Implicit racist message condition	1.952	−0.141	−0.618	7.091
	(6.097)	(5.717)	(6.627)	(25.550)
Perception of Jackson's use of race		22.278**	22.767**	22.902**
		(6.532)	(6.428)	(6.741)
Perception of Herbert's use of race		−24.616***	−25.287***	−24.987***
		(6.672)	(6.596)	(6.796)
Symbolic Racism Scale (SR2K)			−1.243*	−1.657†
			(0.590)	(0.847)
Ideology	−0.431	0.455	1.064	1.075
	(1.931)	(1.837)	(1.829)	(2.404)
Media attentiveness	−0.056	1.642	1.479	1.874
	(3.770)	(3.550)	(3.492)	(4.815)
Condition × ideology				−1.384
				(4.273)
Condition × SR2K				1.029
				(1.340)
Condition × media attentiveness				−0.553
				(6.583)
Constant	−25.504	−29.576	−35.279	−38.615
	(25.075)	(24.542)	(24.287)	(27.680)
N	113	113	113	113
F	0.974	2.353*	2.588**	2.091*
Adjusted R^2	−.002	.126	.154	.134

Note: Coefficients are generated by ordinary least squares regression (standard errors appear in parentheses), processed in four blocks. The dependent variable is a construction of separate feeling-thermometer scores for each candidate (Herbert–Jackson), so that positive values indicate support for Herbert, the Black candidate who invokes the authenticity message in the test condition. Implicit message condition is a dummy variable that represents inclusion in the test condition (as opposed to the control). Perception of candidates' use of race is a dichotomous measure in which 0 = belief that the candidate was "definitely not" making a racial appeal and 1 = belief that he "definitely" did, "maybe" did, or "don't know" if he did. Symbolic racism is borrowed from Henry and Sears 2000; higher values represent greater levels of symbolic racism. Ideology is measured using a seven-point Likert scale, where higher values indicate a greater degree of conservatism. Media attentiveness is measured using a four-point Likert scale that has been coded so that higher values represent greater levels of self-reported attentiveness. The following variables were included as controls in all models: participant's age, gender, education, income, and geographic region of residence.

*** $p < .001$; ** $p < .01$; * $p < .05$; † $p < .10$

negatively correlated with his feeling-thermometer rating ($r = -.255$; $p < .01$), and the belief that Herbert might have appealed to race was negatively correlated with his feeling-thermometer rating ($r = -.349$; $p < .01$). Other demographic and attitudinal indicators, including symbolic racism, did not correlate with the perception of "playing the race card" at a statistically significant level.

AUTHENTICITY IN BLACK AND WHITE

Our investigation of the potential effects of authenticity appeals on Black and White potential voters, to the best of our knowledge, is the first of its kind. Thus, while our results are clear, we do not claim that they provide a final statement about how authenticity appeals might influence Black and White members of the electorate. As the number of Black candidates for office increases, and as the context of those contests shifts (from all-Black races in majority-minority districts to more all-Black and biracial contests in majority-White districts), it becomes increasingly important to understand the dynamics of the communication that takes place in those elections. While previous research on the effect of racist appeals on White voters may inform our study of authenticity appeals, it is clear that these findings are not necessarily applicable to these new situations. First, White voters may assume that candidates of color are appealing to race, even if there is no intent on the part of the candidate to do so. Nearly three-quarters of the White participants in this study perceived that one or both of the candidates was appealing to race, irrespective of the experiment condition they were assigned to, and only 46 percent believed that both candidates had invoked race. Similarly, Black voters may perceive a racial appeal in this context irrespective of a candidate's intent to employ it. In this experiment, a similarly large majority of African American participants (70%) believed that one or both candidates had appealed to race, irrespective of which ads they saw, and 45 percent believed that both of the candidates were appealing to race.

SHIFTING NORMS: AN EMERGING ERA OF COLORBLINDNESS?

One of the reasons that Mendelberg's (2001) model of implicit communication is theoretically attractive is that it is based on the concept of shifting societal norms that have necessitated and produced a dominant new way in which racial prejudices, stereotypes, and resentments are represented in and produced through certain forms of race-related language and images, as we demonstrated in Chapter 1. This is to say that the theory, in much the same way as do theories of "new racism," "symbolic racism," and the like, acknowledges cultural shifts in the sociopolitical landscape and their mutual relationship with certain aspects of the body politic, such as the form and content of political advertising appeals—racist and racial appeals, in particular. However, the lack of direct effects between the racist and racial appeals we test in this and the previous chapter seems to bear out Huber and Lapinski's (2006) conclusions about the relative indistinction between explicit and implicit appeals among members of the White electorate.

While we acknowledge how our findings here are situated within the larger debate between implicit communication theorists and those who do not adhere to that theory so readily, we do not take a position in the debate, as our tests are too distinct to lend support to one side or the other. We previously stated that we are reluctant to do so principally because our theoretical interests differ in that our main concern was with the effects of race-based principles of representative democracy, at least in the descriptive sense. Given our findings, however, it appears that the fact of the matter may be that the debate in some ways is succumbing to the passage of time and the winds of political change. Again, it has been more than a decade since Mendelberg and others first began pursuing the theory of implicit communication as it applies to racial politics and more than two decades since we were introduced to Willie Horton, the example that touched off scholarly interest in the topic. Twenty years of demographic shifts, shifting ideological alliances, and political parties jockeying for varying positions to steer the country have intervened. We have experienced twenty years in which candidates of color have felt the need for, and embraced, the possibilities of competing on a wider and, arguably, more equitable electoral playing field, and we have witnessed twenty years of shifting policy priorities within the nation as a whole and among members of racial minority groups as a whole.

Talk of a shifting new era of American racial politics, in the wake of Barack Obama's historic election and historic electoral firsts throughout the country and at all levels of government, has largely been articulated as a burgeoning post-racialism. Some form of the term or concept made headlines and was included in television news stories some 2,000 times throughout the 2008 election alone. Some may see the results showing Whites' favorable perceptions toward the Black candidate in the fictitious biracial election scenarios we tested in the previous chapter as a testament to the idea that America has somehow managed to get beyond or otherwise circumvent racial reasoning, resentments, and other forms of racial decision making. We strongly suggest that other results highlighted in our studies more accurately reflect the shift that may be taking place in America's contemporary political landscape.

The shift we are currently witnessing in American racial politics reflects what we call a norm of acute colorblindness. We use the term "acute" to signify that fact that the kind of colorblind norm we speak of is, at this point, episodic, taking place within a short duration of time, but is nevertheless intense in its expression. The rumblings of this emerging norm can be seen in a dual set of electoral realities borne out in the results of our studies here and are anecdotally reflected throughout the political landscape. On the one hand, the traditional myth of colorblindness and the contemporary fad of postracial pronouncements appear to be an increasing reality. We have a Black president. The Republican Party's chairman (as of this writing) is Black, and its previous one was Latino. The number of Latino elected officials has increased by more than 75 percent over the past decade. John Liu, the first Asian American to be elected to citywide office in New York City, was elected as comptroller in 2009. In short, these recent milestones reflect a veneer of racial equality, confirming America's ability to look beyond or, perhaps, not even consider race when making political decisions. This is the colorblind ideal as interpreted and rearticulated in conservative rhetoric.

More than signaling an electoral reality free of discrimination, however—that comes with making racial distinctions—this acute colorblindness seems to be reflected in a diminishing tolerance for and growing prohibition not only against making racial distinctions, but against talking about race at all. This emerging norm of acute colorblindness is old wine in a new bottle. The new bottle is an electoral and political landscape that has produced and amassed more substantive evidence that Americans can and have rid themselves of the racial chains that bound them to make discriminatory choices in ways that privilege Whites and disadvantage people of color, especially when it comes to the sphere of electoral politics. The racial successes in the electoral realm in particular, and in the political arena more generally, seem to be producing a reactionary disdain for talking about race altogether, much less suggesting that any kind of racial discrimination is still prevalent or arguing that race should still be part of our public policy deliberations.

We witness this in our studies when both White and Black participants disapprove and punish candidates whom they perceive as invoking race-based appeals. What is more, they seem to detect candidates doing so even when nothing more than the (Black) image of the candidate warrants such a determination. It is a feature of both liberal and conservative racial perception, and the message to both Black and White candidates seems to be: "We are willing to consider you as a candidate, despite your race, so long as you do not even vaguely allude to anything related to race." While this seems to validate the colorblind ideal, it also invalidates the possibility of any racial response—that is, the possibility that candidates may still need to point out, respond to, or otherwise resist the very real fact that prejudice and stereotypical thinking, often at the subconscious level, consistently have been, and still very much are, part of America's collective racial psyche. In the end, this emerging norm of acute colorblindness seems to uphold the norm of racial equality while normalizing oppositional discourse about and prohibitions against all manner of racial conversation that highlight racial distinction for either reason, especially to point out potential differential treatment or effect based on race. We see further evidence of this as we turn our attention toward the way that the news media report the election contests of candidates of color in the next chapter.

4

Competing Novelties

How Newspapers Frame the Election Campaigns of Blacks, Latinos, and Asian Americans

I N CHAPTER 1, we argued that White candidates frequently construct political ads with potential for racist appeal. Further, we argued that the stereotypes and prejudices expressed and codified in those ads greatly influence the image that candidates of color project to the voting public. At that point, however, our assessment of race-based appeals extended only to the visibly produced but not yet broadcast advertising spot. The previous two chapters advanced us to that next milestone in this story: demonstrating that both racist appeals and racial appeals to Black authenticity influence not so much how potential voters evaluate candidates as their perception about which candidate they believe has appealed to race. We conclude this first portion of the book by taking a closer look at mass media coverage of these contests, which represent a different and critically influential dimension of the political communication process insofar as it involves and has a bearing on candidates of color.

Up to this point we have measured the effects of race-based appeals in a relative vacuum, looking first at ad productions and then their potential effects in a laboratory setting. Yet we are all aware that political life does not operate in such an isolated void. More than fifty years since Katz and Lazarsfeld (1955) published their seminal *Personal Influence,* we understand more clearly in our contemporary age that many forms of personal and mediated communications influence public opinion about political issues and our perceptions of political candidates. At the same time that voters may be confronted with race-based appeals by political candidates or interest groups, we simultaneously engage in the stuff of everyday life. We go to work, interact with co-workers, commiserate with friends and family, and daydream. We scan newspaper headlines, amuse ourselves with political cartoons, or take in the opinions of television talking heads who analyze the news of the day. Each of these interactions with people and media sources can and does have a bearing on what happens between the time one is exposed to a race-based appeal and the time that one must make a concrete decision, such as voting. We are interested in one aspect of what occurs in the time in between.

We examined candidates' communications in the previous two chapters to better understand how race-based appeals might influence the racialized electoral playing field in which candidates of color compete. Consistent with our primary interest in how racialized communication affects the electoral hopes of candidates of color, we turn our attention in this chapter to investigating how the news media influences this process. In general, we seek to ascertain whether and to what degree news media impose racial frames in their reporting on election contests involving racial minorities. Further, we desire to understand how racially framed news coverage might serve the electoral interests of certain candidates or contribute to other candidates' disadvantage.

BLACK ELECTED OFFICIALS, BLACK CANDIDATES, BLACK POLITICS

The scholarly story about the relationship between Black politicians and the American news media begins around 1980. The Voting Rights Act passed and took root among the American electorate fifteen years earlier, bearing its first substantive fruit at the beginning of the 1970s when African Americans began to be elected en masse (in relative terms) to the U.S. Congress. Conyers and Wallace (1976) surveyed members of this newly elected class of Black officials, inquiring into their motivations for seeking office and assessing their beliefs about who had helped or hurt them in their pursuit. An overwhelming number of Black elected officials at the time reported having no qualms with how the media treated them, many of them saying that the media provided a great deal of help rather than hindrance. Despite the fact that these officials expressed almost no contention with media reporting, a small study by Anju Chaudhary emerged in 1980 that served to add texture to their claims. Interested in how Black elected officials were portrayed in the news media, Chaudhary investigated whether Black elected officials receive equitable exposure in newspaper reporting compared with elected officials generally. She found, in fact, that Blacks received more coverage than Whites in terms of allotted space in newspapers. Despite finding that White elected officials received better placement and that Black officials received slightly more negative coverage, the report concluded that the news media displayed essentially no systematic bias when reporting on Black officeholders.

In 1984, another brief report emerged, focusing not only on the novelty of Black elected officials in American political life, but also the extreme novelty of a Black candidate vying for office against a White candidate. Interested in many of the same concerns as Chaudhary, Grainey, Pollack, and Kusmierek (1984) presented an in-depth exploration of the mayoral contest between Harold Washington (who was Black) and Bernard Epton, who was White (Jewish), in Chicago in 1983. They found the news coverage of the contest by three Chicago newspapers generally unbiased. The problem, their results showed, was that despite giving Washington equitable coverage, the news media devoted the bulk of its space to addressing race, providing substantially less space for policy issues. Grainey, Pollack, and Kusmierek claimed that this was likely the result of reporters' using "news value" criteria to guide their coverage, as well as time limitations in writing their stories, and they argued that news media overly racialized their treatment of the campaign and especially that of Washington. In doing so, they argued that the news media contributed to the negative racial tenor of the campaign and, potentially, to some of the negative backlash that Washington received from White voters. Washington did, of course, win, becoming Chicago's first (as still only) Black mayor.

In these initial studies, we see a dual focus on how the news media cover both Blacks vying for office and those already elected. One focuses on aggregate numbers of Black elected officials, while another focuses directly on a single case of an individual contest. The dual nature of this focus runs throughout what is a relatively small pool of research in the area as we move into the 1990s and beyond. Barber and Gandy (1990) next took up these questions, sharing the previous researchers' concerns about equity in coverage, balance in treatment, and racial tone. They similarly went on the hunt for news bias in media reporting with respect not only to the media's issue agenda but also to how they frame news coverage of Black elected officials. Like the researchers who preceded them, they are interested not only in whether there is evidence of news bias but also in the motive behind the news media's coverage. At the end of the day, they concluded that the news media do discriminate. Black representatives were more likely to be quoted in stories about local and racial affairs, whereas their White colleagues were more frequently cited as experts on congressional, national, and international affairs. While they conceded that in most areas of reporting, the media were unbiased in their coverage of Black elected officials, they did find that the media's tendency to place candidates' names in headlines more often than policy issues or political problems reflected a more general penchant to focus on "Black American political actors' personalities, personal style, and idiosyncrasies, rather than their professional leadership qualities and abilities" (Barber and Gandy 1990, 224). While they indicated that newspaper headlines and page location were generally the most sensitive index of new bias, they ultimately came up short not only in ascertaining systematic news bias, but also in discerning from their data reporters' motivations for covering the news of Black elected officials the way they did.

In the interval between Grainey, Pollack, and Kusmierek (1984) and Barber and Gandy (1990), three significant events took place concerning Black politicians and the issue of race more generally. In 1984 and 1988, Jesse Jackson, who had held no formal political office, ran for president, and in 1988 he eclipsed most critics' electoral predictions with successful primary wins in both the North and the South. And, as we have mentioned several times, 1988 is the year that allies of the George H. W. Bush campaign debuted Willie Horton. The following year, Doug Wilder, a Black politician in Virginia, became the first African American elected to statewide office in Virginia—the heart of the old Confederacy—and the first Black American to be elected governor in the United States. The demographic contexts and electoral triumphs and tragedies that took place during this period are reflected in the next round of studies that focused attention on the news media's treatment of Black candidates. They primarily deal with the concern of the Black politician competing on a predominantly White playing field. They are more expansive in the number of candidates they consider, more in-depth in their analysis of specific issues of concern, and generally more negative in their assessment and pointed in their criticism of how the news media routinely treat Black political figures.

Arnold Gibbons (1993) produced one of the more scathing indictments of the news media in his study of Jesse Jackson's 1984 and 1988 presidential campaigns. Gibbons pointed out the persistent prejudices and stereotypes that worked against Jackson's election, particularly among America's White (primarily Southern) electorate. Beyond this, however, Gibbons argued that the news media reduced Jackson and his candidacy to a narrow range of racial attributes. He claimed that by overly focusing attention on race, the media induced voters to think about Jackson in purely racial terms, and in so doing, the media also conjured up (and linked Jackson to) many of the negative stereotypes that Whites held about Blacks. As an example, Gibbons demonstrated how the media subtly linked Jackson to issues of crime and criminal activity by featuring photographs of the candidate in close proximity on the page with headlines and stories related to crime.

At this point in scholarly assessments of media reporting on Black candidates, racialization became a primary theme. Scholars became less concerned with finding explicit forms of bias or unequal treatment in covering Black candidates compared with White ones. Instead, they shifted their critical eye to the idea that the most damaging result the news media has on the election hopes of Black candidates is that they fundamentally define Black candidates as *Black candidates,* and that this characterization dominates the nature of their coverage.

Studies by Terkildsen and Damore (1999) and Reeves (1997) reflect this new focus on the tendency for news media to racialize the campaigns of Black candidates. The former look at a set of biracial (Black–White) congressional contests throughout the United States during the 1990 and 1992 election cycles, while the latter looks at the mayoral contests in New York and Seattle, both of which featured Black candidates. Both studies conclude that, when covering election contests involving African American candidates, the news media make frequent and varied references to race to such a degree that race becomes a salient feature of news stories. Terkildsen and Damore presume (as did all previous research in this area), and Reeves goes a step further to actually test, the underlying relationship between the media and voters that make racialized media coverage problematic. In an experiment, Reeves found support for the proposition that racialized coverage of Black candidates can prime White voters' negative stereotypes and prejudices about Blacks and therefore work against the election hopes of Black candidates.

The news media frequently refers to race, framing contests between Black and White candidates largely in racial terms, which prime negative racial attitudes among Whites readers/voters, which in turn adversely affects the Black candidate in the election contest. According to these assumptions, racialized media coverage theoretically operates in much the same manner as the racist appeals we tested in Chapter 2 in that they are said to prime negative racial sentiment primarily among Whites so that those negative attitudes become salient when making voting decisions.

Domke (2001) assesses the priming possibilities of racial cues in media coverage in greater detail, finding that racial cues can produce framing effects, influencing readers to focus on certain political information to the exclusion of other information. Like most research in the area of race and associative priming, Domke's focus is on the priming effects of racial cues on voters' position on policy issues—primarily crime. Nevertheless, he effectively demonstrates that racial cues in news reporting activate and link racial perceptions with political ideology in ways that strengthen participants' ideological identifications (in much the same way that Valentino, Traugott, and Hutchings [2002] found in their study of racial cues in political advertisements). He also finds that racial perceptions and political ideology are particularly linked among more highly educated members of the public. Domke's assessment of the priming possibilities involved with media reporting also includes one novel and extremely important characteristic: He shows that the same associative priming that results from racial cues about Blacks extends to participants' racial perceptions of Hispanics. That is, racial cues similarly activate a linkage between ideology and negative racial perceptions about both Hispanics and Black Americans.

We situate our assessment of racialized news coverage among this long but narrow sphere of research about the relationship between the news media and Black and other politicians of color. Our primary interest is in candidates of color vying for political office rather than in officeholders (except inasmuch as our study includes incumbents who, of course, occupy both positions). We are interested in whether the news media presents barriers to candidates of color getting elected, therefore potentially affecting the descriptive representation of racial minority groups in the U.S. Congress. In line with the latest vein of research, we take up the primary issue of racialization—the propensity for news media to frame, reference, cue, highlight, or otherwise signal race in news stories about campaign contests involving candidates of color running in biracial contests against White candidates and same-race contests that include other candidates of color.

Having tested and affirmed the potential for associative priming to result from racial cues in political advertising, we rely on those results and the results of others' research that point to similar conclusions about the effects of news media (Domke 2001; Reeves 1997; White 2007). That is, we take for granted the possibility that racially framed news stories may prime negative racial attitudes about racial minorities rather than explicitly test that hypothesis here. We are more interested in trying to better understand the degree to which the media actually do frame contests involving candidates of color and whether they do so to such a degree that it would activate racial priming. That is, those who have demonstrated potential racial priming effects have done so in a lab setting, where participants are exposed to stimuli and immediately given the opportunity to make a decision based on what they have read or otherwise were exposed to. In this context, a story's potential salience is manufactured in ways unlike that in the "real world." Thus, while we take the potential for racial priming for granted given previous work, we focus on whether actual news stories are likely to produce the kind of racially salient content that might match that which has been manufactured in a lab.

We are also interested, though to a lesser extent, in trying to address one of the underlying questions researchers in this area have had from the beginning: What is behind the media's coverage? That is, we try to extrapolate from our data what seems to be the dominating news motivation (as opposed to individual reporters' motivations) for reporting on election contests involving candidates of color in the way the news media does.

ASSESSING RACIALIZED MEDIA COVERAGE

One of the limitations of previous research about racialized media coverage of minority candidates is its relatively limited scope and almost singular focus on African American candidates in biracial election contests with White candidates. These studies produced broad theoretical claims and conclusions based on substantial data that was, nevertheless, limiting. By and large, they consist of in-depth case studies of one or two candidates or contests. Those more expansive in scope are still stymied by the few existing cases available for systematic study at the time. Now that both Black and other minority candidates have made significant headway into federal election contests—competing more often, doing so more competitively, and being more successful when they do—we aim to build on the theoretical and practical foundation of previous research by significantly expanding both the size and scope of our data. This provides firm footing for drawing widespread conclusions applicable beyond particular cases of specific candidates and contests.

From a list of candidates and their opponents, we selected election contests involving African American, Latino, and Asian American candidates throughout eight election cycles, between 1992 and 2006. Inclusion in the data pool was predicated on three factors. The contest must have been relatively competitive, defined retrospectively as the winning candidate receiving less than 60 percent of the vote. Stories about the contest had to be available in newspapers found in the Lexis-Nexis database, the source for all of our news items. Finally, each election contest had to produce at least five stories substantively focused on the two major party candidates and their campaigns. While each of these criteria produces some limitations, it is an appropriately systematic method of selection to produce the kind of data necessary to analyze the significant breadth and depth of racialized news coverage of racial minority candidates for federal office.

The story is our primary unit of analysis. Given the criteria described above, we drew stories from a diverse array of election contests. They included biracial contests between White candidates and Black, Latino, and Asian Americans, as well as contests involving two minorities, which, in our dataset, includes contests between either two Latino or two Black candidates. The contests included bids for the U.S. House of Representatives and the U.S. Senate. Ultimately, we selected, and others coded, 2,024 individual stories. We included a number of characteristics of the election contests and stories in Table 4.1.

The stories represent forty different election contests. While 70 percent of the stories were drawn from U.S. Senate contests, a greater number of election contests represented campaigns for the U.S. House of Representatives. Biracial contests involving Black and White candidates account for the greatest percentage of stories included, and biracial contests between Latino and White candidates account for one-third. Multiple independent coders coded the stories in the dataset along four content categories, including election contest and candidate demographics; general identification and structural details about the newspaper from which the story was generated; political and campaign related content; and racial content.[1]

The breadth of our data allows us to assess the nature of racialized news coverage beyond the possible anomalies that might occur in a single election

TABLE 4.1 Election contests, candidate demographics, and number of articles coded

Election contest	Racial composition	Office	State	Year	N
Barack Obama* vs. Alan Keyes	Black–Black	Senate	Ill.	2004	317
Harold Ford Jr. vs. Bob Corker*	Black–White	Senate	Tenn.	2006	313
Dennis Cardoza* vs. Dick Monteith	Latino–White	House	Calif.	2002	215
Ken Salazar* vs. Pete Coors	Latino–White	Senate	Colo.	2004	212
Ron Kirk vs. John Cornyn*	Black–White	Senate	Tex.	2002	200
Mel Martinez* vs. Betty Castor	Latino–White	Senate	Fla.	2004	111
Patricia Madrid vs. Heather Wilson*	Latino–White	House	N.M.	2006	109
Victor Morales vs. Phil Gramm*	Latino–White	Senate	Tex.	1996	99
Carol Moseley Braun* vs. Rich Williamson	Black–White	Senate	Ill.	1992	98
Carol Moseley Braun vs. Peter Fitzgerald*	Black–White	Senate	Ill.	1998	86
Cynthia McKinney* vs. John Mitnick	Black–White	House	Ga.	1996	82
Alan Wheat vs. John Ashcroft*	Black–White	Senate	Mo.	1994	74
Harvey Gantt vs. Jesse Helms*	Black–White	Senate	N.C.	1996	72
Denise Majette vs. Johnny Isackson*	Black–White	Senate	Ga.	2004	66
Henry Bonilla vs. Ciro Rodriguez*	Latino–Latino	House	Tex.	2006	62
David Wu* vs. Molly Bordonaro	Asian–White	House	Ore.	1998	31
Richard Romero vs. Heather Wilson*	Latino–White	House	N.M.	2002	29
Richard Romero vs. Heather Wilson*	Latino–White	House	N.M.	2004	28
Corrine Brown* vs. Bill Randall	Black–Black	House	Fla.	1998	26
Rich Rodriguez vs. Cal Dooley*	Latino–White	House	Calif.	2000	24
Joe Negron vs. Tim Mahoney*	Latino–White	House	Fla.	2006	21
Henry Bonilla vs. Henry Cuellar	Latino–Latino	House	Tex.	2004	15
Stan Matsunaka vs. Marilyn Musgrave*	Asian–White	House	Colo.	2002	14
Bob Beauprez* vs. Dave Thomas	Latino–White	House	Colo.	2004	13
Mark Takano vs. Ken Calvert*	Asian–White	House	Calif.	1992	12
Linda Sanchez* vs. Tim Escobar	Latino–Latino	House	Calif.	2002	11
Mike Honda* vs. Jim Cuneen	Asian–White	House	Calif.	2000	10
John Salazar* vs. Greg Walcher	Latino–White	House	Colo.	2004	10
Michael Steele vs. Ben Cardin*	Black–White	Senate	Md.	2006	9
Bob Beauprez* vs. Mike Feeley	Latino–White	House	Colo.	2002	9
John Sununu* vs. Joe Keefe	Asian–White	House	N.H.	1996	9
Michael Pappas vs. Rush Holt*	Latino–White	House	N.J.	1998	8
Stan Matsunaka vs. Marilyn Musgrave*	Asian–White	House	Colo.	2004	7
Sanford Bishop* vs. Dylan Glenn	Black–Black	House	Ga.	2000	6
Corrine Brown* vs. Jennifer Carroll	Black–Black	House	Fla.	2000	6
Sanford Bishop* vs. Joe McCormick	Black–White	House	Ga.	1998	5
Sanford Bishop* vs. Darrel Ealum	Black–White	House	Ga.	1996	5

* Winning candidate

contest or cycle, within a particular level of electoral competition, or with respect to a single racial group. More important, the scope of the data allows us to assess the two primary issues related to how print journalists cover election contests involving racial minority candidates—the frequency with which they invoke racial references in their coverage and the degree to which their reporting "racializes" or racially frames both the coverage and the candidates involved—particularly candidates of color. In the remaining pages of this chapter, we construct an edifice, brick by brick, of divergent (but parallel) claims about and explanations of how journalists communicate with the American public about candidates of color.

THE FREQUENCY OF RACIAL REFERENCES

The dominant claim offered by most recent studies of racialized media coverage is that the news media frequently rely on a stable of racial references when reporting campaign news about election contests involving candidates of color. Thus, we begin our analysis by addressing this question: How frequently do news stories about candidates of color include references to race, and, frequent relative to what criteria? The second part of this question is, of course, more difficult to assess. We could measure how frequently such references occur in news stories about campaigns involving only White candidates, as we previously have done (Caliendo and McIlwain 2006). But that is likely to yield little useful information, given that, with probably few exceptions, racial discourse and newsworthy racial content almost always proceeds from the presence of racialized subjects, which Whites in general, and White candidates in particular, are not (see, e.g., Zilber and Niven 2000). That is, we do not generally receive, nor do we expect, much racial content from campaigns involving White candidates, especially when the majority of the voters they aim to secure most often are also White. Given few additional alternatives, we assess the relative frequency with which racial references are made in news stories by comparing their presence among and between election contests involving different racial pairs of candidates, as well as by comparing these groups with data on overall frequency.

While there may be many means by which reporters reference race—both implicitly and explicitly—three types of racial references are most common (drawn in part from Reeves [1997] and Terkildsen and Damore [1999]). The first type refers to the race of either or both of the candidates in phrases such as "the first Latino candidate," "Jackson, who is African American," or "Sanchez is Latino, her opponent, White." The news media also refer to race by distinguishing the racial makeup of the voters or district in which the election contest is taking place. At other times, the term "race" itself is used to describe some feature of the contest—for example, when a story says something like,

"Race has been an underlying component of this election." As will soon become clear, we use the number of racial references as the primary basis for each of the assessments of the use of racial references and racialized framing we construct in the remainder of the chapter. This number is drawn from counting these three primary forms of racial references. They are represented in stories that include at least one racial reference in the following way: Eighty percent reference the race of a candidate (the majority of those referring to the candidate of color); 49 percent identify or discuss the race of voters; and 37 percent use terms such as "race," "ethnicity," and "heritage" to make racial identifications.

In Table 4.2, we begin our look at how frequently these forms of racial references appear in the aggregate, among all stories and in stories from contests that include different candidate compositions. We also include several other important comparators that, as previous scholars have pointed out, may be important factors in understanding the role racial content may play in

TABLE 4.2   Election contests and candidate demographics

	% of stories with at least one racial reference (across total stories)	Mean number of racial references (across total stories)	Mean number of racial references (across stories with at least one racial reference)
All contests	25	1	4
Racial composition of contest			
Black–White	30	1.3	4.6
Latino–White	17	0.59 (p < .00)	3.6 (p < .01)
Asian–White	5	0.08 (p < .00)	1.8 (p < .17)
Black–Black	26	1 (p < .09)	4 (p < .28)
Latino–Latino	46	1.4 (p < .88)	3 (p < .02)
	χ^2 = 79, 4df (p < .00)		
Office			
Senate	27	1	3.9
House	19	0.92 (p < .45)	4.9 (p < .00)
	χ^2 = 19, 1df (p < .00)		
Story type			
News	24	0.99	4.2
Editorial	28	0.91 (p < .58)	3.6 (p < .13)
	χ^2 = 5.6, 3df (p < .13)		

Note: Data in the second column are cross-tabulation results; remaining columns are the results of means tests comparing the first-row group with subsequent rows.

news stories. The most important set of numbers to keep in mind throughout the remainder of this chapter is found on the first line of Table 4.2, labeled "All contests." Among all stories in the sample, 25 percent included at least one racial reference. While from one point of view, this proportion appears quite high—one of every four stories one might read about a candidate of color refers to race in some way—we must acknowledge the converse reality: that the vast majority of stories written about the campaigns in which minority candidates have been involved between 1992 and 2006 featured no racial reference whatsoever. One can expect to find an average of one racial reference in each story, when we consider all stories in the sample. When we include only stories with at least one racial reference, reporters use an average of four such references in each. It is telling that in more than 60 percent of stories, this average includes all three forms of racial references. That is, stories identify and focus on the race of one or both candidates, the race of voters, and the subject of race in general.

Using the 25 percent as a baseline, the percentage of all stories that include at least one racial reference differs significantly depending on the racial composition of the election contest. Biracial Black and single-race Black contests exceed this baseline, and contests between two Latino candidates do so to an even greater degree. Despite this sharp difference among the two candidate groups, both biracial Black contests and single-race Latino contests feature somewhere between one and two racial references. These numbers increase dramatically for all groups when we consider only stories that include at least one racial reference. Here, contests involving Black candidates include the greatest number of such references, significantly eclipsing stories that feature Latino candidates in either the biracial or single-race configuration. This initial frequency assessment provides some indication that the presence or absence of racial references may differ depending on the office being sought, while no differences exist between news stories and editorials.[2]

Two dual narratives take shape beginning with our initial assessment of how frequently news stories include racial references when reporting on campaigns involving candidates of color. One side tells a story from a position that acknowledges the reality that racial references are found infrequently in most news stories. In addition, when such references are found, reporters use relatively few of them—an average of one reference in a sample in which the number of references encompassed numbers as few as zero and as many as twenty-three in a single story. The other side of this story provides a glimpse into how racially oriented stories are when they include at least one racial reference. Considering only those stories that included at least one racial reference, reporters more often than not used multiple racial references, most frequently identifying the race of candidates but also often referring to the race of voters and featuring talk about "race" specifically.

Can we conclude anything about racialized media coverage at this point? Yes and no. We can say with some certainty that, while common, racial references are not pervasive in the aggregate. Their usage depends much on the racial composition of the candidates. Such references are more likely to be found and used in greater numbers in stories about Black candidates. This fact notwithstanding, racial references are commonly found in stories reporting on Latino candidates, while very few stories about Asian American candidates do (although few such stories are included in our data). We cannot yet tell, however, what this really means beyond the simple empirical fact of their presence, because counting up racial references can tell us only so much, especially in the absence of any real empirical basis for comparison.

This overall picture of racial references, in and of itself, suggests that while such references are used to signify a peculiar aspect of the campaign in question (both biracial and competitive same-race contests are quite novel in the electorate overall), adopting a common mode of referring to people whose racial distinctions are to some degree "news" is to be expected. In other words, this should not come as much of a surprise; nor should these findings about the prevalence of racial references—in and of themselves—be cause for alarm. That is, if a reasonable cause for alarm is the conclusion that news reporting on minority candidates influences people to think about the campaign and the candidates in racial terms, the evidence here does not rise to that level. We do not, however, want to downplay the significance of the one-quarter of newspaper stories that do invoke racial references and, as we show, often do so more than once in a single story.

Racial references, like any other kind, provide information; knowing the characteristics of candidates and voters—demographic or otherwise—is of public interest and consequently the stuff of news. Racial references are also powerful pointers, drawing our attention and, perhaps, focusing it on certain attributes about candidates and their campaigns. Whether these references have the ability to pervade a story to the point where we can reasonably refer to them as a "racial frame" is a different matter, and one that we take up next.

RACIAL REFERENCES AND RACIAL FRAMING

When we—like many media and political communication scholars—turn a critical eye toward the news media (on racial matters in particular), we do so with the premise that the material we are exposed to by such sources influence the knowledge we have about a given subject, as well as our opinions of it. This is to say, we investigate what we do assuming that media do affect us in important and meaningful ways. To use Walter Lippman's (1922) popular words, we each have a mental picture that represents our reality of the world; we derive these pictures largely from the media we consume, and thus we can conclude that media—news media in particular—shape our reality of public and political affairs. McCombs and Shaw (1972) and other media effects scholars who have studied the impact of news on public opinion have long suggested and substantiated the fact that the news media wield their most unwitting and sometimes insidious influence when stories move beyond merely telling us what to think about to telling is how to think about the subjects. That is, the ability to influence both individual and aggregate public opinion lies in the reality that news media do not merely have the ability to set the public agenda, but they can also frame our understanding of the issues and political players of the day.

Perhaps it is because of the normative belief among scholars in the so-called not-so-minimal-effects perspective of media (Iyengar, Peters, and Kinder 1982) that there is a tendency in the literature to conflate—at least by presumption—racial references and racial frames. That is, scholars interested in probing how the news media cover Black and other candidates of color are motivated by an overarching concern: that racial references will translate into racial readings, and racial readings will translate into racial decisions, principally those that negatively affect the candidate of color vying for election. Racial references have principally been the identifiable evidence of this possibility. As such, framing effects become the bridge between racial references and racial priming of voters. Frequent racial references presumably produce framing effects that then have potential to prime anti-minority stereotypes among readers and influence their political decisions in ways that disadvantage candidates of color. However, racial references do not necessarily constitute racial frames. We believe that by distinguishing between them, and analyzing them as separate constructs, we can more reliably and broadly assess the degree to which news coverage might in some way negatively influence minority candidates' electoral success or failure. As we have shown, racial references are just that: referents that generally identify attributes about candidates, the voters who must elect them, and the political issues raised in the course of persuading them to do so. Whether this constitutes racial framing—of either a news story or a candidate—is, quite another question. McCombs (2004, 88) puts it best, describing frames as "an attribute of the object under consideration because it describes the object. . . . [N]ot all attributes are frames. If a frame is defined as a dominant perspective on the object—a pervasive description and characterization of the object—then a frame is usefully delimited as a very special case of attributes."

Racial references have the potential to become, but are not in and of themselves, racial frames. A racially framed news story or candidate within it, in our estimation, is one in which racial references are not merely present but *pervasive*. In the following pages, then, we investigate the pervasiveness of such references in news stories about minority candidates. Of course, there are many ways one can define "pervasive" in this context. Thus, we use a variety of criteria to test our hypotheses on this matter.

HEADLINES AND SECTIONS

In several previous studies, story placement has been used as a marker of differential racial coverage between Black and White officeholders. Headlines and story placement may be important measures of pervasiveness inasmuch as they indicate the relative importance of specific stories or story content (placement) or provide a suggested frame of reference for reading the story (headlines). As an initial measure of racial framing, then, we are interested in where racial references appear in newspapers and how often such references are highlighted in story headlines. When we look at the data in Table 4.3, we get a clear picture about story placement. The overwhelming majority of stories that included racial references were located in the front two sections of newspapers. While stories in the A section tended to feature a slightly greater number of such references than section B stories when all stories were considered, that number and the difference between the two sections was slight. This is consistent with the fact that racial references appear relatively infrequently in news stories as a whole. Looking only at stories with at least one racial reference, the average number of references per story again increases, with no difference in section A and section B stories. Section C stories, however, featured the greatest numbers of racial references.

To some degree, section location loses meaning when we consider that in some newspapers, sections can include as many as thirty to forty pages. Also,

TABLE 4.3   Racial references and story placement

	% story placement (across stories with at least one racial reference)	Mean number of racial references (across total stories)	Mean number of racial references (across stories with at least one racial reference)
Section A	60	1.1	4.3
Section B	32	0.68 (p < .00)	3.8 (p < .18)
Section C	7	2.3 (p < .00)	7.6 (p < .00)
Section D	2	0.96 (p < .81)	5.9 (p < .34)
	$\chi^2 = 13$, 4df (p < .01)		
Front page	17	3.2	4.7
Other page	83	2.4 (p < .00)	4.0 (p < .15)
	$\chi^2 = 6.9$, 1df (p < .01)		
Headline	16	8.6	8.6
Not in headline	84	0.68 (p < .00)	3.3 (p < .15)
	$\chi^2 = 295$, 1df (p < .00)		

Note: Data in the second column are cross-tabulation results; the remaining columns are means tests comparing the first-row categories with subsequent rows. N for all stories = 2,424. N for stories with at least one racial reference = 599.

story placement is somewhat idiosyncratic in that in some papers, section A is the "politics," "state," "local," or other such section, while others may locate such stories in section B, D, or G. So in some respects, the most meaningful difference—and the one in which we place the greatest stock—is singular: Does the story appear on the front page or not? Most of the time, stories that make one racial reference or more are not located on the front pages of newspapers. In the few instances that they do appear on the front pages, stories (considering them all) feature between three and four such references, and when we consider only those stories with at least one reference, that number increases to between four and five.

References to race in headlines may be the most salient single indicator of racial framing because the very purpose of headlines is to tell readers, "This is what this story is about." Thus, the mean number of racial references included in all stories speaks volumes. In the relatively rare instance that a racial reference is indicated in a headline—in all stories and in only those that include at least one racial reference—the story includes close to nine racial references.

At this juncture in our unfolding story about the news media's propensity to racially frame election contests that include candidates of color, results continue to indicate dual readings. Are racial references pervasive when we consider the placement of the stories in which they are found and the degree to which such references are featured in headlines? Overall, no, but sometimes yes. In sum, results thus far indicate that journalists infrequently impose a racial frame on stories involving candidates of color; they select only certain stories to consciously and explicitly highlight the racial dynamics of the candidates themselves and their campaigns. Before we can answer the question about racial framing more definitively, however, we must consider other measures of racial pervasiveness in stories.

THREE MEASURES OF RACIAL SALIENCE

The frequency of racial references in individual news stories and the placement of such stories within newspapers may be initial indicators of potential racial framing. However, the mere practice of reading tells us that racial references alone do not necessarily enact a racial filter by which we interpret an entire news story. The salience with which race and racial references appear when reading stories about election contests involving minority candidates is the best measure of pervasiveness, of determining the degree of racial framing that exists and the potential for such frames to produce framing effects among readers. We argue that racial salience is highly dependent on three key factors: the length of an individual story; the presence of nonracial content in a single story; and the racial content of all stories over the period of time readers may read them. We developed several Racial Framing Indexes (RFIs) to test these three elements of racial framing in news stories.

Racial Framing and Story Length

First, we argue that the racial elements of a news story are more prominent when the ratio of racial references to story length is high to low, respectively. Simply put, a person is more likely to think racially about a two-hundred-word story that makes four racial references than he or she would when reading a one-thousand-word story with the same number of racial references. Our first Racial Framing Index (RFI-1) measures the depth of racial content in stories by adding together the total number of racial references in a story and then dividing it by the length of the story (measured by the number of words).[3] Scores on the scale range from 0 to 100 (though the vast majority of scores fall between 0 and 11.11), with higher scores reflecting greater racial density.

Consistent with the presence and number of racial references found in all stories (compared with only those stories that include at least one racial reference), the mean RFI-1 score is .20 for the former and .85 for the latter (Table 4.4). When we look at the racial density of news stories where the racial composition of the candidates in the contest differs, we see that biracial Black stories are more racially concentrated than all others, irrespective of whether we consider all stories or only those with at least one reference. In every instance

TABLE 4.4 Racial framing and story length

	Total stories		Stories with at least one racial reference	
	Mean RFI-1 (sample mean = 0.20)	N	Mean RFI-1 (sample mean = 0.85)	N
Racial makeup of contest				
Black–White	0.33	1,048	1.14	300
Latino–White	0.09 (p < .03)	827	0.55 (p < .09)	139
Asian–White	0.01 (p < .00)	83	0.28 (p < .02)	4
Black–Black	0.14 (p < .27)	349	0.56 (p < .09)	87
Latino–Latino	0.22 (p < .29)	88	0.47 (p < .05)	40
Latino–White	0.09 (p < .00)	827	0.55 (p < .32)	139
Office				
House	0.15	764	0.82	144
Senate	0.23 (p < .26)	1,631	0.87 (p < .84)	426
Story section				
Front page	0.13	331	0.43	98
Not front page	0.22 (p < .09)	2,064	0.94 (p < .02)	472

Note: Data are the results of means tests comparing the first row of each set with subsequent rows, with one exception: The last row under "Racial makeup of contest" compares Latino–White contests with Latino–Latino contests.

except one (Latino versus Latino contests), scores for the biracial–Black contests exceed the sample mean, while the others fall well below.

Stories that do not appear on the front pages of newspapers are also more racially concentrated than front-page stories. It is important to note that index scores of stories found beyond the front page also exceed the sample mean, similar to the mean scores for biracial Black contests. Thus, when we measure racial framing as a ratio of numbers of racial references to story length, we again find that the density of racial content in most news stories is quite diffuse. However, when we exclude stories with no racial content, the racial content of most news stories is somewhat dense (though still quite low)—stories about Black candidates running against White candidates in particular.

Racial Framing and Nonracial Content

Like the racial concentration or density of stories, we argue that the degree of racial salience in a given story is likely enhanced by the absence of nonracial content. Like many of the preceding studies of racialized news coverage, we contrast the presence of racial content in news stories with arguably more important and pertinent content about candidates seeking to represent por-

TABLE 4.5 Racial framing and nonracial content (issues)

	Total stories		Stories with at least one racial reference	
	Mean RFI-2 (sample mean = 0.51)	N	Mean RFI-2 (sample mean = 1.97)	N
Racial makeup of contest				
Black–White	0.63	550	1.91	182
Latino–White	0.33 (p < .00)	485	1.83 (p < .81)	88
Asian–White	0.05 (p < .01)	55	0.86 (p < .06)	3
Black–Black	0.90 (p < .12)	147	2.82 (p < .05)	47
Latino–Latino	0.35 (p < .24)	43	0.93 (p < .09)	16
Latino–White	0.33 (p < .91)	485	1.83 (p < .14)	88
Office				
House	0.37	387	2.34	62
Senate	0.58 (p < .04)	893	1.87 (p < .21)	274
Story section				
Front page	0.68	188	2.0	64
Not front page	0.49 (p < .12)	1,092	1.9 (p < .88)	272

Note: Data are the results of means tests comparing the first row of each set with subsequent rows, with one exception: The last row under "Racial makeup of contest" compares Latino–White contests with Latino–Latino contests.

tions of the American public in public office: substantive policy issues. Our second Racial Framing Index (RFI-2) measures racial salience in terms of the ratio of racial references to policy issues mentioned. We constructed the RFI-2 by subtracting the total number of issues mentioned in a story from the total number of racial references the story included. Higher scores indicate potentially greater racial salience, while lower scores indicate potentially higher issue salience. The mean RFI-2 score was .51 for all stories and 1.97 for stories with one racial reference or more.

Considering racial salience as a comparison between the prominence of racial versus issue content, we see in Table 4.5 that the story changes in several respects. First, biracial Black contests shift to second place behind contests including two Black candidates (in both samples). Second, contests including Latino candidates rise higher on the ladder, with biracial Latino contests scoring equally with biracial Black contests in both samples and same-race Latino contests in the sample of all stories. Third, among all stories, Senate contests score higher than those about House candidates. The backdrop to each of the individual group scores, however, is the caveat that the index scores are extremely low. Potentially scoring as high as 18, the average story in these samples does not exceed 2 points.

Racial Framing and the News Campaign

By using RFI-1 as a measure of racial framing, we argue that a reader is more likely to think of race when reading a story that is three paragraphs long with many racial references than when reading a ten-paragraph story with the same number of racial references. With RFI-2 we argue that a racial framing effect is more likely to occur when a reader reads a story with many racial references and no substantive political issues than when he or she is reading a story that has the same number of racial references but also talks about education, health care, or the environment. With our third measure, RFI-3, we argue that we should consider the racial salience of all of the stories in a given contest. That is, it makes sense to measure the degree of racial framing that exists of the "news campaign" as a whole. If story length and nonracial content mitigates racial salience, the total number of articles written about each individual campaign may also influence racial salience, especially for those who might read stories throughout a given campaign cycle. In addition, the length of the time period in which these stories appears is likely to be a factor. Thus, we composed our third Racial Framing Index (RFI-3) by dividing the total number of racial references in each story by both the number of total stories included about each contest and the length of the news campaign cycle, measured as the difference between the month of the first and last stories.

TABLE 4.6 Racial framing and the news campaign

	Total stories		Stories with at least one racial reference	
	Mean RFI-3 (sample mean = 0.59)	N	Mean RFI-3 (sample mean = 2.5)	N
Racial makeup of contest				
Black–White	0.75	1,048	2.6	300
Latino–White	0.16 (p < .00)	827	0.94 (p < .03)	139
Asian–White	0.26 (p < .02)	83	5.4 (p < .08)	4
Black–Black	1.1 (p < .28)	349	4.6 (p < .14)	87
Latino–Latino	0.78 (p < .88)	88	1.7 (p < .53)	40
Latino–White	0.16 (p < .00)	827	0.94 (p < .00)	139
Office				
House	1.1	764	6.0	144
Senate	0.33 (p < .00)	1,631	1.3 (p < .00)	426
Story section				
Front page	0.48	331	1.6	98
Not front page	0.60 (p < .37)	2,064	2.6 (p < .31)	472

Note: Data are the results of means tests comparing the first row of each set with subsequent rows, with one exception: The last row under "Racial makeup of contest" compares Latino–White contests with Latino–Latino contests.

Here again (Table 4.6), contests between two Latino candidates and any contest that included a Black candidate produced the highest scores throughout a campaign cycle, indicating that stories about these campaigns more consistently feature racial content than others. This reflects several types of campaign news scenarios. On the one hand, it might be a contest like the congressional race in Georgia between Sanford Bishop and Dylan Glenn (RFI-3 score of 53)—two Black candidates—in 2000 or against Darrel Ealum (RFI-3 score of 49), a White candidate, in 1996. The news campaign lasted for three months in the former and four months in the latter. The first contest included six stories; the second, five; and the average number of racial references per story in each campaign was 10.6. Here we have a news campaign with higher racial salience because of the high average number of racial references within a concentrated time frame. On the other hand, RFI-3 results also reflect a contest like the congressional race between Henry Bonilla and Henry Cuellar (RFI-3 score of .33), two Latino candidates in South Texas, in 2004. In this case, there was an eight-month news cycle in which racial references appeared an average of 4.5 times per story in a news campaign that consisted of only fifteen stories—not proportional with the time frame compared with the Bishop campaigns.

Again, although we cannot compare these scores to any objective measure of racial framing, we can say that when we think about the possibility that news reporting on campaigns involving minority candidates are racially framed, the likelihood is greatest for those contests to have higher RFI-3 scores. That is, voters are exposed to news media over a period of time prior to making a voting decision about particular candidates. The degree to which that decision will be filtered through a racial lens depends highly on the degree to which news reporting consistently focuses on racial elements of the contest over that full period of time. Of course, it is certainly possible for a reader to pick up the paper only days before an election and therefore be influenced by the racial nature of coverage in such a way that it forms a basis for his or her decision.

However, we believe that this possibility is greater if one has been exposed to and has developed a racial frame of reference for the election contest that has been solidified over a period of time. Race is more likely to be a conscious influence on the voting decisions of those who have read news coverage through a racial lens over three months of a campaign cycle than for those who have read several racially framed news stories the week prior to an election. That is, the primacy effect will be greater than the recency effect because initial racially framed stories about the campaign would be followed by consistent racially framed coverage, where consistent, continual coverage strengthens the cumulative effect of the articles read first (see Hovland 1957).

A Multidimensional Model of Racial Framing

We use three different measures of racial framing. Each on its own sheds significant light on how we might determine whether and to what degree stories and election contests are framed in racial terms. These are different analytical methods for measuring the kind of pervasiveness indicative of consistent and durable news frames. Given the relative change with each new measure, we combine the three to form a model of racial framing that takes into account the number of racial references in stories and across all stories throughout an individual election contest, the length of each story, and the amount of non-racial content that accompanies racial references. Putting these dimensions together provides as clear a picture as possible. Our fourth Racial Framing Index (RFI-4) accordingly is computed by adding the scores on each index and dividing by the total number scores included in the calculation (three).

The resulting scores are shown in Table 4.7. Here we have a final set of pictures reflecting the degree to which we consider stories about minority

TABLE 4.7 Multidimensional model of racial framing

	Total stories		Stories with at least one racial reference	
	Mean RFI-4 (sample mean = 0.87)	N	Mean RFI-4 (sample mean = 3.3)	N
Racial makeup of contest				
Black–White	1.1	550	3.2	182
Latino–White	0.48 (p < .00)	485	2.6 (p < .19)	88
Asian–White	0.15 (p < .01)	55	2.8 (p < .52)	3
Black–Black	1.8 (p < .05)	147	5.5 (p < .02)	47
Latino–Latino	0.71 (p < .14)	43	1.9 (p < .19)	16
Latino–White	0.48 (p < .27)	485	2.6 (p < .15)	88
Office				
House	0.88	387	5.5	62
Senate	0.85 (p < .91)	893	2.8 (p < .00)	274
Story section				
Front page	0.98	188	2.9	64
Not front page	0.85 (p < .50)	1,092	3.4 (p < .30)	272

Note: Data are the results of means tests comparing the first row of each set with subsequent rows, with one exception: The last row under "Racial makeup of contest" compares Latino–White contests with Latino–Latino contests.

candidates to be racially framed. With a maximum possible score of 53, the average score for each sample fell shy of even 1 point among all stories and just exceeded 3 points among only those stories that included at least one racial reference. That is, no matter what category of stories we consider, the pervasiveness of racial content in news stories in the aggregate is extremely low. Stories about campaigns that included two Black candidates were more racially salient than all others, and when it came to just those stories in which one or racial reference or more were found, contests for the House were more racially salient than those for the U.S. Senate.

If "pervasiveness"—whether measured by the story or by the election contest—is the primary criteria we use to determine whether racial references can and do constitute racial frames, then the results thus far strongly indicate that the frequency of racial references alone is not an adequate representation of racial framing. But this is not sufficient cause to close the book on racial framing just yet. We want to consider one additional aspect that may figure into racial framing and revisit another before we provide an explanation for these results overall.

CANDIDATES' CHARACTER, POLICY ISSUES, AND RACIAL FRAMING

We measure racial framing primarily as a constellation of factors—how many racial references are used in a story, how long the story is, how much nonracial content is present, and the total number of stories written about the campaign—whose paths might coincide in such a way so as to make race a prominent, if not the most prominent, feature of a story. But there are other things to consider. As we mentioned earlier, including a photograph of a candidate—particularly a minority candidate—is also a means of referring to race. In addition, at some point in a campaign the voters are quite likely to come to know that one of the candidates is a racial minority. Even if they are not reminded of such in the actual text of news stories, they are reminded when they see a photograph. Image of candidates appeared in more than one-third of stories overall and in half of the stories that included at least one racial reference.[4]

We point this out as a way to say that news stories can refer to race in at least one other way than we have considered in our measures thus far. If a reader knows full well, for instance, that Harold Ford Jr. is Black, the news story that he or she reads may take on some racial dimension given that fact alone. That is, readers will bring their own racial knowledge about candidates (information and feelings drawn from advertisements and other communications, for instance) to bear on how they read and interpret stories even if the stories do not make racial references. What this means is that news media might unwittingly reinforce societal presumptions or prejudices about minority candidates by featuring certain forms of nonracial content. One of the ways this may be done is by focusing coverage on character-related issues either in addition to or instead of referring to race.

In Chapter 1, we demonstrated that character content is often the way in which subtle racial appeals are deployed in candidates' political ads. That is, racial stereotypes are often mobilized through the medium of character attacks. While they are not likely framed as attacks against a given candidate by the media in news reporting, character content may nevertheless serve as an associative cue for those who are aware that a racial minority candidate is involved in the contest. Thus, if we know the degree to which character content is present in news stories about minority candidates, we may be able to evaluate the broader significance of the media's use of racial references in news reporting and whether there is adequate cause for concern.

To fully assess this, we must answer several related sets of questions. First, how frequently is a candidate's character mentioned in stories, and to what degree is the presence of character content related to the racial makeup of contests and the presence and number of racial references included? The

TABLE 4.8   Racial references in stories with character content

	Stories in which character is mentioned		Number of racial references in story	
	% of stories	N	Mean	N
All stories	31	2,424		
Racial composition of contest				
Black–White	33	1,051		
Latino–White	20	830		
Asian–White	23	83		
Black–Black	53	351		
Latino–Latino	36	88		
$\chi^2 = 132$, 8df (p < .00)				
Stories with at least one racial reference	36	599		
$\chi^2 = 8.6$, 1df (p < .00)				
Character mentioned (across all stories)				
Yes			1.2	747
No			0.87 (p < .00)	1,646
Character mentioned (across stories with at least one racial reference)				
Yes			4.4	208
No			4.0 (p < .16)	362

Note: Chi-square tests were used to compare the percentages of stories with character content among each group of contests, and between stories that had at least one racial reference versus those that did not. Means tests were used to compare the numbers of racial references found in stories that had character content versus those that did not.

overall presence of character content in stories provides a basis for comparing the presence of particular minority group candidates and the presence of character content; it also informs us about whether character content in stories is more pronounced when minorities are the sole subject of election news coverage. We see these results in Table 4.8. Candidates' character is mentioned in 31 percent of all stories and only slightly more in stories with at least one racial reference. Stories about same-race Black contests contain a significantly greater proportion of references than all others. This means that the number of racial references in stories moderately increases when character content is included. The correlation between the racial makeup of contests and character references is significant, though not extremely strong, except for stories about those contests in which both candidates were Black.

TABLE 4.9   Racial and character references in stories with issue content

| | Stories in which at least one issue is mentioned | | | | Number of issue references in story | |
| | Across all stories | | Across stories with at least one racial reference | | | |
	% of stories	N	% of stories	N	Mean	N
Racial composition of contest						
Black–White	54	1,067	64	319		
Latino–White	59	831	64	143		
Asian–White	66	83	75	4		
Black–Black	43	355	57	93		
Latino–Latino	49	88	40	40		
Character mentioned	61	748	32	209		
Story includes at least one racial reference						
Yes					1.8	574
No					1.2 (p < .00)	1,816

Note: Frequency data are presented for the presence of issue content among each group of contests. Means tests were used to compare the numbers of issues discussed in stories that had at least one racial reference versus those that did not.

Before we draw any conclusions about what these findings mean, one additional set of questions is worth pursuing. Consistent with our earlier thinking, references to candidates' character are likely to be more salient when they are the most significant element of a story. Thus, one way to discern whether the discussion of character may take on a negative tone is to determine the degree to which it does or does not appear alongside political content that many Americans consider most appropriate in political discourse (i.e., discussion of substantive policy issues). Table 4.9 speaks volumes in this respect. On the whole, stories featuring character content also feature almost twice the number of policy issues. Almost half of the stories about same-race Black contests in the full sample and more than half in the sample limited to stories with one racial reference or more also included at least one mention of an issue. Further, the average number of issues mentioned increased when character references were included alongside racial content.

Character references appear fairly frequently in news stories about minority candidates. However, based on these data, the propensity for news stories to feed the racially associative activity of readers does not appear to be great. These results suggest that when character references do come up, they are likely to accompany a racial reference. However, the existence of more references does not suggest protracted attention to a candidate's character. Further, the degree to which racial and character references are used is highly mitigated by the number of policy issues present.

RACIAL FRAMING: WHAT IS REALLY GOING ON?

Whether we consider the presence of racial references alone or the degree to which their salience is mitigated by the length of stories, the presence of nonracial content, the number of stories produced across the duration of the news campaign, or with respect to character or issue content, we draw the following unequivocal conclusion: A widespread pattern or practice of creating durable and consistent racial frames does not exist when it comes to how journalists report on federal election contests involving candidates of color. When we consider the available stories across the racial and electoral spectrum from the past eight election cycles, the proportion of racial references included in such stories is relatively small, and their salience is likely even lower when we consider all of the factors that might influence the potential that readers will be led to read, interpret, and judge stories and the candidates and campaigns they report on through the prism of race.

The data do not, however, suggest that none of the stories, or even election contests, is racially framed by the journalists who cover them. In fact, the evidence here strongly demonstrates that, while racial frames on a whole are not prominent features of news stories, journalists do select certain stories, certain contests, and certain categories of contests to report on through at least a moderately racial lens. The evidence shows a distinct pattern in the frequency, density, and likely salience of racial content that leads us to conclude that journalists make this choice consciously and deliberately. That is, the evidence suggests that, more often than not, journalists say things like, "We are going to cover the racial dimension of this contest in this story," rather than decide up front or throughout a campaign that "this contest *is* about race." Further, the evidence here not only provides insight into the empirical patterns of content found in news stories, but also gives us some inclination about the potential motivations or interests underlying the ways journalists convey information about minority candidates to the news-reading public.

Looking at the evidence on the basis of individual contests provides further corroboration of the conclusion that certain contests selectively produce stories with greater and more salient racial content, as opposed to racial content being a general feature of news stories about candidates of color. Table 4.10 lists the RFI scores for each contest, beginning with and sorted in descending order based on the RFI-4 scores, our overall measure of racial framing. From simple visual observation, the contests break out into five tiers, with

TABLE 4.10 Mean Racial Framing Index (RFI) scores by election contest

Election contest	Mean RFI-4	Mean RFI-1	Mean RFI-2	Mean RFI-3
Tier 1				
Sanford Bishop vs. Darrel Ealum	30.54	1.93	6.5	53
Sanford Bishop vs. Dylan Glenn	30.32	1.06	1.2	49.07
Tier 2				
Sanford Bishop vs. Joe McCormick	9.09	0.20	2.75	7
Michael Steele vs. Ben Cardin	6.02	1.07	1.12	25.92
Corrine Brown vs. Bill Randall	2.33	0.23	1.22	3.55
Tier 3				
Ron Kirk vs. John Cornyn	1.92	0.18	1.34	0.14
Harvey Gantt vs. Jesse Helms	1.70	1.69	1.24	0.57
Victor Morales vs. Phil Gramm	1.67	0.37	1.26	0.31
Carol Moseley Braun vs. Rich Williamson	1.41	0.42	0.83	0.18
Cynthia McKinney vs. John Mitnick	1.31	0.71	0.81	0.57
Mike Honda vs. Jim Cunneen	1.20	0.06	0.44	0.5
Mel Martinez vs. Betty Castor	1.05	0.17	0.68	0.59
Alan Wheat vs. John Ashcroft	1.05	0.16	0.57	0.74
Tier 4				
Henry Bonilla vs. Ciro Rodriguez	0.92	0.28	0.44	0.95
Barack Obama vs. Alan Keyes	0.71	0.11	0.56	0.03
Stan Matsunaka vs. Marilyn Musgrave	0.68	0.04	0.06	2.04
Rich Rodriguez vs. Cal Dooley	0.51	0.13	0.27	0.54
Denise Majette vs. Johnny Isackson	0.48	0.13	0.21	0.42
Harold Ford Jr. vs. John Corker	0.44	0.10	0.35	0.02
Carol Moseley Braun vs. Peter Fitzgerald	0.39	0.10	0.28	0.08
Richard Romero vs. Heather Wilson	0.26	0.09	0.16	0.31
Patricia Madrid vs. Heather Wilson	0.25	0.02	0.19	0.03
Stan Matsunaka vs. Marilyn Musgrave	0.19	0.01	0.1	0.17
Joe Negron vs. Tim Mahoney	0.19	0.00	0.08	0.22
Ken Salazar vs. Pete Coors	0.14	0.03	0.10	0.03
Corrine Brown vs. Jennifer Carroll	0.11	0.01	0.04	0.16
Dennis Cardoza vs. Dick Monteith	0.10	0.02	0.07	0.00
Tier 5				
David Wu vs. Molly Bordonaro	0	0	0	0
Richard Romero vs. Heather Wilson	0	0.05	0	0.29
Michael Pappas vs. Rush Holt	0	0	0	0
Linda Sanchez vs. Tim Escobar	0	0.05	0	0.41
John Sununu vs. Joe Keefe	0	0	0	0
John Salazar vs. Greg Walcher	0	0	0	0
Henry Bonilla vs. Henry Cuellar	0	0.03	0	0.33
Mark Takano vs. Ken Calvert	0	0	0	0
Bob Beauprez vs. Mike Feeley	0	0	0	0

tier-one contests reflecting an extremely high degree of racial framing (relative to the other contests); tier-two contests, a moderately high degree; tier-three contests, some degree of racial framing; tier-four contests, little racial framing; and tier-five contests, no racial framing at all. So what about the contests at each level can tell us anything about what may have contributed to the high or low degree of racial framing?

Racial Novelty, Racial News

When Sanford Bishop, a newcomer to congressional politics, ran for office for the first time in 1992 and ran for re-election in 1994, he defeated his Republican opponents by 64 and 66 points, respectively. During that time, Georgia's Second Congressional District was a newly apportioned majority-Black district. He defeated his 1996 opponent, Darrel Ealum, but not as handily, winning by a margin of only 8 points. But this was also not the same district it had been in 1994. When he was first elected, Bishop, who is Black, represented a mostly Black district. By 1996, the Supreme Court had overturned the ruling that had created Bishop's majority-Black district. So when he ran against Ealum, who is White, Bishop had to compete for the votes of a new majority—60 percent of the new district's White citizens. This was quite a novelty at the time (and still is). When Bishop faced Dylan Glenn in 2000, the campaign was distinguished in another way: Glenn was also Black. Here were two Black candidates—one a Democrat, the other a Republican—vying for the votes of mostly White citizens. (Bishop won by 6 points.) Thus, in these two cases, racial novelty about the candidates and the voters likely contributed to the highly racially framed stories. Adding to the racial drama was the probable hurdle that Bishop—and, later, Glenn—would have to clear to persuade the majority White citizenship of a rural Georgia district that Black men could represent White folks' interests (and in Bishop's case in 1996, that he could do so more effectively than a rural White Georgia citizen).

We also see Bishop atop the tier-two contests. Again, the Black–White makeup of the contests and vying for the votes of mostly White citizens—as well as the electoral history of Bishop and the district—provided some measure of novelty. A different but somewhat similar set of novel circumstances surrounded the race between Corrine Brown and Bill Randall in 1998. Brown and Randall are both Black, as are the majority of the citizens in Florida's Third Congressional District. As we theorized and demonstrated in the previous chapters, this kind of contest was ripe for the kind of discourse that was frequent fare throughout the campaign, in large part emanating from the candidates themselves. That is, much of the conversation was about which Black candidate was more authentic and could lay claim to the interests of the district's Black voters. Randall, who might have been seen as somewhat of an outsider because of his Republican Party affiliation, previously had been the president of the Jacksonville chapter of the National Association for the Advancement of Colored People, boosting his community credentials among Blacks and strengthening his rhetoric about authenticity. The candidates' debate over racial authenticity was the subject of many of the news accounts throughout the contest.

Electoral Passing

On the lowest tier, we find a set of contests with equally identifiable circumstances that may have contributed to their lack of racialized coverage. In the cases of David Wu, John Sununu, and Mark Takano, we have Asian candidates who—as a group—are not racialized or stereotyped in American political discourse in the same negative ways that Blacks and Latinos have been. The fact that each of these candidates ran in districts with small Asian populations meant they did not have to appeal specifically to other Asian Americans for their vote (which we saw in the ads by Asian American candidates examined in Chapter 1). Given the relatively positive (though nevertheless stereotypical and in some respects damaging) perception of the character of Asian Americans among the White population, these candidates' appeal for White votes also did not need to take the form of a racial appeal (i.e., a counter-stereotype appeal).

Another group of candidates in this tier are Latino candidates, who are distinguished in one of two ways. Some, such as Michael Pappas and Bob Beauprez, do not publicly identify themselves in racial terms—a particular luxury afforded to people whose racial heritage does not extend beyond their surname or whose light (or White) skin tone does not cause anyone to think of them in terms of their racial heritage. Others, such as Henry Bonilla and Henry Cuellar and Linda Sanchez and Tim Escobar, ran in overwhelmingly Latino districts in which the Latino majority was, and has long been, a known quantity. That is, the demographic and congressional history of the districts—their voters and candidates—normalized Latino ethnicity in ways that perhaps made it unnecessary to point out (and certainly made it unnecessary to focus on the fact) that the candidates, voters, and opinion leaders were Latino. This is not the case, that is, unless and until one or both of the candidates find it strategically necessary to do so, particularly by making appeals to racial authenticity, as was the case when Ciro Rodriguez (top of RFI-4, tier four) challenged and ultimately defeated the incumbent Henry Bonilla for Texas's Twenty-third Congressional District seat in 2006.

Thus, we argue that the heightened attention to race drawn out in news stories about election contests involving racial minority candidates is in large part due to a sense of racial novelty and the journalistic presumption that *what is new is news,* so that journalists consider the racial dynamics of certain election contests newsworthy. Competitive contests between Black candidates in majority Black districts are quite novel, given the electoral history (and, by and large, the current reality) in which the real contests in majority-Black congressional districts are found in party (primarily Democratic Party) primaries. Historically, candidates—especially Black candidates—elected in this context have tended to hold their seats for a very long time. When those seats are relinquished, successors often have been hand-picked and groomed so that the resulting "open" seat is not really competitive. Frequently, these successors are children of the incumbent officeholder, as has been the case with former Congressman Harold Ford Jr. of Tennessee, William "Lacy" Clay of Missouri, and Kendrick Meek of Florida. Thus, when we begin to see highly competitive contests emerge, in general elections or primaries, it is the competitiveness and the fact that both candidates are minorities that make the contests newsworthy. The primary election contest for the seat of the retiring African American Congressman Major Owens, a Democrat from New York, in 2006 is a good example. That contest made national news on more than one occasion because of the fierce competition among several other Black candidates, including Chris Owens, the former congressman's son, and a notable White contestant, David Yassky, a Democratic city councilman. A similar set of circumstances surrounded the contest in western Tennessee, also in 2006, for the seat Harold Ford Jr. vacated during his bid for the U.S. Senate. That contest featured similar circumstances, in which Ford's brother ran for the seat but ultimately lost to a White (Jewish) candidate, Steve Cohen. Another Black candidate—Willie Herenton, former mayor of Memphis—challenged Cohen in the 2010 Democratic primary, appealing mostly to his belief that the mostly Black district would be better served by a Black congressman.

We also argue that another basis for racialized coverage is the content, tenor, and tone of racial rhetoric produced by the campaigns that the news media cover (i.e., the racial appeals made by candidates). We want to speak to this further, but before we do, we offer a more general explanation for racialized media coverage. We believe that the evidence suggests certain factors that are likely to affect whether, and the degree to which, journalists choose to report on certain election contests through a racial frame of reference.

A COMPETITION/NOVELTY HYPOTHESIS OF RACIAL FRAMING

Most studies of racialized media coverage of minority candidates and officeholders have tested a number of factors that contribute to how the news media cover candidates of color (Black candidates and elected officials specifically), demonstrating the empirical reality of differential and various forms of

race-related coverage. However, few have offered much in the way of definitive, testable explanations for or insights into the underlying motivations
behind the way journalists cover candidates of color. Some studies have cited
systematic news bias as a likely explanation but have not been able to validate
such claims empirically (Barber and Gandy 1990), while others seem to fall
back on veiled forms of implicit communication theories in which journalists' individual racial attitudes, stereotypes, and predispositions seem unconsciously to find their way onto the page when they report about candidates of
color (Zilber and Niven 2000). Still others (Terkildsen and Damore 1999)
do not speculate directly about journalists' motivations, choosing instead to
focus on the media's dual role of minimizing candidates' racial rhetoric while
highlighting Black candidates' racial characteristics in news stories. Perhaps
the closest attempt at a full explanation for racialized media coverage is
Reeves's contention that the news media are motivated toward racialized coverage to heighten a sense of racial conflict. We agree . . . sort of.

   We argue that alongside the racial novelty of particular campaigns and
candidates, competition and competitiveness (rather than conflict, insofar as
conflict is part and parcel of competition) explains a great deal about the motivations behind what appear to be very conscious decisions journalists make
about how to cover some minority candidates' political campaigns. While
there is some overlap here with Reeves's theoretical suggestions (and the two
certainly would not necessarily be mutually exclusive in some instances), our
argument is different in that it does not rest on evidence that demonstrates
what Reeves and others have referred to as racially polarized coverage: the
propensity for the media to zero in on the racial characteristics of Black candidates to the exclusion of all else. We argue that, rather than being fueled by
the need to create and sustain racial controversy, the media seeks to enhance
and maintain electoral competition and a public sense of competitiveness
that by and large lends itself to increased racialized coverage, though not necessarily (in fact, not often) in terms of racially polarizing conflict.

   In a final analysis, the results of which are found in Table 4.11, we test
three models of racial framing. The first is what we refer to as the *racial novelty
model,* which holds that the degree of racial framing is influenced by the pecu-
liarities of specific election contests—the unique contests themselves, something about the racial composition of the contest, or something about the
race of the candidates and the office they seek. The second is what we call the
racial competition model, which asserts that horserace-type coverage within the
story will strongly predict the degree of racial framing that occurs. The final
model is the closest we can come to modeling Reeves's conflict hypothesis. It
presumes that greater racial content in stories will be driven in part by focusing on personal character issues to the exclusion of substantive issue content.
That is, a conflict model of racial framing, as we operationalize it here, says

TABLE 4.11   Three models of racial framing

Racial novelty model		Racial competition model		Racial conflict model	
Unique contest	.032*** (.006)	Horserace content	.450** (.185)	Character content	.320** (.113)
Contest makeup	.254*** (.086)	Vote margin	.008 (.007)	Total issues	.080*** (.029)
Chamber	.779*** (.236)	Month of story	.040 (.051)		
Constant	−.173*** (.032)	Constant	.108 (.505)	Constant	.773*** (.073)
N	1,280	N	1,280	N	2,383
F	10.22	F	2.43	F	9.11
Adjusted R^2	.021	Adjusted R^2	.003	Adjusted R^2	.007

Note: Coefficients were generated by ordinary least squares regression (standard errors appear in parentheses). The dependent variable in the first two models is the RFI-4 score. The dependent variable in the third model is the total number of racial references in stories.

*** p < .001; ** p < .01

that coverage of minority candidates will frequently focus on racial content, candidates' character, and few substantive issues.

The data in Table 4.11 support both the racial novelty and competition models. Each of the predictor variables in the racial novelty model are significant at the highest levels, demonstrating that the unique election contest, the racial composition of the candidates in the contest, and the office being sought all strongly influence levels of racial framing. Each of the variables corresponds with a significant increase in RFI-4 scores. In the competition model, we conceptualized competitiveness using factors external to actual stories, such as margin of victory in each contest and the month in which the story was published (given the presumption that competition increases the closer one gets to election day). Neither of these, however, significantly affects levels of racial framing. The one critical variable related to actual story content, however—the presence of horserace coverage (including reporting on polls, lead changes, campaign strategy, fundraising, and the like)—does significantly influence the degree of racial framing in stories, increasing RFI-4 scores by .34 points above the constant. When we look at the racial conflict model, we see that while character content and the number of issues present in a story do influence the prevalence of racial content in stories, they do so in a way that would contradict the presumptions of the conflict model. That is, when character and issue content is factored in, racial content decreases.

CONCLUSION

Our objective in this chapter was to reinvestigate whether the news media rely on racial references when covering campaign contests that involve candidates of color. Our more specific object was to determine how prominent these racial references are in news stories and whether their use amounts to what we would refer to as a racial frame. Underlying these questions is our shared concern with previous scholars that racialized news coverage might adversely (and unfairly) affect candidates of color by prompting readers to consider and judge candidates of color through the prism of race, thereby potentially priming negative racial attitudes, stereotypes, and resentments held primarily by White voters.

We find that racial references appear in news stories infrequently overall. However, stories about Black candidates are more likely to include at least one, and overall higher numbers, of racial references. We also found that on the relatively rare occasions that stories do make racial references, the stories are generally found off the front page. Despite this fact, the front-page stories that do make racial references tend to include multiple references. Similarly, race is rarely mentioned in story headlines, yet when it is, the headlines are remarkably indicative of the racialized coverage to come in the full story. The potential salience of relatively infrequent racial references is further diminished when we consider factors that influence how prominent certain story content might be in the minds of readers, such as the length of stories, the presence of nonracial content, and the number and duration of stories that appear throughout a campaign news cycle. Thus, when we consider the general practice of journalistic reporting on campaigns involving candidates of color, we find no evidence to suggest that racialized coverage is a widespread problem that is likely to present a definitive barrier to the electoral success that candidates of color seek. In fact, of the most highly racially framed contests in our data, 60 percent corresponded with electoral victories for the candidate of color, and seven out of eight of these included candidates in biracial contests against White opponents.

This does not mean that candidates of color have nothing to fear or consider when it comes to how the media will report the news of their candidacies and campaigns to potential voters. Our results show that journalists are quite willing to delve into racial discourse surrounding candidates and campaigns when they believe it is warranted. Further, the journalistic obsession with competition and horserace type coverage of elections indicates that highly competitive contests involving candidates of color will particularly pique journalists' interest, attention, and scrutiny. In a country whose electoral history has only relatively recently witnessed competitive biracial contests, and even fewer competitive contests involving only candidates of color, journalists, at least in the near future, are likely to continue to see race definitely as a newsworthy characteristic of such contests.

Our broad analysis indicates that such coverage will most likely focus on the racially competitive aspects of campaigns—for example, the circumstances that propelled candidates of color to electoral prominence, their fitness to compete for the votes of racial insiders and outsiders, and how America's racial history and the history of particular states and districts might influence the candidates' success. But this does not guarantee that it necessarily has to be or always will be in all or even most cases. Candidates and their campaigns can exercise some control over coverage relating to their specific choices to deploy race-based appeals and refer to themselves and their opponents in racial terms. That is, given the media's penchant to view competitive contests involving candidates of color as the stuff of news, they are likely to latch on to candidates' race-based appeals in such a way that the news media are not the progenitors but the purveyors of racialized coverage, not originating racialized coverage but obliged to extend it when candidates provide ample justification.

This fact notwithstanding, whether racialized coverage in and of itself tends to have a negative influence on the outcome of elections that involve candidates of color is an open question. In fact, we argue in Chapter 7 that in some cases, such coverage may even be relatively positive. Before we get there, however, we begin Part II by revisiting our initial subject of candidates' appeals with a case study of how candidates construct racist appeals through various combinations of racial language, imagery, and issue content.

Part II

Case Studies in
Race Appeal

5

Racializing Immigration Policy

Issue Ads in the 2006 Election

I N CHAPTER 1, we focused our attention on the primary forms of race-based appeals that have appeared in political campaign advertisements over the past three decades. We specifically described how race-based appeals were communicated through various combinations of racialized language and images. We discussed the electoral circumstances that gave rise to their deployment and speculated on the ways that such ads might intentionally or unintentionally disadvantage one candidate or another or work to frame sponsoring candidates in the best possible light to voters. In other words, we considered race-based appeals primarily within the particular context of an election but focused our discussion on how such ads potentially affect candidates directly.

In the midst of that, we pointed out that substantive policy issues were mentioned infrequently in both racist and racial appeals. However, in some cases, policy issues can be the vehicle for deploying race-based appeals. That is, there are times when an issue, rather than a candidate of color, becomes the reference point for various racial stereotypes, images, and language that may be used in an ad. Further, we expect that, given the challenges and potential negative reactions candidates might receive from voters when making a racist or racial appeal, candidates may increasingly target issues rather than candidates of color specifically when lodging specific kinds of race-based appeals—racist appeals in particular.

Thus, the case study we present in this chapter provides an opportunity to accomplish two things: first, to consider in more depth and detail how language and images in political ads become racialized; and second, to demonstrate how this is accomplished in and through policy discussion. We demonstrate how race-based political campaign ads racially frame policy discussions in ways that have the potential to appeal to negative racial stereotypes, prejudices, and resentments generated by the issues themselves rather than by candidates. That is, by focusing on the issue of immigration, we demonstrate how racialized issues may stand in for candidates of color as a means by which negative racial attitudes are drawn out.

Standard issue-oriented political advertisements focus on one or more substantive policy issues, and sponsoring candidates attempt to align themselves with what they believe is the preferred position on the issue or issues in question while negatively associating their opponents with the less desirable position. While the electoral interests of candidates are still the most salient concern in issue ads, calling attention to certain issues and issue positions frames not only the candidates but also the issue that is the principal subject of the ad. Thus, in this chapter we are less concerned with how race-based appeals are constructed to advance candidates' electoral hopes than with how racialized language and imagery related to immigration—replete within a corpus of ads spanning multiple elections in a given election year—racialized a policy issue in such a way to create the potential for ads' sponsors and candidates to appeal to race through the vehicle of policy debate.

IMMIGRATION ADS IN THE 2006 ELECTION

Public attention to immigration skyrocketed in the year preceding the 2006 midterm elections, as seen in the frequency with which the issue found its way into news reports in that year. From 2000 to the end of 2004, immigration was cited in the headline or lead paragraph of 2,423 stories in U.S. newspapers and wire service reports. In 2005, however—just one year—we found virtually the same number of stories reporting on immigration issues as in the previous four years combined. Immigration issues increasingly dominated the television news agenda, as well. In fact, Lou Dobbs, formerly of CNN—who, some assert, single-handedly elevated the issue of immigration to the national stage—featured a story on immigration in almost every episode of his nightly show, *The Lou Dobbs Report*.[1]

Immigration's newfound position atop the media agenda shaped both the public agenda (the percentage of the population citing immigration as an issue of greatest concern) and the agenda of congressional and state-level lawmakers. By the end of 2005, 40–80 percent of American citizens surveyed (depending on the poll and the specific wording of the question) reported that immigration was on the list of issues that most concerned them. The year also ended with a prominent, hotly debated immigration bill: the Border

Protection, Anti-terrorism, and Illegal Immigration Control Act of 2005 (H.R. 4437). The legislation passed with the support of 203 Republican members, while only 36 Democratic members voted for it.

Those who supported the bill, such as Representative James Sensenbrenner, Republican of Wisconsin, emphasized the enforcement aspect of the bill as one of its chief attributes. While explaining the significance of the bill, Sensenbrenner referred to "those breaking the law, whether they are smugglers, . . . employers hiring illegal workers, or alien gang members terrorizing communities."[2] In addition, a large number of states, including Georgia, Tennessee, New Mexico, Texas, Nevada, California, Oklahoma, Arkansas, and many others, began their respective legislative sessions with immigration-related bills to consider. It is within this context that the debate about immigration began in 2006.

By the 2006 election cycle, video-sharing sites such as YouTube became a standard repository for candidates' political advertisements. These online vehicles allowed candidates to showcase their persuasive appeals in a venue that was free of cost and that served as a forum attracting politically engaged citizens who, among many things, might do the campaign the favor of further disseminating the ad to the online public, essentially supplementing the candidates' paid advertising budgets. For this reason, we used YouTube as the source of the immigration ads by candidates and third-party interest groups that make up our case study in this chapter. We selected the ads because they singularly focus on the immigration issue. They are derived from a diverse set of sponsors in terms of the political office sought by the candidates, their political party affiliations, and the states in which they ran. In all, we use twenty-four ads in our case study, the characteristics of which are included in Table 5.1.[3]

THE LANGUAGE OF IMMIGRATION

We begin the case study by focusing on the language used throughout immigration ads. We display several sets of terms and phrases in a series of tables that depict their relationship to one another in a way that, we argue, functions as one component in a larger racialized narrative about immigration. These tables convey every substantive term used in each of the ads that make up the pool. Each substantive term used in a given ad was recorded, then reduced to thematic categories. We open the analysis with a brief description of the five thematic categories that characterize the linguistic content of the advertisements: (1) immigrants; (2) candidates; (3) Americans; (4) issues; and (5) immigration. Each of the five categories contains closely associated terms used within each of the ads.

TABLE 5.1 Immigration ads, 2006

Sponsor	Party	Opponent	State	Office	Length	Focus
Arizona Republican Party	Republican	Clarence Boykins	Ariz.	N.A.	:40	Opponent
Art Olivier	Libertarian	Phil Angelides–Arnold Schwarzenegger	Calif.	Governor	:60	Candidate
Asa Hutchinson	Republican	Mike Beebe	Ark.	Governor	:30	Candidate
Ben Nelson	Democrat	Pete Ricketts	Neb.	U.S. Senate	:30	Candidate
Betty Boyd	Democrat	Vicki Stack	Colo.	State Senate	:60	Candidate
David Magnum	Republican	Tammy Baldwin	Wis.	U.S. House	:30	Candidate
J. B. Van Hollen	Republican	Kathleen Falk	Wis.	Attorney-General	:30	Candidate
J. D. Hayworth	Republican	Harry Mitchell	Ariz.	U.S. House	:30	Both
Jim Barnett	Republican	Kathleen Sebelius	Kans.	Governor	:30	Both
Jim Bryson	Republican	Phil Bredesen	Tenn.	Governor	:30	Candidate
Jim Pederson	Democrat	Jon Kyl	Ariz.	U.S. House	:30	Opponent
John Kline	Republican	Coleen Crowley	Minn.	U.S. House	:30	Both
Max Burns (ad 1)	Republican	John Barrow	Ga.	U.S. House	:30	Opponent
Max Burns (ad 2)	Republican	John Barrow	Ga.	U.S. House	:30	Opponent
National Republican Congressional Campaign Committee	Republican	John Cranley	Ohio	U.S. House	:30	Opponent
NumbersUSA	N.A.	N.A.	N.A.	N.A.	:60	N.A.
Peter Roskam	Republican	Tammy Duckworth	Ill.	U.S. House	:30	Opponent
Randy Graf	Republican	Gabrielle Giffords	Ariz.	U.S. House	:30	Candidate
Republican Party of Florida	Republican	Keith Firzgerald	Fla.	U.S. House	:30	Opponent
Sean Burrage	Republican	Ami Shaffer	Okla.	State Senate	:45	Candidate
Tammy Duckworth (ad 1)	Democrat	Peter Roskam	Ill.	U.S. House	:30	Candidate
Tammy Duckworth (ad 2)	Democrat	Peter Roskam	Ill.	U.S. House	:30	Candidate
Tessa Hafen	Democrat	Jon Porter	Nev.	U.S. House	:30	Opponent
Van Taylor	Republican	Chet Edwards	Tex.	U.S. House	:30	Opponent

Terms that target immigrants describe specific immigrants (e.g., Gustavo Reyes), a particular immigrant population as a whole (e.g., Mexicans), or specific types or classes of immigrants (e.g., "undocumented workers"). Language focused on candidates—whether by the ad's sponsor or his or her opponent—described specific character traits (e.g., a leader), positions (e.g., "oppose"), or ideas or actions (e.g., "crackdown") that the candidates promise to perform vis-à-vis the issue of immigration as a whole or a specific aspect of it. Some of the ads specify "the American people" as their principal subjects and include descriptive terms characterizing who they mean by the phrase, what such "people" value, and what they prioritize. Other language is directly tied to secondary policy issues related to immigration, often suggesting a relationship between immigration and a related policy area. For example, an ad's language might argue that immigration adversely affects the Social Security System. Such language specifies a range of related issues caught up in the nexus of immigration policy. Finally, language is used in the ads to broadly describe and characterize the issue of immigration. These terms, few as they are, reflect how the candidates view, and how they suggest viewers should see, the immigration issue.

In the following pages, we look at each of these thematic categories—first separately, then as a whole—to understand the mutual web of associations and connotations they invoke with regard to the issue of immigration. Throughout our analysis of the narrative language used in these ads, we address two underlying questions: How might the language used to talk about immigration frame thinking about the issue? And how does this language produce a set of racialized connotations that ultimately frame the issue of immigration as a racial issue? In short, how does language work to racialize the immigration issue?

The "Criminal" Mass

The ads here focus on "immigrants," a specific category of individuals or groups of such individuals, more than on any other category. This language dominates the content of ads both in sentiment (the immigrants are of primary interest) and in terms of the sheer number of words used to describe the population. Just who, then, are these "people," these immigrants? What do they look like, act like, symbolize, or otherwise represent in the minds of political candidates whose interest in and perspectives on immigration policy is so fundamentally shaped by the answers to these questions?

The terms listed in Table 5.2 tell much of the essential story that demonstrates how immigration policy has become racially framed. The language speaks of two general types or classes, descriptively defined as the immigrant population (specific individuals and groups as a whole). Immigrants are first

TABLE 5.2   Terms candidates' ads used to describe "immigrants"

<table>
<tr><td colspan="4" align="center">Criminal</td></tr>
<tr><td>Criminals</td><td>Danger</td><td>Illegal</td><td>Kill</td></tr>
<tr><td>Arrested</td><td>Deported</td><td>Immigrants</td><td>Rape</td></tr>
<tr><td>Bad</td><td>Drunk</td><td>Illegals</td><td>Murder</td></tr>
<tr><td>Break laws</td><td>Gang members</td><td>Illegal aliens</td><td>Terrorists</td></tr>
<tr><td>Crime</td><td>Gustavo Reyes</td><td>Illegal immigrants</td><td></td></tr>
<tr><td>Crime rate</td><td>Hurt</td><td>Undocumented</td><td></td></tr>
<tr><td>Heinous crimes</td><td></td><td>workers</td><td></td></tr>
<tr><td>Bail</td><td></td><td></td><td></td></tr>
<tr><td>Released</td><td></td><td></td><td></td></tr>
</table>

<table>
<tr><td colspan="2" align="center">Masses</td></tr>
<tr><td>Millions</td><td>Open borders</td></tr>
<tr><td>60,000</td><td>Out of control</td></tr>
<tr><td>11 Million</td><td>Mass</td></tr>
<tr><td>12 Million</td><td>Enter</td></tr>
<tr><td>50 Million</td><td>Overwhelm</td></tr>
<tr><td>66 Million</td><td>Spilling over</td></tr>
<tr><td>300 Million</td><td>Stream in</td></tr>
<tr><td>400 Million</td><td>Uncontrolled</td></tr>
<tr><td>Fastest growing</td><td>Crowded</td></tr>
<tr><td>Quadrupled</td><td>Mexican</td></tr>
</table>

grouped according to their pervasive criminality. These terms are not implicit; they describe exactly what they mean, frequently using the actual term "criminal" or some form of it.

In some instances, terms directly denote the nature of immigrants' crimes or the outcome of committing them (such as being "arrested" or "deported.") In other instances, the language describes immigrants' criminal nature by using terms that suggest the feelings their crimes are said to signify, such as "danger"; the criminal entities that evoke that same sense of danger and fear, such as "gang members"; or specific criminal acts, such as "kill," "rape," and "murder." Several examples convey the context in which these terms are evoked and deployed. For instance, an ad by Democratic Senator Ben Nelson of Nebraska, opened with the line, "Drug dealers, gang members." A similar ad by the Republican congressional candidate Randy Graf of Arizona warned, "Drugs, criminals, terrorists—we just don't know." In another example, an announcer in an ad from the Republican congressional candidate Van Taylor of Texas remarked, "Worse, Chet Edwards [Taylor's opponent] voted to protect [those] arrested for crimes from deportation, allowing them to be released on bail. Some have committed heinous crimes, including rape and murder."

The language of criminality used to describe the immigrants represented in these advertisements is not only negative in tone; it goes above and beyond that, linking immigrants to the most deplorable crimes imaginable. Terms used to denote immigrants' criminal behavior are often repeated several times, firmly embedding immigrants' felonious image in the minds of viewers. No one would argue that there are gradations of criminal significance among the long list of potential crimes one might commit. However, because it is not specific, the criminal language used here leads one to associate even the petty criminal with the most villainous—the immigrant who might grab an extra roll of toilet paper from the house she cleans with the street thug who kills at will.

But the story continues. This first set of language links immigrants to a variety of criminal enterprises and behaviors. Another thread in this pattern of criminalizing language is the term ads most often use to describe immigrants: "illegal." These ads rarely distinguish various categories of immigrants. In fact, the vast majority of references to "immigrants" is preceded by "illegal" or, in many instances, immigrants are simply referred to as "illegals." In many respects, these referents are more negative than those used above to denote explicit criminal acts. The terms "illegal immigrant" and, especially, "illegal" cast immigrants as lawbreakers by definition (the latter strips them of all humanity, as well). Generally, the immigrants referred to in these ads have no name of their own; rather, their name is a collective one that fundamentally defines them as being outside the law, lawbreakers. The associative damage done by the kind of language that fails to distinguish "illegal" immigrants from "legal" ones is clear: All immigrants are connected to criminality and the most feared types of violent criminality, at that.

The term "alien" carries with it a similar set of problematic connotations. Rather than signifying fundamental criminality as a lawbreaker, "alien" has long been part of the legalistic language the American government uses to denote non-native-born Americans—foreigners. As Ngai (2004) points out, the term "alien" also signals a wide variety of otherness, whether based on racial differences or differences in national origin. Thus, when the candidates in these ads use the term "alien," they signify immigrants' foreignness, the sense that they are simply not like "us." Using language alone, the ads considered here infrequently specify illegal immigrants' national origin. Only in one instance is the term "Mexican" used as a national, racial, or cultural identifier. If these were radio ads in which only the language or tone was communicated, one might get the sense that the "criminal" label used to describe immigrants applies to all immigrant groups equally, irrespective of their national origin. We will see later why this is not the case.

Before we get there, however, another clear category of language is used to describe the immigrants who occupy center stage in these political ads. Individual illegal immigrants are sometimes used to dramatize and further concretize immigrants' collective association with criminality—their villainous nature and the danger they pose. However, the language addresses immigrants more frequently in the abstract, substituting individuals and individual names with the concrete language of numbers. The second branch in Table 5.2 signifies the ads' pervasive sentiment about the "mass" immigrant population in the United States. The first column, read from top to bottom, reveals that the increasing numerical values create the sense of a ubiquitous immigrant threat. "Annual immigration numbers have quadrupled," an ad from one non-candidate interest group warned. "Over 50 million immigrants and dependents are already crowded into our communities." In some ads, numerical precision (e.g., "60,000") was replaced with exponentialized and abstract designations such as "millions"; such spots were ambiguous about whether this meant 2 million or 500 million. In other ads, such as several run by Max Burns, a former congressman from Georgia, against John Barrow, hyperbolic numbers were replaced with the alarmist statement, "Illegal immigration is out of control." Other language in ads conveys this view, describing how immigrant populations get to this country and the impact they have on the population. In some of the ads, they "spill over"; in others, they "stream in," "crowd," or "overwhelm."

There is no reason to care about the cumulative expressiveness of the ads that use this language if what we are concerned with are individual-level effects they might have on any given audience member who might be exposed to only one of them in a particular state or district during the election cycle. But we are concerned with a broader scope of meaning here—a narrative—that is communicated and the ways in which it both expresses and influences our general posture toward immigrants and the issue of immigration. In this respect, when one watches all of these ads together, one gets the sense of a mounting hysteria reminiscent of the *War of the Worlds* radio broadcast in 1938 in which listeners were compelled by the apparent reality that an invading alien mass (of the extraterrestrial kind) had insidiously and spontaneously emerged to destroy world civilization. The dominant portion of the linguistic narrative introduces us to a dangerous population defined inherently as criminal and characterized by the specific heinous crimes they interchangeably commit. All other language categories (and later, images) refer to this group in some way.

Thus far, we have looked only at the range of associations the ads' language evokes about the immigrant population. We are building here—tearing apart and reconstructing the various layers of meaning communicated with each linguistic brick that makes up the ads' collective narrative structure. The first layer consists of the advertisers' and candidates' descriptions of immigrants themselves, those who are the central figures in this issue drama. We move now to the next layer, beyond specific immigrants and the immigrant population, to the "issue" of immigration itself, including the language that these candidates used to characterize the issue of immigration and the terms they used to describe themselves vis-à-vis the issue.

Immigration Problems and Candidate Solutions

It should come as no surprise, given the aforementioned characterization of America's immigrant population, that the political candidates here framed the general issue of immigration as a "problem." The "border"—another term frequently used in the ads, especially when talking about the immigrant masses—was often used as a catalyst for or facilitator of this spillover, leakage, or flood of immigrants into the United States. It is how they stream in and thus crowd the existing population. Invoking Lou Dobbs's metaphor, the borders are fundamentally "broken." As shown in Table 5.3, many of the immigration ads adopted the metaphor of the "broken border" to define the danger posed by immigration and illegal immigrants. When we consider many of the terms that are synonymous with "broken"—from "fractured" to "destroyed," "faulty" to "failed"—the term "broken borders" signals a range of connotations. Borders are broken in the sense of being porous, allowing the immigrant masses to enter. They are broken down—destroyed—in part by the immigrant masses who overwhelm them, and in part by a U.S. government that fails to keep them strong. They are broken in the sense that they do not work; the broken border does not fulfill its purpose in keeping people out. Finally, the term "broken border" calls to mind the image of a physical wall, erected to defend those on one side from those who threaten from the other. In this sense, the broken border is a security threat, placing those

TABLE 5.3 Terms candidates' ads used to describe immigration and themselves

Problem	Law	Character	Action
Broken borders	District attorney	Soft	Fight
Border	Prosecutor	Strong	Talk
Challenges	Sheriffs	Truth	Penalize
Mess	Rules	Tough	Justice
Hard	Judgment	Leader	Punish
State	Enforcement	Leadership	Beef up
		Decide	Fix
		Dedicated	Crack down
			Change
			First
			New ideas
			Plan

on one side in imminent danger. Like the language describing immigrants, none of the language invoking the broken borders metaphor specifies which border is the problem. That is, in language alone, one is presented with the reality that the U.S. borders to the North and the South are equally problematic.

Something broken begs to be fixed. Thus, the candidates in these ads emerge—having framed the issue of immigration as a fundamental problem—as poised to solve it (in the case of attack or contrast ads, the opposing candidates are cast as those who cannot or will not solve the problem). Table 5.3 shows three related sets of terms. In relation to the immigrant problem, candidates trumpet either their past experience as an officeholder or individual character attributes that make them best suited to solving the immigrant problem. Most important, however, is that they linguistically describe a variety of actions they are prepared to carry out to solve the problem.

This important promise of action—whether it is "fighting," "leading," "planning," or otherwise—is framed in relation to the immigrants themselves. Hence, the broken border is inextricably linked to the immigrant masses. A border is an inanimate object without agency. When ads speak of "broken borders" and the like, it is clear that immigrants—not the border—are the real problem. This is why candidates in the ads describe themselves as a response, not directly to the language of "the border," but to that of the immigrant hordes. J. B. Van Hollen, a Republican candidate for Attorney-General from Wisconsin, is a "tough as nails former federal prosecutor (who will prosecute actual people, not a physical border)," while J. D. Hayworth, a Republican candidate for the House of Representatives from Arizona promises to "beef up enforcement." Randy Graf says he will "secure" the border, and Asa Hutchinson, a Republican gubernatorial candidate from Arkansas, says he will "crack down" on illegal immigrants. Others highlight their law-enforcement credentials, promising the kind of justice that will "punish," "penalize," and mete out swift "judgment" on illegal immigrants and those who aid them. Candidates frame themselves as solutions to a border problem characterized by illegal immigrants whose criminal threat demands a legal remedy. "Illegals" are the lawbreakers; the candidates are law enforcers.

Thus far, we have considered three of the layers in the communicative edifice of immigration ads: the immigrants themselves, who are deemed fundamentally criminal; the broken border, framed as the fundamental problem of immigration; and political candidates, portrayed as the enforcers of American law, those who would punish the immigrant hordes. Illegal aliens are the threat against which candidates defend. The question that remains in this narrative is: Who are the candidates protecting, and what, specifically, are they protecting us from?

Protecting "Our" Way of Life

It seems obvious that candidates who hold themselves out as defenders against the immigrant hordes seek to protect the American people, citizens of the United States, a sovereign nation with a collective set of values and national interests. But the real question is again one of language. We know in the abstract who and what America is, but how is the American public specifically characterized in this narrative, in which criminal immigrant populations thus far are the primary characters—the villains? What attributes—individual and collective—are foregrounded in this linguistic network that frames immigrants, the issue of immigration, and the candidates who seek to deal with the issue in mutually referential ways? In addition, what other political matters fall under the broad umbrella of the immigration issue in these ads, and how are they descriptively linked to the people that these political candidates seek to protect?

Table 5.4 includes the terms repeated throughout the ads to describe "Americans"—who we are, what we need, what we stand to lose in the face of the immigrant threat. We have already alluded to the preponderance of protectionist language in the immigration ads we consider here. Most often, this language is encapsulated into the now familiar trope "security." This is no small point. That the language of security—instead of "protection"—dominates these ads is crucial to their racial framing. More specifically, it provides convenient cover for potential underlying motivations about why these political candidates frame the immigration issue the way they do. By invoking the term "security," candidates are able to link the issue of immigration to broader national security issues—concern that extends into America's foreign policy, beyond the country's Northern and Southern borders.

The trope also links immigration policy to the terrorist attacks in the United States on September 11, 2001. That is, the days following the September 11 attacks led to an increasingly amplified discourse about security.[4] This linguistic sleight of hand has several consequences. First, it amplifies the fear and pervasive sense of danger already communicated in the language describing the immigrant masses that threaten to overrun us at any time. Second, it is a form of geopolitical misdirection, erroneously leading one to believe that the "immigrant" threat is a terrorist threat by those whom Americans have largely come to associate with terrorism—individuals from the Arab/Muslim world. As a result of the first, the third consequence of framing the immigration issue in terms of "security" is that it allows politicians to argue that we should devote the same amount of resources to "protecting our borders" as we do, say, fighting the Iraq or Afghan wars. George H. W. Bush and conservatives had an alibi when Willie Horton emerged in their ads in the 1988

TABLE 5.4   Terms candidates' ads used to describe "Americans" and issues

Americans		
Protect	America(n)	Family
Secure	Tax-paying citizens	Children
Defend	Us	Father
Escape	Citizens	Mother
Safety	We	
Security	Communities	
Strengthen	Our	
	Side	
	Population	
	Nation	

presidential contest: The issue was not one of race but, rather, of crime policy. Evoking the security trope in immigration ads is the foundation for another such alibi: The protectionist stance against immigration is not about race; it is about national security. We return to this point later in the chapter.

What is most interesting about the language related to the American population in these ads is that they are generally not descriptive at all. Unlike the immigrants who were described in very explicit language as criminals, deceivers, drug dealers and the like, no such attributes are used when talking about the American people. Looking at Table 5.4, what we see used over and over again are first-person plural pronouns that identify the collective ("we," "us," and "our")—terms connected to others denoting the American collectivity, such as "our communities" or "our families." Because they are the presumed and preferred in-group, "Americans" need no definition here. Being American brings with it an assumed goodness. In the not-so-subtle "us-versus-them" framework presented in the language of these ads, the immigrants represent the extreme criminal threat; "we" are simply "Americans." We need no further definition because we are defined by our opposite.

What is at stake, what we Americans need protection from, is frequently expressed in the form of economic or cultural issues. Illegal immigrants threaten our way of life. In addition to threatening our safety, "they" threaten our culture, our economic interests, and our individual financial livelihood. The language in many of the ads is concerned with immigrants' threat to America's economic interests. Though "American" almost always stands alone, when a modifier precedes it, that modifier most often is "taxpaying." In the ads, paying taxes, contributing to the national economy, is a defining attribute of what it means to be a citizen. Citizens pay taxes. Government benefits such as health care, Social Security, and education are taxpayer-funded programs, and since

TABLE 5.5 Terms candidates' ads used to describe "issues"

Issues	
Government benefits	Official language
Benefits	Amnesty
Handouts	Assimilation
Social Security	English requirement
Health care	Citizenship
Welfare	
Food stamps	
Hospitals	
Jobs	
Schools	
Driver's licenses	

only Americans pay taxes, only Americans are entitled to benefit. Thus, part of the threat immigrants pose is that they will avail themselves of benefits that they do not deserve, benefits for which they have not worked. Language related to immigrants' access to government services is listed in Table 5.5.

To those looking back on the scholarship on race and welfare policy rhetoric—especially in the administrations of Ronald Reagan and Bill Clinton—this sentiment about the "undeserving poor" and its association with African Americans is familiar. However, there is a critical distinction between the Black welfare queens of the 1980s and 1990s and the immigrant hordes represented in these ads—those who benefit from programs funded by taxpayers to which they do not financially contribute. When Martin Gilens (2000) wrote about this phenomenon, he was speaking about African Americans who, though many paid no taxes because they had little or no income, were nevertheless citizens. By virtue of their citizenship, they have the right to access government benefits. Blacks were characterized by the participants in Gilens's study as freeloaders because they took advantage of services they were entitled to but did not deserve.[5]

What is different about the immigrants on whom these ads focus is that they are cast as non-citizens, non-American, aliens. They are fundamentally defined by their criminal nature. Thus, when they receive taxpayer-funded benefits such as free medical care, it further underscores their criminal character. They are not lazy like Black welfare moms with three (or more) children who refuse to look for a job. They are quite the opposite in that respect—that is, they are quite willing to work. But being hardworking, ironically, makes them worse in this context. They are hardworking, industrious *thieves*. Though the benefits are freely given (i.e., illegal immigrants who do receive benefits do so through some legal mechanism), the immigrants are literally taking things that do not belong to them (Niemann 2001). To be clear, this is what we are saying. The language used in these ads characterizes immigrants as *fundamentally* criminal (as opposed to individuals who commit crimes). The same language casts them as the out-group, opposite of American citizens who are described only in terms of a national and communal collective that needs no further definition. It is because of these two factors that the pervasive language of these ads communicates the identity of immigrants as thieves rather than mere freeloaders when it comes to economic benefits.

The "us" versus "them" comportment of immigrants and American citizens (in these ads) carries through in a different way with respect to the immigrant threat to American culture. The presumption of the "immigrant hordes" language spoken of earlier insinuates that they pose a threat both from without (hence, the need to fix the border) and from within. As the ad discussed earlier stated, "50 million are *already* here. The only way to deal with this threat is to deport the immigrants or assimilate them. Candidates who use law-enforcement language typically favor deportation; those more willing to deal with existing immigrants in a non-criminal way stress assimilation, principally by requiring immigrants to learn and conduct all facets of daily life in English. Thus, in addition to candidates' need to protect the financial well-being of American citizens, their language indicates a strong desire to protect so-called American culture. The importance of language is implicitly highlighted in this respect. Those looking to protect America from threats that legal immigrants pose aim primarily to diminish the degree to which immigrants retain their primary language.

The Linguistic Foundation of Race-Based Appeals

Having separately discussed each category of linguistic content within immigration ads run in the 2006 midterm elections, we now pull back to examine the bigger picture to see the categories of terms as a whole. This is included in Table 5.6. A couple of points about language are in order before we summarize what the language of these immigration ads tells us about how political candidates frame the immigration issue and those involved. First, language—words, more specifically—are imbued with a range of signification. In Roland Barthes's (1978) conception of the semiotic system, this expressive range can be described as the plane of denotation/connotation in which signifiers and signifieds either closely correspond to each other or the range of possible signifieds for a single term is extensive. Put differently, some words mean what they say, while others mean more than what they say. We could also say that language exists on a range of explicitness–implicitness. A codified definition of a term represents the most explicit end of this scale, while the other end is considered "code."[6] Understanding what determines one end of the spectrum from the other is required to decipher the meaning of the given term.

TABLE 5.6 Full list of main terms used in immigration ads

Immigrants

Hordes

Millions	Open borders
60,000	Out of control
11 Million	Mass
12 Million	Enter
50 Million	Overwhelm
66 Million	Spilling over
300 Million	Stream in
400 Million	Uncontrolled
Fastest growing	Crowded
Quadrupled	Mexican

Criminals

Criminals	Danger	Illegal	Kill
Arrested	Deported	Immigrants	Rape
Bad	Drunk	Illegals	Murder
Break laws	Gang members	Illegal aliens	Terrorists
Crime	Gustavo Reyes	Illegal immigrants	
Crime rate	Hurt	Undocumented workers	
Heinous crimes			
Bail			
Released			

Immigration

State	Action
Problem	Law
Challenges	Fix
Border	Change
Broken border	
Hard	
Mess	

Americans

Protect	American	Citizens
Secure	Taxpaying citizens	Children
Defend	Us	Father
Escape	Citizens	Mother
Safety	We	
Security	Communities	
Strengthen	Side	
	Population	
	Nation	

Related issues

Government benefits	
Benefits	Official language
Handouts	Amnesty
Social Security	Assimilation
Health care	English requirement
Welfare	Citizenship
Food stamps	
Hospitals	
Jobs	
Schools	
Driver's licenses	

Candidates

Law	Strength
District attorney	Fight
Prosecutor	Soft
Sheriffs	Strong
Rules	Talk
Judgment	Truth
Enforcement	Tough
Penalize	Leader
Justice	Leadership
Punish	Decide
	Dedicated

Explicit language requires little explanation; one need only be familiar with the singular or small number of possible definitions the word or phrase possesses because it has a predictable set of possible and commonly accepted meanings. Deciphering code, by contrast, necessitates context. It involves being immersed in a particular symbolic world that provides specific inside knowledge that opens up a world of possible meanings for a given linguistic sign (Geertz 1977). What matters most in distinguishing the two is whether or not one is immersed in such cultural space or, at least, familiar with the symbolic world in which a linguistic sign is more code than it is a mere referent.

Returning to our short discussion of African Americans and welfare policy earlier will serve as a useful example of what we mean. The common referent "welfare queen" has a literal meaning that does not extend beyond the most common or literal definitions of the two terms combined, leading one without any background to believe that a "welfare queen" is someone who is the maternal head of social well-being or the matriarchal administrator of government aid programs. With added knowledge and context, one might extend the range of meanings expressed in this term to refer to a mother persistently on welfare, one who dominates the system. This is less literal but not yet code. However, "welfare queen" refers to lazy, *Black* mothers, primarily in urban ghettos, who remain on welfare by resorting to extreme tactics such as continuing to have more children than they can financially support (Davis and Silver 2003; Hancock 2004; Zucchino 1999). This is code because understanding this connoted meaning requires not only that one be familiar with the term and the actual people to whom it refers, but also be immersed in a symbolic universe in which the social circumstances are ripe for this person to exist (i.e., a welfare system of government benefits available to mothers and tied, to some degree, to children). It also requires immersion in a system that is fundamentally racist in the sense that it is not unusual for skin color to invoke a powerful, valuative distinction between Black women on welfare compared with similarly situated Whites. One must be immersed in a social milieu in which stereotypes are interpreted as such (whether one espouses them or not). In another simple example, when someone tells a joke about an Irish American drinking and getting into a brawl, the question is not whether one laughs or not; it is whether one understands the joke. If one is socialized in a sociopolitical context in which "welfare queen" makes sense in the sense that we know what it means, we understand the code—again, regardless of whether we consciously accept or reject the sentiment or belief that underlies it.

What stands out about the immigration ads analyzed here is that, by and large, the language is *not* coded. This seems peculiar when we think about racial coding in any media that relies, in whole or part, on language. When we think about the hundreds of ads we analyzed for Chapter 1, racially coded language was often part and parcel of race-based appeals where they were found.

Some of these examples included how the term "liberal" is often code for "Black radical" and "urban schools" is code for "poor, Black or Latino schools," and the like. They are coded descriptors of a given object, person, individual characteristic, or social situation. However, terms such as "millions," "criminals," "government benefits," "undocumented workers," "citizens"—the vast majority of substantive terms used in these ads—are quite literal; they are clearly explicit, expressing exactly what they mean.

So why does this seem odd compared with other ads that make race-based appeals? It is odd—and significant—when we consider the purpose of coded language. As shorthand, code is efficient. Inasmuch as code changes our perception of the thing coded, it is potentially subversive (consciously or unconsciously). But often, especially when deployed in an explicitly purposeful manner, code is used to conceal, to say something without saying it. The need to do this implies some moral or strategic prohibition against using explicit language to refer to people, places, things, or circumstances in a particular way.

The history of commonly used racially coded language used in the United States shows that it has been used largely to characterize African Americans. When Mendelberg (2001) talks about the "norm of racial equality" that emerged in and around the Civil Rights Movement of the 1960s, she is generally referring to an expression of the dominant belief in the equality of all people. However, it is generally understood that, given the time in which this shift emerged, it is connected to African Americans who were the central figures in the fight to secure civil rights. African Americans are similarly the central group about whom issues of social desirability emerged with respect to survey research (Davis and Silver 2003). We mention this because it demonstrates that racial code words were in a large part developed as a covert vehicle for Whites to talk negatively about Blacks without appearing to violate the norm of racial equality or communicate general socially unacceptable sentiments about African Americans (whereas they had been extremely explicit and widely accepted as such). The fact that the immigration ads considered here generally rely on explicit characterizations of the referents they aim to describe suggests no similar filtering mechanism is in place that would necessitate coded language to refer to the groups to which the language in these ads refer.

The second point about language that needs to be made has to do with the social power of language. Should the fact that certain kinds of language are used to describe various facets of the immigration issue be our only concern? Or is there greater cause for alarm when we think about how this language might influence how we think about immigrants and immigration policy? We take the theoretical position about language expressed by Austin (1963) and commonly adopted by cultural studies scholars and critical legal theorists such as Butler (1997) and Matsuda (1993). This theoretical position about language espoused to varying degrees by them all is the view that language and speech constitute an illocutionary act. It is the view that language not only describes but also performs; language is imbued with power and force irrespective of a given speaker. In a sense, it is a form of magical incantation that calls something into being by speaking the word (Gebser 1985).

While some scholars emphasize that certain words may not only lead to but may also constitute their own violence, we focus on what we believe to be the more important illocutionary aspect of language: its constitutive power to enact particular relationships among and between people based on perceived or actual power differentials. Butler (1997) points out that one of the most potentially damaging acts of language is naming. When we name something or someone—such as an individual or groups of immigrants as "illegals"—the named and the one naming are interpolated in a context in which the former are subordinated in relationship to the latter. This interpolation constitutes a set of mutually referencing, static dichotomizations in which the named is defined by who he or she is not. As we have mentioned, when we consider language alone, no racial appeal is made in the immigration ads we look at here. This is largely due to the fact that no clear and explicit racial referent is identified in any of the language. The fact that the language used in these ads generally comprises explicit referents rather than code does not mean the language is racially neutral. In fact, the reality that the language is not coded is the strategic foundation for the racialization of the ads, which is not complete until there is a clear referent. As we will see, this referent is expressed not in language but through visual images.

THE IMAGES OF IMMIGRATION

Thus far, we have looked primarily at the language used in the immigration ads insofar as they characterize and frame the central figures within and motivations behind immigration policy. Ultimately, we argue, the ads appeal to race as a basis for their persuasive appeal. In this regard, we have been concerned with how the language in the ads not only frames and describes the objects to which it refers, but the role it plays in shaping the underlying race-based appeal. While we argue that language is central to the construction of the race-based appeal, the underlying message is not generally conveyed by language alone. In this case, it is the expressive specificity of the visual image, in combination with language, that distinguishes a race-based appeal from all others. That is, in Chapter 1 we demonstrated that one of the critical characteristics of race-based appeals is the presence of a visual image that serves to evoke a set of racial associations. In the following pages, we focus on the expressive qualities of visual images in much the same way we did with the linguistic content of the ads. While the images correspond to the thematic categories we used to analyze the language of the ads, they are more restrictive. That is, common image tropes are used throughout the ads—frequently used images that signify meanings that pervade several thematic categories. To frame the remainder of our analysis, we begin with a brief description of what these image tropes are.

Iconic Images of Immigration

We divided each of the ads in our analysis into distinct image frames so that we created a still frame each time substantively new content was added to the moving image. From these, we distinguished twelve image types, each with unique characteristics, even though they frequently overlay one another. These image categories include fences and fence jumpers; borders and border crossers; hordes; flags; "us"; candidates; opponents; language; law enforcement, crime, and jails; money; government; "legal" immigrants; and classrooms. We proceeded with three primary questions in mind: (1) What is the range of meaning associated with each category of images? (2) How do the images supplement, complement, conflict with, or otherwise relate to the language of the ads in terms of offering a description of how the issue of immigration is framed? and (3) How does the combination of these images and this language constitute a race-based appeal? Because space does not allow us to fully describe each of the image categories outlined, we focus primarily on those categories most germane to accomplishing our purpose with this chapter. We should also repeat that we are interested less in any single ad's potential effect on any given viewer than in the way in which the ads collectively produce a racial narrative that frames immigration as fundamentally a race-based issue. Thus, when we consider the image content of these categories, we do so by examining a set of composites composed of similar images found throughout all of the ads under consideration.

Fences, borders, jumpers, and crossers. We begin with this category because the argument trajectory of most ads follows a problem–solution format. That is, by and large the ads begin with images that represent the sponsor's view of what (and who) constitutes the problem, followed by, or incorporating, the sponsor's perspective about the problem's significance (to whom and what it is detrimental), and ending with the solution to that problem. The ads also depict images of the border and those who move about it as the central problem. So this is where we begin.

The first image composite includes images of borders, border crossers, fences, and fence jumpers. They are split into two separate composites, the first shown in Figure 5.1. Besides candidates and flags—which we consider later—the images in Figure 5.1 represent the border as an object. What we see is the physical, geographical terrain. In some images, the border stands singularly

FIGURE 5.1   Fences and borders

alone, a seemingly benign, blank landscape. But these images provide a critical geographical clue. The terrain in these images is dry. Vegetation is absent
in some, while in others what does appear is clearly dead or dying. It is desert
terrain; the effects of long seasons of prolonged, direct sunlight and high
temperatures are apparent in the color of the soil. This is important because
between the two U.S. borders, one is clearly signified in these images: It is the
Southern border separating "us" from Mexico, not the Northern border separating "us" from Canada.[7]

Still looking at the composite in Figure 5.1, two types of objects appear on
the border: fences and law-enforcement vehicles. The first signify the idea of
and need for separation. In this respect, both the chain-link fence in one
instance and the wooden fence in the other refer to and qualify the problem:

The fences are either insufficient (the relative flimsiness of the chain-link fence) or unfinished (in the sense that the wooden fence is still under construction). In both instances, the fences are inadequate to fulfill their purpose. We say "separation" because that is the only thing a fence signifies. It is a demarcating object separating two geographical areas, a means to determine where the one side begins and another ends. It is not until we consider the second set of images on the border—law-enforcement vehicles—that the meaning of the fences, and the significance of their inadequacy, is fully realized. The presence of law-enforcement vehicles signals the protective function of the fence. The fences not only separate the two physical sides; they are meant to protect one side from encroachment by the other.

The border landscape image is part of the issue alibi in this discourse of immigration policy. It points to the border and its protection not only as the central issue but also as a natural issue in the history of U.S. national and international affairs. It is natural for a sovereign nation-state to mark its territory and protect its border if its citizens feel that this territory is being compromised. Who can argue? Like the largely explicit, code-free language we discussed earlier in the chapter, there would be no significant criticism to lodge at these images in the ads; they look like any other issue ad we have come to recognize in the course of American political campaigns. However, when we move from the first composite to the one in Figure 5.2, we see that the first set of images do not tell the complete story of the border.

Figure 5.2 reflects the greater number of images of the border found in these ads. With only one distinguishing addition from those in Figure 5.1—that of people—the icon of the border takes on a drastically different shape. These images transfigure the desert and deserted border, and the inadequate fences that occupy them, from a statement about an issue or problem into a targeted characterization of the real threat. The real significance of an open border with inadequate boundaries is not the inadequacy of the physical objects (fences, walls, etc.) themselves but their inability to protect actual people on one side from actual people on the other. The problem is not the border; it is the people who cross it. The set of images in Figure 5.2 characterizes these fence jumpers and border crossers in a singular way: They are criminals.

The first set of images represented the problem of the border. The addition of law-enforcement vehicles to the border landscape signified the framing of the problem as a security matter. These images form the foundation for how those who cross the border are framed: They are criminals who threaten our national security. A common motif in each of these images is bound up with the fact that these images are photographs. The subject is the unseen eye on one side of the camera, while the fence jumpers and border crossers are visually objectified in the still photograph. These images suggest that the objects on the other end of the camera are not simply being photographed

FIGURE 5.2   Border crossers and fence jumpers

but also are being watched, monitored, surveilled (Shapiro 1995). Apparent in each of these images is the feeling that a hidden, all-seeing eye (again, we never see someone *taking* the photograph) is lurking in the shadows. A Foucauldian panopticon (1995) exists in which unsuspecting criminal trespassers trying to make their way across the border are simultaneously aware and unaware that someone is watching. But the full story of how these ads frame the problem of immigration by characterizing the immigrants who cross the border is exemplified in the image in the second row, second column. The subject behind the surveillance device is not participating in a passive act of covert surveillance but is making an active attempt ostensibly to aim a weapon at the objectified immigrants poised to cross the border. The immigrants are made into targets, signified by the crosshairs in the infrared scope. This image suggests that those who cross are not only criminals in the sense that they are illegally crossing national boundaries without permission, but that they constitute a real threat. They are dangerous, an imminent security threat so significant that police, even military, action is necessary.

Thus, the images of the border replete in these ads frame the problem of immigration as an imminent threat that begins at the Mexican border and is constituted in the bodies of objectified, trespassing immigrants. Although they are often represented by multiple individuals in single-file lines that give the illusion of a never-ending stream of individuals trekking across the border, and although they are often shown scurrying as if acknowledging their criminal deeds by trying to evade capture, one can never quite make out any of the immigrants' faces. None of the corporeal images that would transform them into subjects—especially eyes—are present. They are a faceless enemy threat that justifies the need for in-kind solutions.

These objectified images of criminal immigrants conceal the motivations that might lie at the heart of any one of these individuals' decision to brave the border. There are no desperate sons among these border crossers hoping to find work as day laborers at some corporation's factory outside Laredo so they can support ailing parents back home. There are no mothers among these fence jumpers making a last-ditch effort to try to support hungry children with just a little more than slave wages in a sweatshop on this side of the border separating (old) Mexico from New Mexico. There are no dreams or dreamers among these images. There are only criminals. The criminal threat posed by illegal immigrants begins with these images of the border. This perceived threat is compounded in the next set of images that we consider, which purport to show the truth about what these immigrants do when they arrive.

Criminal hordes. Immigrants who cross the Mexican border in the fashion imagined in the photographic images displayed in these ads are already criminalized; they have jumped a fence, walked across a border, or otherwise breached the national boundary to arrive in the United States. Images such as those in Figure 5.3 further develop this visual criminalization of Mexican immigrants in two significant ways. As we saw in the previous section, the criminal nature of Mexican immigrants is coded in the images of border crossers and fence jumpers—the depiction of national borders and those crossing it, and the depiction of law-enforcement images, form the criminal code. In the images, criminal status is explicitly labeled by overlaying the images of immigrants with linguistic images bearing the terms "criminal," "arrested," and "break our laws," or through explicit symbols of criminality—a jail cell, crime tape, law-enforcement personnel, or police cars. Again, because the immigrants in these photographs have no names, no history, no context, and no individuality, they have no identity except the label. "They" are *all* fundamentally criminals. The only exception to this, the one image that bears one's name, serves not to personalize or humanize the named individual immigrant but to make more pronounced his criminal nature. Gustavo Reyes is the iconic representative of "they."

There is a second difference between these images and the border images we examined earlier. The criminal images here intensify and heighten the threat posed by the criminal aliens not only by making their criminal nature

FIGURE 5.3 Criminal aliens

more explicit, but also by localizing the geographical location of their criminal acts. The images of the border terrain—barren and absent of life, except for a uniform, nondescript fence, law-enforcement vehicles, and a steady trickle of faceless jumpers and crossers—is essentially nowhere. Except for signaling its location as the American border between Mexico, it is located outside the geographical parameters in which everyday American life takes place. The border region could be anywhere from the far east of the Gulf of Mexico to the southwestern tip of California. Because it could be almost anywhere, it is, for all intents and purposes, nowhere at all in terms of the viewers' perception of its proximity to them.

The images of the border signify a national threat, while the images of the criminal aliens in Figure 5.3 evoke a more personal danger. There images show real people in the sense that we can see some of their faces. Border-patrol vehicles are the law-enforcement accoutrements for the border, but police cars are the vehicles that patrol communities and neighborhoods, and the officers in them are recognizable among the people who live there. The kind of spotlighting depicted in the first column, second row, of Figure 5.3 is not the scoping technology to surveil border crossers; it is a tool used to find criminals in terrain populated and crowded by people, office buildings, homes. People who live in populated neighborhoods and communities are more likely to see police

FIGURE 5.4   Immigrant hordes

tape than a fenced border. The tape itself marks a crime scene, meant to protect evidence from the possibility of damage by passersby. In short, the images of criminals that are displayed transport the immigrant threat from the border to our backyards. The threat is no longer just an ephemeral national one, like the threat of global warming, that we do not (cannot) see and recognize day to day. The threat is real, signified by criminal aliens with visible faces who commit crimes against real people whom we know in our own communities.

Another set of images that depicts crowds of immigrants further intensifies the criminal threat posed by illegal Mexican immigrants. While the set of images we just considered worked to localize this perceived threat, the images of crowds of immigrants suggest the pervasive, insidious growth of the threat. The double-layered images of crowds and linguistic images of numbers in the composite in Figure 5.4 best illustrate this reality. Because these photographs have been extracted from one context and placed into an ad, we only see crowds of immigrants. Although one might guess from the surroundings of several of the images that they are protesting, it is not entirely clear, and, even if they are, we do not know what it is they are protesting. The significance of these images is not so much that they signify the underlying criminality of the immigrants gathered, although both the scope and other surveillance images in the middle row allude to this fact. The most prominent aspect of these images is in how they characterize the magnitude of the problem represented by those featured in the crowds. The crowds themselves signify something of the omnipresent immigrant threat. They are depicted as unruly mobs, in one instance requiring police presence. This, along with the fact that they are often pictured with Mexican flags, open mouths, and arms thrust into the air, conjures a sense of inevitable national confrontation.

But the images of numbers really tell the whole story here. We have moved from a steady trickle of individuals jumping across the border to an organized mass of immigrants. "Twelve million are *already* here" in once instance; "50 million," in another. The precision of the number does not matter when what really needs to be communicated is the sense of an imminent and expanding threat. The term "already" pictured in two of the images adds a dimension of insidiousness to the threat, as if the millions already present are organized—as in the crowds in which they are depicted—secretly plotting, planning, at any moment ready to carry out some grand Mexican offensive against the United States. The threat grows and is more imminent with each passing year, with the addition of the next million immigrants, the next 30 million, the next 100 million. These invasion-laced images, when read alongside the criminal images before them, transpose the localized, personal threat communicated in the former into an increasingly pervasive reality for every local community across the country.

The images we have considered thus far tell a story. The narrative begins at the U.S.–Mexican border, where ubiquitous surveillors and border-patrol agents in enforcement vehicles keep continual watch over a steady stream of Mexican immigrants who cross the border into the United States. Once here, they inevitably become involved in lives of crime, and in concert with millions of their cohorts, their insidious criminal invasion grows, spreads, and spirals out of control. The remainder of the story is told by the most significant remaining set of images left out of the narrative thus far. We know where the threat begins; we know who constitutes the threat; and we know how pervasive the threat is. But what—and, more important, whom—do these people threaten most? We know who *they* are that threaten, but who is this *we*?

The royal "we" and the vulnerable "us." The images in Figure 5.5 are a linchpin to our underlying argument about the transformation of immigration policy discourse from being race-neutral to being race-dependent. But we should start at the beginning: Who is the "we" identified in these ads as those who stand to be harmed from the insidious threat posed by criminal aliens; who are those who demand protection, those who are on the threshold of being overrun? Two categories of people are shown in these ads: immigrants (the focus of our analysis thus far) and non-immigrants—Americans, "us." Whether candidates or otherwise, non-immigrant individuals signify the royal "we," those pitted in opposition to immigrants and who stand above them in the

FIGURE 5.5   "Us" and "we" (Americans)

privileged position of citizen. As seen in Figure 5.5, "we" have many faces. Often "we" are represented by the smallest among us, children. Born in some images, yet to be born in others (the pregnant woman in the image in row one, column five), our children are presented as innocent, carefree, and most vulnerable. In other images, "we" are the face of the elderly—also vulnerable but, beyond that, signifying the national legacy. They are old; they built this country and made it what it is. This country belongs to them. They have much to lose if the nation is taken away from them. "We" are families: mothers, fathers, sisters, brothers. The repetitive images of family signal not only a collective unit but also a set of collective values: goodness, unity, strength, interdependence, and self-reliance. The immigrants are masses of individuals; "we" are family. "We" are also a way of life, imaged in the serene scene of the pristine farm, the quiet suburban community, the safe playground, and the places where we meet for civic gatherings.

But most important of all—"we" are White. Again, the images in these ads represent "them" and "us," Mexicans and Americans. Perhaps the most overarching and significant characteristic of these ads is that of all the images of "us," only one includes someone who appears to be non-White.

The Racist Appeal in Immigration Ads

Now that all of the pieces of the puzzle are here—the language that describes and the images that visualize for us the nature and relationship between immigrants and citizens, Mexicans and Americans, the problem of the border, and the candidates purporting to remedy it—how do they fit together? How and why do the language and images of these ads constitute a racist appeal? First, the racist appeals discussed in Chapter 1 differed from the way language is used here in terms of the role that language played in constructing the racist appeal. In candidates' ads, where much of the racial appeal is wrapped up in a stereotypical character attack, language more often than not is coded. Racially coded language serves as its own alibi, concealing the explicit racial basis of the appeal.

As previously mentioned, the language used in immigration ads is largely explicit, neither concealing nor trying to conceal an underlying racial basis. Whether in the term "criminal," "illegal," or "illegal alien," the language clearly characterizes immigrants fundamentally as lawbreakers, and the language of invasion in the ads explicitly communicates the sense that they constitute an imminent threat. No prohibition against this labeling exists; thus, there is no need for code, because other language used in the ads makes it explicitly clear what the problem with immigrants is. It is a problem of the border. It is a national threat. It is a national security issue. In issue ads such as these, it is the issue itself that provides the alibi that conceals the underlying basis of the racist appeal. One can talk explicitly and often about immigrants as criminals; no racial implication is involved when the language appears to target and characterize all immigrants from all nationalities and backgrounds equally and when the overriding "issue" is a security issue, a geopolitical issue, not a "racial" issue. In short, while candidates would have us believe that their (and our) real concern with immigration is about national security, the persuasive basis of the appeal lies in evoking the sense of danger and fear that comes with a particular racial characterization of immigrants.

The second point to be made about the racial nature of these appeals relates to the relationship of language and the visual image. Again, in candidate-centered ads, racially coded language provides the concealing alibi (as we noted in Chapter 1), and the visual image is used as a cipher. That is, when a candidate refers to an "inner-city school," it is the visual image of a dilapidated school building with black and brown children playing in the playground that—subtle as it may be—tells the viewer how to interpret the term. In addition, in candidate-focused ads, the racial ethos is transposed onto the opposing candidate, especially when that candidate is a racial minority.

In the immigration ads we focus on in this chapter, the interpretation of language is not dependent on but exponentially enhanced by the visual image. In the case of these ads, the essential racializing component comes with the visual representation of who the immigrants are, what the real problem of the border is, and, most important, whom these immigrants threaten. We argue that the underlying racist appeal in these ads comes through in the visual depiction of "us" and "them," immigrants and American citizens. It is with the visual images that we see clearly that the border is the southern one that divides the United States from Mexico. It is with these images that we get a clear picture of who these immigrants are. They are Mexican immigrants. We know this from the language of the ads and the immigrants' visual comportment as an organized mass of criminals threatening America and American citizens. But it is no insignificant point that nearly 100 percent of the images of American citizens in these ads have White faces. We know that American citizens represent every racial, cultural, and national background in the world, including a large and continually growing number of Mexican and Latin American descent. Many are legal immigrants. But in these ads, we do not see Mexican Americans or African Americans or Native Americans or any other racial/ethnic group other than Whites represented. In these ads, White America stands in as the visual personification of the nation—its ideals, its values, those whom America holds itself out to be.[8] These values, ideals, and national identity erase all traces of difference such that it is *White* America that is threatened by the immigrant "other"—the Mexican, the illegal, the criminal (Holmes, Smith, Munoz, and Freng 2008; Zatz 1987). The underlying racial appeal in these ads is not transposed so much onto the opposing candidates, though this does happen. In fact, opposing candidates are most often pictured alongside the Mexican immigrants in the ads. However, in ads such as these, in which a single issue dominates, the underlying racial antipathy against Mexican immigrants is transposed onto the whole of the issue of immigration.

In the end, the immigration ads construct a narrative whose underlying racial basis is constructed from those elements we identified in Chapter 1 as the primary characteristics of race-based (primarily racist) appeals. That is, a person (a candidate in the ads from Chapter 1) or group of people (Mexican immigrants in immigration ads) is characterized according to a prevailing stereotype about the group. The stereotyped group is visually depicted in a manner that either implicitly or explicitly highlights the individuals' or groups' racial features, and the group is both linguistically and visually represented as a (racial) outsider, while Whites are depicted as consummate insiders. The immigration ads we focus on in our analysis contain each of the principal characteristics we use to determine whether a race-based appeal is present in a given political advertisement. But this also begs a critical question we must address: Can immigration ads be nonracial? The short answer to this is yes.

The language and images from the immigration advertisements we included in the bulk of our analysis are predominately racist in the ways we outline above. However, a scant few other immigration ads that ran during congressional elections in 2006 were clearly nonracial, in our analysis. That is, the language, images, and general framing of immigration in the ads did not fit into the dominant racial narrative about the imminent racial threat posed by Mexican criminal aliens. A couple of examples suffice to demonstrate how nonracial ads differ from the racialized ones. The first example is an ad by Tammy Duckworth, a Democratic House candidate from Illinois, that aired in Illinois. It accused her opponent of distorting her record on immigration and claimed she wanted to set the record straight. She pointed out that she opposed "amnesty for illegal immigrants" and supported increasing the number of border-patrol agents. She highlighted the fact that she had been a pilot in the armed forces and risked her life to defend the country, so people therefore could be assured she would fight to keep the country secure.

Perhaps the most important distinction between Duckworth's ad and the racialized immigration ads we discussed is that Duckworth used very little imagery. When she spoke about amnesty and illegal "immigrants" (not "illegal aliens," or "illegals"), the viewer was looking at her, not at images of shady figures hopping a fence or committing crimes. That is, while talking about immigration, she—not the immigrants to whom she referred—were the central focus. When she referred to illegal immigrants, she did not attempt to represent or amplify who they were with images of borders or fences or hordes of illegal aliens crossing into the country. She said as much as others have in their ads without inciting any race-related thinking about the issue itself or about those toward whom it is targeted.

A second example is an ad by Tessa Hafen, a Democrat who ran for Congress in Nevada against Jon Porter. The ad began by pointing out that Porter agreed with George Bush almost 100 percent of the time, "even when it comes to illegal immigration." As in Duckworth's ad, however, the narrator in this ad used the terms "illegal immigration," "illegal immigrants," and "amnesty." Hafen charged that her opponent had done nothing to penalize employers for hiring them. Again, the imagery in the ad was nonracial. When immigration-related terms were used, the image on the screen were of Porter, Bush, and an American flag—not a Mexican flag, not Mexican people, nothing racial whatsoever. And again as in Duckworth's ad, the focus was on a candidate—Hafen's opponent, in this case. When Hafen talked about immigrants, she did not imply that they were to blame; she faulted Porter for not doing enough to punish employers who hired them, not the immigrants themselves looking for work.

CONCLUSION

This chapter demonstrates through another lens the simple, yet sophisticated, ways in which race-based appeals are constructed. Although the racist appeals deployed in candidates' issue-focused advertisements and those used in the candidate-focused ads we looked at in the previous chapters are similar in many ways, we have seen that there are some subtle but significant differences.

The most salient aspect of the racial appeals in the immigration ads we considered in this chapter is their singular and unified characterization of the central players in the immigration arena. In almost every ad, regardless of party affiliation or ideological position of its sponsor, immigrants were Mexican, with visibly different skin color. Overwhelmingly, they personified the problem of the border, the essential flaw in American immigration policy. They were almost always described or visually depicted as criminals, as an insidious threat to American ideals—family, hard work, responsibility, and commerce. The language and visual images myopically signified White America as that which needs to be protected. Americans—White Americans—were always the righteous, the virtuous, the vulnerable.

The real threat here is that these ads produce a particular discourse about immigration and immigration policy. The danger goes beyond the success or failure of a given candidate who may have become erroneously entangled in a web of associations with these illegal, criminal, Mexican aliens. The real danger is that these ads produce a discourse about immigration that irrationally frames how we view the issue and colors the measures we propose to solve the problem. This is to say, it leads us to view the issue of immigration as fundamentally a problem, and a problem about a monolithic mass of racialized others who, because of their innate criminal character, threaten the system of White supremacy on which America was founded. It is an emotional appeal that exemplifies the worst of Walter Lippman's fears about the public and its ability to support political remedies based on reasoned deliberation. The real consequence of such racial appeals is that public policy, which no doubt is heavily influenced by this racial framing of the immigration issue, will reflect an emotional will that targets, dehumanizes, and disenfranchises a group of people based on a fever pitch of errors that the producers of immigration discourse have deployed to gain public support.

As we noted at the outset, however, direct messages are only one form of communication to which potential voters are exposed during the course of a campaign. While such messages are important to understand because of the potential for direct effects, the mediated messages voters receive help to shape and place such messages into context, which creates a complex political environment. It is precisely this type of contextualization to which we turn next as we consider the ways that media outlets tend to reinforce, perpetuate, and exacerbate racialized campaign communication emanating from the candidates or their surrogates.

6

Harold Ford Jr., Mel Martinez, and Artur Davis

Case Studies in Racially Framed News

W HEN WE REFER to race-based appeals, we largely refer to communications that emanate from the candidates and their surrogates or
supporters. However, as we noted in Chapter 4, the news media
often buttress these appeals in the way that they frame their reporting of election contests. That is, when the mass media go beyond simply conveying candidates' appeals to racialized framing, they may often work to support or
undermine race-based claims made by candidates. In keeping with their
"watchdog" function, news media can especially be involved in bolstering or
mitigating race-based appeals, particularly with regard to accusations of who
"played the race card."

In this chapter, we closely examine three contests from the first decade of
the twenty-first century as case studies of campaign communication about
race—both direct and mediated. These contests were chosen because of their
diversity with respect to the seats sought (we examine two U.S. Senate races
and one race for the U.S. House of Representatives) and racial composition
(one contest features a White candidate running against a Black candidate in
a general election; one features a White candidate running against a Latino
candidate in a general election; and one features two Black candidates running against each other in the Democratic Party primary for a seat in a heavily
Democratic and majority-Black district). This approach gives us the opportunity to provide a deeper analysis of television ads and newspaper coverage of
each of these contests, paying particular attention to the themes that emerged
from our quantitative analysis of the larger group of similar contests in previous chapters.

THE TENNESSEE U.S. SENATE RACE, 2006

Although the stereotype of Whites in the Southern United States is that they are more bigoted than Whites in the North, Black candidates for high-profile statewide office have fared equally poorly in both areas. Through the 2008 elections, only two Black governors (Douglas Wilder in Virginia and Deval Patrick in Massachusetts) and three Black U.S. senators (Edward Brooke in Massachusetts and Carol Moseley Braun and Barack Obama in Illinois) have been elected since Reconstruction.[1] In 2006, a number of Black candidates—many of them Republicans—sought statewide office, and though only Patrick won, their combined presence contributed to the increased normalcy of Black candidates' running for high-profile statewide office, which can only have helped Barack Obama in winning a statewide plurality in enough states to secure the Electoral College vote for president two years later.

Harold Ford Jr., a Democrat, was a popular five-term member of the U.S. Congress from Tennessee's Ninth District (Memphis). He resigned in 2008 to run for the state's open Senate seat. His father had been the first African American to represent Tennessee in Congress and had served that district for the twenty-two years that preceded his son's election. Ford Jr. has an Ivy League education (he earned his bachelor of arts from the University of Pennsylvania) and a law degree from the University of Michigan. His opponent in the race, the Republican Bob Corker, who is White, was educated at the University of Tennessee and had a career in business and construction before serving as a public official. He was mayor of Chattanooga for five years before he sought the Senate seat. Corker is married with two children, while Ford is single, a fact that would become as least indirectly relevant as the campaign took shape. Corker defeated Ford by a margin of 51–48 percent in the general election in November.

Two prominent race-related themes emerged during the campaign: Ford as "the other" and Ford as having questionable character. For his part, Ford worked to inoculate and defend himself against the attacks by using counter-stereotype language and images while attacking Corker for being uncaring and out of touch with ordinary Tennesseans because of his wealth. We provide a detailed analysis of each theme below.

The "Other"

One of the characteristics of a biracial election is that race is inherently a factor, irrespective of the participants' intent. Despite the persistent claims of "colorblindness" in America, everyone understood that Corker was White and Ford was Black and that Ford would have to win a significant amount of White support to be elected.[2] In previewing the contest after the primaries had been decided, the *Chattanooga Times Free Press* noted that Ford was "trying to become the first black senator in Tennessee, a state with a relatively small minority population outside the metropolitan centers."[3] An article in the *Memphis Flyer* raised the possibility that, even during the primaries, national Democrats were backing Ford, as they wished to capitalize on his "storyline that runs something like this: 'Can a bright young charismatic African-American congressman overcome racial bias and his family history to win back a Senate seat for the Democrats in the swing state of Tennessee?'"[4]

The racial rhetoric shifted quickly from explicit to implicit after the primaries, however, with code words that we discovered and discussed in Chapter 1 making numerous appearances. One of the ways this happened was through the "otherness" frame, where a subconscious norm of Whiteness can be relied on for a baseline from which difference can be inferred without pointing out race explicitly.[5]

Corker, his surrogates, and a supportive press consistently referred to Ford as "liberal," both as an adjective to describe him and his voting record and as a noun (e.g., the headline "Conservative Bob versus a Liberal").[6] Corker's campaign consistently referred to Ford as "the most liberal member" of Tennessee's congressional delegation.[7] Ben Mitchell, Corker's campaign manager, was quoted as saying that Ford should "explain [his] liberal votes."[8] As we noted in previous chapters, "liberal" is often used to attack candidates of color in a biracial contest. While the claim is also used by conservative candidates against White opponents, the effect is different because the connotation of the word, particularly with conservatives, suggests support for government handouts, permissive sexuality, and the general eschewing of traditional moral values, all of which are encompassed in stereotypes of African Americans and Latinos. Early in the race, the executive director of the Tennessee Republican Party quipped, "Congressman Ford is a darling of the Eastern liberal establishment, and every opportunity he has to go up to D.C. and raise money, he takes advantage of it."[9] This attack has two components that play into the "other" frame: liberal ideology and outsider, East Coast, inner-city proclivities that ostensibly are at odds with the values embraced by White, rural Tennesseans.

Corker ran a number of television ads designed to enhance his rural/insider credentials. Fred Thompson, the actor and former U.S. senator from Tennessee, filmed a number of spots for Corker, and rural settings characterized a number of Corker's ads. Ford, too, tried to employ rural imagery in his ads, having White folks provide a testimonial in a spot called "Partners." The ad opened with a middle-aged White woman, identified as Dixie Taylor Huff, speaking in a thick Southern drawl: "I was asked a few weeks ago, 'What in the world's a country girl like you doin' for Harold Ford Jr.,' and I said, 'We need change.'" A man on a tractor—Johnny Dodson—appeared next, saying in an even thicker accent, "I'm not a Democrat or a Republican. I vote for the man who has the ideas." Tennessee's Democratic Governor Phil Bredesen spoke, and then Dodson returned to say, "Harold Ford is the one for the job." One Black man, a preacher identified as the Reverend Melvin Charles Smith, spoke for two seconds at the twenty-one-second mark of the thirty-second spot, and the ad closed with Ford himself looking at the camera and asking for support for a few seconds until Bredesen returned, saying, "Harold will make us proud." Such an effort is a clear attempt at inoculation against—or, in this case, defense against—accusations that a person of color cannot look out for the interests of Whites. Tennessee voters certainly were aware that Ford, as well as his father, represented the only majority-Black district in the state, so an effort to send a clear signal of concern for people in the rest of the state had heightened importance. When a prominent White Tennessean uses "us," it signals to those who identify with him as a "real" Tennessean that Ford, too, can be counted on to represent "our" interests.

"Family"—particularly Ford's family—was a considerable sub-theme throughout the campaign. Many of the attacks against Ford mentioned his family, despite Corker's explicit claim early on that this would not be an issue in the campaign.[10] Less than three weeks after that proclamation, Corker was publicly expressing concern about the "Ford political machine" in Memphis, alleging that politics was the Fords' "family business."[11] In fact, three members of Ford's family have been indicted;[12] his father was acquitted, but one uncle was convicted and another was awaiting trial as the campaign took shape.[13] Attempts to link Ford to such unpopular activity would be effective in any context. It is important to remember, however, that the stereotypical association of African Americans with criminality and lack of trustworthiness makes the effect of such accusations disproportionate when leveled against the Black candidate in a biracial contest.

Corker put forth further accusations that Ford's votes were influenced by his father's work as a lobbyist for Fannie Mae, the government-sponsored mortgage company. A television ad called "Too Close for Comfort" featured a split screen with father and son appearing, moving in slow motion, while a narrator explained that Harold Ford Sr. had been hired as a lobbyist for Fannie Mae three months after his son was seated on a congressional committee with oversight responsibilities for the entity and that Ford Jr. had sponsored four bills that were advocated by Fannie Mae. The narrator concluded, "Troubled family ties—that's the real Harold Ford Jr." as the text "That's the real Harold Ford Jr." appeared on the screen. Ford challenged Corker's attacks on his family in a debate held a month before the election,[14] and he ran a television ad in which he looked directly at the camera and said, "Look, I love my family, and I won't speak ill of them, but I hope you'll judge me by what I do. My ideas, right and wrong.... This election *is* about family—yours. And I'll never forget that."

The attempts to lump Ford in with his powerful family is consistent with the "otherness" frame. In this case, Ford is portrayed as not being authentically

Tennessean. In one contrast advertisement, Corker juxtaposed his back-ground with Ford's via a narrator: "Harold Ford Jr. grew up in D.C.; Bob Corker, in Tennessee." An image of Ford in front of the Capitol, followed by accelerated footage of a busy city street, accompanied the language about him, while a picture of Corker walking in front of a tree and a still image of a heavily foliated riverbank accompanied the comment about his upbringing. The narrator continued: "Harold schooled at Penn. Bob chose UT." The texts "University of Pennsylvania" and "University of Tennessee" accompanied images of Ford and Corker, respectively. Ford's image was always in slow motion; Corker's was at full speed. "Harold inherited a life of politics. Bob Corker built a business, a family, helped secure affordable homes for thou-sands, and built a city. Harold's lived politics, and Bob Corker's lived a Ten-nessee life." Besides the obvious contrast that Corker sought to draw, it should be noted that "inherited" is also a reference that plays into the "unde-serving" stereotype that so often characterizes attacks on candidates of color, especially as contrasted here with Corker, who "built" (worked for) what he had accomplished. Further, this "outsider" frame touches on the second major theme of the campaign—character—as it carries with it an inherent implication that Ford is trying to deceive Tennesseans into thinking he is someone he is not. In short, Ford is not to be trusted.

Character

An editorial in the *Chattanooga Times Free Press* immediately after the primaries had been decided provides interesting foreshadowing of what would come in this regard. The editorial board referred to Ford as "articulate," which is often considered insulting when applied to African Americans, as it suggests that this characteristic sets the target individual apart from African Americans as a whole. The newspaper also noted that Ford was "a spell-binding and well-informed speaker."[15] A recurrent theme in Corker's campaign was that Ford was "slick" and untrustworthy and that he was hiding who he really was.

The *Chattanooga Times Free Press,* in fact, contributed significantly to this frame, referring on numerous occasions to these characteristics. An editorial published on October 3, made a reference to "the articulate Ford," and other articles commented on Ford's "well-crafted delivery" and "flashy image and smooth talk."[16] Republican Congressman Zach Wamp said that Ford was "a friend who has 'charisma coming out of his ears,' but [is] a political chame-leon. 'If he's in one particular audience, he's going to say just what they want to hear, and then when he's in another audience, he's going to say just what they want to hear."[17]

Many of Corker's television ads focused on this theme. The tag "The <u>Real</u> Harold Ford Jr." was used in most of the attack ads (with the word "real" underlined in the on-screen text), which varied by type of alleged lie, "stretched truth," or "unanswered question." In one spot, Corker alleged, by way of a narrator, that Ford was traveling around the world on taxpayer money, missing votes. "He doesn't show up for work. That's the real Harold Ford Jr.," his ad said, and "That's the real Harold Ford. Things aren't always as they seem." In another ad, the narrator noted that Ford needed to clarify his record on a number of issues, including claiming he was a lawyer when he had not passed the bar exam: "Exaggerations and questionable judgment—that's the real Harold Ford Jr."

Perhaps the most striking ad on this theme came from the Republican National Committee (RNC) and featured 1970s-style funky disco music in the background as a narrator said:

> Harold Ford Jr. He's slick. He's smooth. But his record? A little shaky. Ford is Tennessee's most liberal congressman. He campaigns in a church but took cash from Hollywood's top X-rated porn moguls. Ford talks values but voted to recognize gay marriage, voted for taxpayer-funded abortions ten times, and wants to give the abortion pill to our schoolchildren. Harold Ford. Smooth talk, Hollywood values.

The images in the ad ranged from unflattering pictures of Ford to a large "XXX" image over the iconic Hollywood sign and a girl in a school uniform looking invitingly toward the camera as the narrator talked about the abortion pill. Although the most controversial ads did, in fact, come from the RNC, Corker worked to reinforce the themes. In one of his spots, the handsome Corker feigned self-deprecation by saying, "I might not be as good-looking. I may not be as articulate. And I may not be able to do those slick commercials. . . . We'll do it the way Tennesseans want it done."

No advertisement in the 2006 national election cycle got as much attention as the now infamous "Playboy" ad that was run by the RNC. The Playboy angle did not start with this ad, however. As early as mid-August, Ford had made news by returning $3,600 in campaign contributions from representatives of Playboy Enterprises and adult film studios.[18] But in late October, the RNC ad surfaced both on the air in Tennessee and on the Internet, raising allegations of racism that would be vociferously denied by RNC representatives.

The spot was designed to be amusing, with fake person-on-the-street testimony sarcastically signaling support for Ford because he "looks nice. Isn't that enough?"; because "terrorists need their privacy"; and because "When I die, Harold Ford will let me pay taxes again." A man in camouflage says, "Ford's right. I do have too many guns." If the ad ended there, it might have been used for years in Campaigns and Elections classes as an effective parody. What happened next assured that it would be used for quite another reason, however. A blonde White woman who appeared to be naked except for a gold necklace but who was standing on a street (which leads one to suspect she was wearing some sort of revealing top or dress that was simply out of the camera's frame) says in a high-pitched, peppy voice: "I met Harold at the Playboy party." After a series of other claims by fictitious supporters, including a man in sunglasses insinuating that everyone has taken money from "porn producers" ("I mean, who hasn't?"), the text "Harold Ford. He's just not right" appeared on the screen. Finally, after the disclaimer, the "Playboy" woman returned—the only character to appear twice in the spot—looked directly into the camera, and whispered, with her fingers to her ear in a mock telephone, "Harold, call me," and winked.

In fact, Ford did attend a Super Bowl party sponsored by Playboy in 2005 but claimed never to have attended a party at the Playboy Mansion in California. A number of writers and public figures, including former Secretary of Defense and Republican Senator William Cohen, pointed out the implicitly racist nature of the attack.[19] Members of Corker's staff said that the ad was "tacky" and "over the top," and Corker himself publicly asked the RNC to pull it.[20] By the end of October, though, just days before the election, the ad was still running, which drew the ire of the *Chattanooga Times Free Press*: "This ad visibly illustrates Republicans' real core values: their ready willingness to trade on sex, race and the Old South taboo against interracial relations and miscegenation to attack Mr. Ford."[21] On NBC's *Meet the Press*, Ken Mehlman, chairman of the RNC, defended the spot, bending over backward to deny that any racism was intended or could be inferred because he had shown it to "African American folks [and] Hispanic folks . . . and [they] did not have that same reaction to it."[22]

The argument over whether the spot is or is not "racist" is largely semantic. That is, for critical race theorists and those who understand "racism" to be systemic and to work most prominently in the subconscious, there is no question that the ad is likely to have an effect that is heightened as a result of America's racist history and the lingering concerns in many parts of the nation—particularly in the Deep South—about interracial romance. For those who believe that only use of the "N word" or overt, individual-level bigotry rises to the level of "racism," there is nothing in the spot to support such a claim. After all, no overtly racial words are used; both Black and White individuals appear in the ad; and Ford is not even depicted. Yet if we divorce the notion of racism from intent, instead focusing on effects, it is nearly impossible to deny that the ads' racist potential is clear and strong.

Explicit Race Talk

Of course, one of the important caveats from the implicit–explicit literature is that once an implicit appeal to race is made explicit, it is rendered ineffective and, in fact, can backfire.[23] Candidates of color running in majority-White districts have a difficult task because they wish to appear to be "post-racial" but cannot allow implicitly racist attacks to exist under the radar because they have such potential to be effective. Barack Obama faced this dilemma when the controversy surrounding the Reverend Jeremiah Wright's alleged racially inflammatory remarks emerged in early 2008, and he chose to deal with it by giving one speech centered firmly on race (as we discuss in detail in the next chapter). Harold Ford Jr. gave no such speech. It is impossible to know whether he would have won the election if he had, but it is clear that the degree to which he and his surrogates sought to shed light on racist appeals were not effective. As we surmised in Chapter 3, it is possible that Ford saw that he had much more to lose by explicitly defending himself against racist attacks.

In early October, Ford was complaining about a different RNC ad that included what he called "a dark, shadowy figure" intended, Ford believed, to represent him. He told the *Chattanooga Times Free Press,* "I think [that the ad] injects a little race in this thing, the way they have me pictured."[24] This would be the only direct public mention of race from Ford during the campaign. A *Time* magazine article reported on the "shadowy figure" spot, pointing out parallels to the "Willie Horton" ad; it noted that Ford's skin had been artificially darkened and that "phrases including 'purports,' 'pretends,' and 'passes himself off as'—all terms once used for light-skinned blacks who pretend to be white"—had been used. The *Time* article quoted the head of the Tennessee Republican Party as dismissing allegations of racism, while the executive director of the Baptist Center for Ethics noted that "the only plausible reason to use [an artificially darkened] picture is to play the race card."[25]

About a week later, an independent group called Tennesseans for Truth ran a sixty-second radio ad that Corker called "outrageous" and demanded to have pulled. In the first twenty-four seconds of the ad, the word "Black" was used six times, accusing "Ford of favoring African-American issues above others. 'His daddy handed him his seat in Congress and his seat in the Congressional Black Caucus, an all-black group of congressmen who represent the interests of black people above all others,' the narrator says."[26] The narrator in the ad went on to question whether Ford was capable of "representing all of us without discrimination."[27]

By the end of October, race was being discussed openly and more frequently, at least in the local press. Ford's surrogates did what they were supposed to do: They played down accusations of race to avoid the perception that Ford fit the stereotype of the hypersensitive African American who turns everything into an issue of race. Klyde Allen, a Black supporter of Ford, told the *Chattanooga Times Free Press* (in an article not facetiously titled "Race Could Be a Factor in Corker–Ford Contest") that he thought "Americans ha[d] grown up, and they [we]re not that shallow anymore." A White Ford supporter, however, indicated that he had seen quite a bit of racism as a result of his support for Ford.[28] Three days later, the *Chattanooga Times Free Press* seemed more sure that race would, in fact, matter in the election. In an editorial entitled "Race Will Matter in U.S. Senate Contest," David Magee wrote, "No factor outside political party affiliations will affect the outcome of this closely contested campaign more [than race]." Magee pointed the finger at Blacks for supporting Ford at a 90 percent rate while noting that many Whites, too, were supporting Corker because of race. The journalist claimed that he could "empathize" with Blacks' unity because of the history of racism in the South, but he bemoaned "racism in reverse":

> Not once during this race, for instance, have I heard a white Tennessean utter a racial derogation or seen a white Tennessean roll an eye. It has happened, I'm sure, but I have not seen it. Conversely, I have had several White Tennesseans state clearly that they like Bob Corker but are voting for Harold Ford Jr. because they want to see the state send to Washington a signal of change—a black Senator from a majority-white state.[29]

After the election was over, in late November, an editorial in the *Memphis Flyer* mocked the mainstream media's obsession with the race issue, praising a *New York Times* article by Adam Nossiter arguing that many factors, including race, had been at work in the election. As long as the "consensus among national pundits" that race was the deciding factor holds, the editorial staff wrote, "any point of view expressed by us local yokels may be deemed irrelevant by the big boys in the well-appointed offices up yonder. After all, are we not suspect witnesses, having perhaps drunk of the bigot's brew ourselves?"[30]

THE FLORIDA U.S. SENATE RACE, 2004

To date, there have been six Hispanic or Latino members of the U.S. Senate. At the time of this contest, none were currently serving, although by January 2005 two would be sworn in: Ken Salazar, a Democrat from Colorado, and Mel Martinez, a Republican from Florida.[31] Martinez, a Cuban American, was educated at Florida State University (bachelor's and law degree) and had a successful law career before being named secretary of housing and urban development by President George W. Bush in 2001. The Democrat Betty Castor, who is White and is a native of New Jersey, holds degrees from Glassboro State College and the University of Miami. She served in a number of local offices in Florida from the early 1970s through the early 1990s and was the first woman to be president of the University of South Florida. Martinez won the general election contest by a margin of 50–48 percent.

This contest was complicated by the fact that it took place during a presidential election year, one year after the U.S. invasion of Iraq. Both President Bush and Vice President Dick Cheney campaigned for Martinez, and Castor was outspoken about her support for the Democratic presidential challenger Senator John Kerry. Bush carried Florida by 5 percentage points, so there is a possibility of a "coattails effect." Regardless, this very expensive contest clearly took a back seat to the presidential race, particularly because of Florida's position as a swing state and its controversial role in the previous presidential election.[32]

The racial dynamic here hinged on two factors. First, Mel Martinez was the only racial minority featured in this chapter to run as a Republican. Thus, he was able to craft a message consistent with conservative ideology that mitigated some racist stereotypes about Latinos. Some of the conservative message is rooted in policy preferences, but other aspects are rooted in the abstract notion of "patriotism," as we discuss below. Further, Martinez's Latino heritage was effectively framed as a strength rather than a liability, stemming at least in part from the fact that he had been born in Cuba rather than Central or South America. These unique factors render Martinez's efforts distinct from those of Harold Ford Jr., as Ford's heritage was de-emphasized because of the need to secure votes among an overwhelmingly White electorate. In that race, Bob Corker made very little attempt to tap into what he must have understood to be solid African American support for Ford.

In this context, then, Martinez was able to compete for Latino voters in ways that Republicans in many other areas could not. He alternated between English and Spanish when appropriate and was not shy about noting the historic nature of his campaign.[33] One local newspaper article noted, in fact, that his ethnicity would be a benefit to the state—more so than Castor's gender:

> If Martinez wins, he would become one of the nation's most prominent Hispanic political figures. As the first Cuban-American senator, he would be in demand by Republicans in areas with large Latino populations, such as New York, Texas and California. No such stage awaits Castor, though she would be only the second woman to hold a Senate seat from Florida.[34]

It is important, however, to take into consideration the unique demographic landscape of Florida, where the racial composition resulted in a more complicated electoral landscape than was in place in Tennessee. Martinez's championing of his "story" (as it was so often called) was not designed simply to solidify votes on the basis of identity politics. Florida is 20 percent Latino, but there is a mix of national origins within that category, including the highest concentration of Cuban Americans in the nation. Cuban Americans historically have identified and voted as Republicans in greater numbers than other Latinos, but Martinez could not count on even a majority of the Latino vote for a number of reasons. A story in *USA Today* notes the following scenario: "For Castor, the challenge is to hold her own among the 14% of voters who are Hispanic. Her odds have improved. Florida's Hispanic community, once 80% Cuban, is now 50% Puerto Rican, Mexican and other non-Cuban Hispanics. Martinez hopes they will cross party lines to elect a fellow Spanish speaker."[35]

Further, young Cubans supported Democratic candidates more than their senior counterparts did, at least in Florida in 2004.[36] Some of the friction was a result of attitudes about the U.S. embargo of Cuba. Young Cubans have been more supportive of ending sanctions and permitting travel, while older Cubans—many of whom were born in Cuba—continue to support sanctions. Martinez not only supported continued sanctions; he was influential in the Bush administration's policy toward Cuba.[37]

Martinez therefore could not take for granted the support of Latinos in the way that Harold Ford Jr. was able to take for granted the Black vote in Tennessee or the way that Latino Democrats in California are able to count on an overwhelming level of support in their communities. In fact, Betty Castor did compete for votes from Latinos and was successful. She ran ads in Spanish and, in an otherwise English-language spot, featured a Black child (who may or may not have been Latina) saying, "Gracias, Betty!" for her work on behalf of children's health care. Exit polls reveal that 15 percent of those who voted in Florida in 2004 identified as Latino, and 40 percent of those voters chose Castor (CNN 2004).

Florida also has a sizable Black population (15.3%), and while Democrats enjoy overwhelming support from Black voters generally, some aspects of identity politics theory and the voting behavior literature would allow for Martinez to receive a minority solidarity vote from African Americans.[38] Several newspaper articles referred to the battle for minority voters, particularly in what is known as the "I-4 corridor":

> In a tossup race, both candidates are reaching beyond traditional sources of support to groups seen as essential to their rival's success. They are doing it with both issues and images. With Hispanics accounting for one of every seven voters in Florida, Castor must cut into Martinez's base of Latino support, with non-Cuban Hispanics in the Interstate-4 corridor, most of whom are Puerto Ricans who lean Democrat. At the same time, Martinez, a self-made Cuban immigrant, pitches his Horatio Alger–like story to black professionals, who are less likely than their parents to be loyal supporters of the Democratic Party.[39]

A radio advertisement from the Human Rights Campaign criticized Martinez for his opposition to hate-crime legislation by invoking the image of James Byrd, a Black man who was dragged to his death in Texas in 1998.[40] Attempts to depict Martinez as bigoted and insensitive were lost in his "story."

That does not mean, however, that Martinez did not have to contend with systemic racism. Parts of Betty Castor's message certainly might have had increased effectiveness because her opponent was a person of color. For instance, Castor consistently implied or stated that Martinez was dishonest. Early in the campaign, for instance, she criticized his behavior in the Republican primary in an ad with a narrator who said, at the end, "Can we believe anything he says?"[41] At one point, Castor quipped, "Oh, Mel. Give us all a break. Tell the truth."[42] In the last few days of the campaign, Castor stepped up her attacks on Martinez's honesty and integrity, accusing him of having a conflict of interest with respect to some decisions he made as Secretary of Housing and Urban Development. She combined that criticism with an indictment of how he had run the campaign, as well, saying, "The issue now . . . is whether or not Mr. Martinez is capable of being an honest representative because I think the way you campaign says an awful lot about the way you will perform in office."[43]

It is possible that such messages about dishonesty resonated with voters disproportionately to how similar attacks on White candidates would because of Martinez's heritage. In the end, however, he was able to leverage his partisanship, his history, and the racial diversity in the state to achieve electoral success by effectively framing his narrative within the notion of the "American dream" and by seizing control of the most salient issue in the election—national security—by arguing that he, not his White opponent, was more devoted to American principles and values.

The "American Dream"

Unlike what we saw in the previous chapter, but certainly related to the same underlying racist principles, Mel Martinez was not to be defined by the "otherness" that so often characterizes depictions of Latinos in campaign communication. Martinez traveled around in a bus on an "American Dream Tour."[44] The phrase "American dream" and references to his "story" were repeated in ads by Martinez and by his supporters. Rudy Giuliani, former mayor of New York City, told a group of Martinez supporters, "[Mel Martinez] is going to be a great senator whose story is a story that ennobles America."[45]

A number of Martinez's advocacy and contrast ads used the phrase "Mel escaped communism," often preceded or followed by "as a child" or "as a teenager."[46] The phrase "escaped communism" is effective on a number of levels. First, it alerts voters to the fact that Martinez is Cuban American, which means that his arrival in the United States is seen as positive. He was never an "illegal alien," and he broke no U.S. laws to cross the border. On the contrary, by leaving a nation that is an official enemy of the United States, Martinez has been awarded a sort of hero status. Further, the word "escaped" is preferable to "fled" or "defected," as "escaped," too, connotes strength, signaling that even the oppressive chains of communism could not hold such a strong leader who is committed to the fundamental values of American democracy. His story plays into the American meta-narrative about freedom and independence that, perhaps ironically, constituted the "us" position in the ads discussed in the previous chapter. Unlike those "aliens" infiltrating from across the U.S.-Mexican border, Martinez is the "good kind" of immigrant. He sought out America not to exploit "our" resources and opportunities but to find a way to contribute to the nation's financial well-being. He celebrates "our" spirit of liberty and is willing to sever all ties and allegiances to his native country.

One Martinez ad featured an endorsement by Giuliani, whose very presence, particularly after the attacks in 2001 and before his bid for the White House in 2008, connotes American values for millions. With footage of Martinez speaking at Ground Zero rolling in the background, Giuliani noted that Martinez was the "clear choice" for the greatest issue facing the American people—"winning the war on terror"—because "Mel Martinez escaped communism and knows what it is like to live without freedom." Giuliani claimed that Martinez would "fight every day to defend the America we love."

Yet another ad began with video footage of President George W. Bush speaking at a rally in support of Martinez, calling him "a great American" as an American flag waved across the screen and footage of Martinez shaking Bush's hand in the Oval Office was shown. As a narrator took over, a picture of a young Martinez was displayed over what appeared to be either trash or a stack of papers: "Mel escaped communism as a young boy, alone, and fell in love with America and freedom." As a large American flag waved, a picture of Martinez in a baseball uniform (a quintessential symbol of America) appeared. There are no fewer than seven separate flags waving in this thirty-second spot, not including the one in his logo.

These types of appeals are racial in the sense that they potentially serve as inoculating mechanisms against a predisposition toward Latinos that they, in fact, are a threat to American values. There is no implicit attack on Castor here, either, because there is no accusation (explicit or implied) that she is any more hostile toward "our" common values than any other candidate of an opposite political party. Neither her gender nor her race contributes to a negative impression of her with respect to this claim.[47]

Castor, however, did try to turn the "American dream" theme against Martinez, particularly by continually noting that he was extremely wealthy and out of touch with ordinary Floridians. One month before the election, she criticized his opposition to raising the minimum wage by saying:

Here's a guy that's in the top 1 percent, he's making over $400,000 a year now as a lobbyist for a law firm, but he doesn't want to have the people that clean the office make a dollar more in wages. That's wrong for Florida. We need to treat all people who work in this state with a fair wage.[48]

By arguing that the people who would benefit the most by her proposed one-dollar increase in the minimum wage were women and Latinos, Castor used Martinez's language against him, arguing, "He wants to deny them the American dream."[49] The next day, she continued with the theme, again referring to Latinos: "It's not enough to say, 'I am the American dream.' We have to make the American dream happen for everyone."[50] Finally, just days before the election, Castor told a group of Black supporters at a campaign stop that Martinez had "forgotten his roots."[51]

Patriotism

Martinez did, however, try to "out American" Castor by juxtaposing his own story with a high-profile case in which Castor was involved. While Castor was president of the University of South Florida, a computer science professor named Sami Al-Arian was suspected by the federal government of being a leader of the Palestinian Islamic Jihad.[52] Interestingly, Castor had first mentioned Al-Arian in a series of ads aired in October in which she attacked Martinez, who supported President Bush's election efforts in Florida in 2000 by showing images of Bush campaigning with Al-Arian in Florida.[53] Martinez shot back with a story that ended up having more staying power: He argued that Castor had allowed Al-Arian to operate under protection of academic freedom at her university for six years. Subsequent arguments—in the press and during debates—ensued with respect to whether Castor had "disciplined" Al-Arian by putting him on paid administrative leave, but the resulting narrative was more harmful to Castor than to Martinez, as it fit nicely into the frame that he was more patriotic—essentially "more American"—than Castor.

For instance, Martinez was able to parlay the controversy into a portrayal of Castor as soft on terror: "She gave [Al-Arian] pay raises and hoped the problem would go away. Terrorists seek to harm us and they masquerade as college professors while Betty Castor tries to be politically correct."[54] A television advertisement on the issue began with video footage of a man presumed to be an Islamic extremist shown with a caption, in translation, saying, "Damn America . . . damn Israel . . . until death." A narrator said, "What is Islamic Jihad? A murderous band of terrorists who hate America." The spot went on to criticize Castor's handling of the Al-Arian situation, followed by criticism of Castor's statement that America was the "the bully of the world." The claim referred to a statement Castor had given in 2003 at a Democratic

Party picnic, where she was quoted as saying, "I don't think we can continue to be the bully of the world. I do wonder if a little more diplomacy . . . if that would have done more."[55] The "bully" comment was introduced immediately after the discussion of the terror cell at the university, leaving open a possible interpretation that Castor not only was soft on terrorism but, perhaps, even somehow involved or complicit in a plan, or in plans, for terrorism in America. Because Castor was critical of the administration's handling of the war in Iraq, Martinez continually argued that she would have been happier if Saddam Hussein was still in power,[56] a claim that also left open the possibility that her allegiance to the United States could be questioned.

When such a narrative about Castor is contrasted with Martinez's story, he is able to shift any possibility of an "other" frame being applied to him as a racial minority to Castor by suggesting that she could not possibly be as committed to American values as he is. In this way, Martinez was able to inoculate himself against being "othered" in part by positioning himself more closely than his White opponent to what the voters would perceive as authentically American.

This effect was enhanced by the repeated use of traditional symbols of American pride throughout his advertisements. While these are standard fare in most candidates' spots, their effect was different in this context, as they were at once framed and helped to frame Martinez's compelling story. In one spot, for example, Martinez appeared on the screen, looking directly at the viewer, and said, "I'm Mel Martinez. As a teenager, I escaped communism." The image transitioned to black-and-white footage of an airplane landing with a large, waving American flag superimposed over it. As his logo appeared at the end of the spot, the lower case "L" at the end of his first name served as a flagpole for another waving American flag.[57]

Partisanship is another mitigating factor for candidates of color, and in this case, it, too, was helpful to Martinez's message of patriotism. In a general election, partisanship matters; Martinez thus was able to rely on some votes on that basis alone, and he would not have been able to capture others, no matter what he said or did. For White voters, it is possible that the "otherness" of a candidate of color can be softened, all other things being equal, by identification with the Republican Party. Because Democrats since the 1960s have been perceived as being most supportive of the rights of ethnic and racial minorities, Republican candidates of color command a presumption of independent-mindedness that is attractive to voters who do not have strong party attachments (as well as, of course, to Republicans). Having a candidate of color run as a Republican serves to reinforce the notion among Republican-leaning voters that the GOP is not in fact a bigoted party or made up of only Whites who disdain people of color. Finally, Mel Martinez's "story" of growing up as a racial minority in a foster family but working hard to pull himself up by his bootstraps and embrace the American dream is attractive to most voters, irrespective of party identification or ideological orientation. Put another way, if Mel Martinez were a Democrat, he would largely blend into the ethnic background that is the Democratic Party, and because he would likely favor stereotypically minority-favored policy positions, he would have to work to overcome that prejudice. As a Republican, however, he garners attention from party insiders (as chair of the Republican National Committee, Martinez was the first Latino to head a major political party in America), as well as from voters.[58] Further, Republicans have been successful in "owning" the notion of patriotism in the past half-century, as defenders of conservative principles have effectively framed the term "liberal" as "anti-American" (see Liu and Hanauer 2008; Sullivan, Fried, and Dietz 1992).

This is not to say, however, that racial minorities have a better chance to win if they run as Republicans. Black Republicans, for instance, have not been particularly successful in seeking elected office, and most Latino members of Congress have been and are Democrats. In Florida, however, with a large (though shrinking) concentration of Cuban Americans in the Latino population, the anticommunist outlook has resulted in a disproportionate level of conservatism compared with Latinos in other parts of the country and from other national backgrounds.

It would be interesting to see how the communicative elements of this contest would have played out if the election had been held in 2006, amid the high level of attention being paid to the issue of immigration. None of the ads we considered in Chapter 5 was run by or against Latino candidates. Thus, it would have been interesting to see, in a political context in which immigration was higher on the issue agenda and the issue was framed in the same way (as an issue that fundamentally criminalizes Latinos), whether the framing would have carried over to anti-Martinez sentiment. Similarly, it would have been interesting to see whether, in such circumstances, individuals likely to be influenced by the anti-Mexican immigration frame would have discerned the distinction between Martinez's Cuban American national origin and the Mexican focus of racialized immigration discourse in the 2006 elections.

THE ALABAMA SEVENTH
CONGRESSIONAL DISTRICT RACE, 2002

While Cory Booker was unsuccessfully battling Sharpe James's political machine in the mayoral contest in Newark, New Jersey, a less visible but equally heated race was taking place in Alabama. The parallels to the Booker–James race are notable and characteristic of a number of all-Black electoral contests in the first decade of the twenty-first century.

In 2002, Earl Hilliard was seeking his sixth term as a member of Congress from western Alabama. Hilliard was the first Black official to represent Alabama since 1877, aided in 1992 by the purposeful creation of a majority-Black district.[59] The sixty-year-old Hilliard, educated at historically Black universities in the 1960s, was challenged in the Democratic Party primary by two African American men in their early thirties: Artur Davis, a Harvard-educated lawyer who had run unsuccessfully against him in the Democratic primary in 2000, and the locally educated lawyer Sam Wiggins, who was making his first run for elected office. While Wiggins eventually garnered 11 percent of the vote, it was Davis who posed the greatest challenge to Hilliard's reelection and thus was the prime target of media attention and of the Hilliard campaign. Davis earned enough votes to force a runoff with Hilliard in the Democratic primary, which Davis won. He then sailed to victory (opposed only by a Libertarian Party candidate) in the general election in the heavily Democratic, majority-Black district. He took the oath of office in January 2003 and was reelected in 2004, 2006, and 2008. He stepped down in 2010 to (unsuccessfully) run for governor of Alabama.[60]

The dynamic at work in this contest has become familiar: A bright, energetic, often light-skinned, Ivy League–educated African American from a generation that was not involved in the Civil Rights activities of the 1950s and 1960s challenges the establishment by running against a seasoned Baby Boom–era political veteran with deep ties to the local community. With the exception of the age difference, this situation played out in the contest for Georgia's Fourth Congressional District in 2004, when Denise Majette challenged the incumbent Cynthia McKinney, as well. That race included strong allegations that Majette was not Black enough to represent the district.[61] Similarly, Sharpe James and his supporters repeatedly referred to Cory Booker as "boy" (in one instance, James called him "faggot White boy"),[62] and Jesse Jackson was famously caught making a derogatory comment about Barack Obama on a microphone that he had not realized was turned on.[63]

There is one overarching narrative in these electoral contexts: that the new generation of Black leaders has not paid its dues, is perhaps not as respectful of the previous generation's pioneering accomplishments, and is "jumping the line" by challenging the Black establishment. Communication emanating directly from the campaigns, as well as that which came through the press, embody this dynamic in similar ways.

Candidate Communication: Television Advertisements

Unlike the U.S. Senate races discussed above, the contest for Alabama's Seventh Congressional District seat in 2002 did not feature many televised campaign commercials. Rather, mailers, personal appearances, and other grassroots tactics were the most prominent forms of campaign communication. Still, we can get a glimpse of the type of messages that characterized the campaign by looking at the ads that were produced and run during the weeks leading up to the primary and runoff elections.

In "For Sale?" Earl Hilliard's campaign suggested that Artur Davis was corrupt, with imagery that suggested criminality and dishonesty. This spot is unique in that it contained racist and racial appeals, both directed at questioning Davis's character and allegiance to the Black community. It opened with a black-and-white still photograph of a Black woman with her arm around a teenager and the words "For Sale" stamped in red letters across the image. The narrator asked, "Are you for sale?" adding, "Artur Davis thinks you are." The image then faded into a picture of a Black teenager, arms crossed, with an angry look on his face, just as the words "Artur Davis" were spoken. A picture of two White children appeared and quickly faded into a screen-wide "$270,000" in white lettering on a black background as the narrator said, "The price? $270,000. From 290 people and businesses in New York, 63 checks from New Jersey and California, money from Connecticut, New Hampshire and Maryland, money from Republicans who support George Bush." Black-and-white still images of children (both Black and White) rotate throughout the spot, with a photograph of a suitcase full of money appearing on the screen as the narrator says, "A huge fortune."

While any accusation of criminality can spell trouble for a candidate, as we have noted throughout, the preexisting stereotype that links African Americans—particularly, African American men—with criminality has the potential to render such attacks on a Black candidate more effective even with African American voters. Systemic racism is powerful because it affects the subconscious and can lead to self-loathing or "too little self-love" (West 1993, 93) among members of racial minority groups. It is unlikely that Black Americans would acknowledge increased concern about Davis's lack of character on the basis of this stereotype any more than White Americans would. Rather, the accusation primes a racial schema in a way that a similar attack against a White candidate does not. In this way, an attack of this sort is racist in nature, irrespective of any intent to invoke race.

The racial appeal is more pronounced, and it came in two forms. The first was the moving, real-time image of a middle-aged White man in a suit coat and tie, lighting a cigar with a $100 bill and laughing as he looked directly at the camera, arrogantly taunting the viewer with his self-assuredness as the narrator said, "From 290 people and businesses in New York." This leaves open the possibility that the viewer will consciously or subconsciously interpret that the man is Jewish, which was an important theme in the campaign, as we describe below. In any case, he was not "one of us" in a district that was majority-Black. The association of Davis with such a crass, uncaring, manipulative character worked to bolster Hilliard's claims that Davis was an outsider and not "Black enough" to represent the interests of the citizens in the district.

The racial nature of the appeal came more clearly into focus as the image of the White man's face digitally morphed into Artur Davis's face, leaving no room for speculation that the accusation was that the fictitious, scheming White man and Davis were one in the same. The image of Davis, also grinning and looking directly at the viewer, holding the cigar and flaming $100 bill, was frozen on the screen for maximum effect. In fact, the morph was repeated at the end of the spot, this time with the word "sold" stamped in red across Davis's face as an auctioneer shouted, "Sold!" This could refer to the colloquial expression "sold out," which suggests individuals have departed from their roots or have failed to "keep it real." Further, the visceral association with slave auctions in the slave-rich South was not likely to have been lost on many of the district's Black citizens, especially those who charged that Davis was bought by and serving his primarily White backers. This message was reinforced by the second form of racial appeal, which came in the form of an association with another "other" in a majority-Black district: Republicans.

After reporting the litany of states from which Davis received campaign contributions (most of which were on the East Coast and were perceived to be the home to very few African Americans), the narrator noted that Davis had also accepted "money from Republicans who support George Bush," with the accompanying text "$ Republicans Who Support George Bush" on the screen. This is an appeal to "party authenticity." Since the 1960s, the Democratic Party has come to be perceived as the party that cares about African Americans, so associating a Black Democrat with Republicans in a district that is overwhelmingly African American serves as a surrogate for saying that the opponent is "not Black enough."

For his part, Davis also suggested in his television advertisements that Hilliard was untrustworthy and possibly even criminal. One of his spots argued: "For five years, Congressman Earl Hilliard failed to pay his taxes: $100,000 in property taxes, personal income and Social Security taxes. Maybe he thought members of Congress only raised taxes, but Earl thought wrong. Now he's at it again. Ghost employees, dummy contracts. Running his congressional office like a family business." Another ad hit the same theme, but with fewer words. It began with a black screen with large white lettering, a metallic "bang" interrupting the silence at four-second intervals, as the words "Earl Hilliard's," "Unanswered," and "Questions" were displayed one at a time to correspond with each jarring sound. With "Questions" still on the screen, a black-and-white image of Hilliard, back toward the camera, appeared and filled up the entire screen. He then turned around in slow motion as the bangs continued to sound at a consistent, rhythmic interval. With each sound, a new newspaper headline was shown that questioned Hilliard's ethics: "No Sign that U.S. Taxes Filed for Hilliard Insurance Firm," "Hilliard Visits Off-Limits Libya," and "Hilliard Being Probed by Ethics Committee." Between each headline, the image of Hilliard turning toward the viewer became clearer and more menacing, zooming in on his face, and then fading again as the next headline appeared. After the last headline, Hilliard was looking directly at the camera, still moving in slow motion and looking through the "Ethics Probe" headline as the words "Re-elect Earl Hilliard?" appeared in white text in the middle of the screen. The screen then faded to black as large white letters spelling "Why?" appeared. The banging sound was reminiscent of a slamming jail cell door; it, combined with the mug-shot-style picture of Hilliard, his slow motion movement, and his looking over his shoulder as if to see whether anyone was watching, sent a clear message of criminality that would be more effective as a result of stereotypes about African Americans.

Finally, Davis ran an ad that tapped into allegations that Hilliard was anti-Semitic and supported terrorist regimes. Hilliard had, in past campaigns, accepted campaign donations from the Arab American Leadership PAC, and he was one of only a handful of House members to oppose nonbinding resolutions designed to indicate U.S. support for Israel.[64] Further, Hilliard was very vocal in his condemnation of Davis's clear support of Israel and his acceptance of donations from Jewish groups and individuals. One Davis ad contained the following verbal script:

> In the weeks following September 11, the children of Alabama saw firefighters from Heflin to Montgomery travel to Ground Zero, while at the same time their congressman, Earl Hilliard, was writing a law to force the United States to drop sanctions against terrorist states—drop all sanctions against countries that support and finance international terror networks. Not one member of Congress supports this law.[65]

Such attacks can be perceived as racist in some contexts, although their effectiveness here are likely to rest with more widespread sentiments about national security and patriotism than a deep resentment of Muslims or Arabs. After all, Hilliard had been consistently vocal about his opposition to unequivocal U.S. support for Israel, and the history of tension between African Americans and Jewish Americans is well understood in both communities (West and Lerner 1996). Rather, the message in this spot is consistent with Davis's broader claims about Hilliard's being out of touch with Alabamans, as demonstrated by his alleged corruption and untrustworthiness.

Mediated Communication: Newspaper Coverage

Local coverage of the Davis–Hilliard contest featured a number of stories that explicitly centered on race, although the discussion was largely rooted in campaign communication that used support for Israel or party loyalty as code for Black authenticity. In fact, the bulk of local newspaper stories about the race focused on cleavages in the Middle East and the corresponding support from each of the two candidates. A national story in the *New York Times* went as far as to assert that the contest had

> become a surrogate battle—waged with contributions from New York lawyers, Detroit doctors and Silicon Valley CEO's—between supporters of Israel incensed by Mr. Hilliard's maverick views on the Middle East, and grateful Arab-Americans and Muslims who are eager to flex their political muscles.[66]

Davis is on record as being a strong supporter of Israel, and Hilliard has said that he does not support either side in the conflict, though, as noted above, he has links to Arab groups (including campaign contributions and a well-publicized trip to Libya in 1997). He also spent a great deal of time during the campaign criticizing Davis for taking contributions from pro-Israel groups and individuals.

The most visible signal of the influence of Middle East politics in the contest was a flyer that surfaced in early May. The flier, titled, "Davis and the Jews: No Good for the Black Belt," clearly did not originate from the Hilliard campaign, even though it was made to appear as if it had.[67] In fact, Hilliard, calling the flier "deplorable," alleged that Davis's supporters might have printed it themselves to "inflame the Jews who are supporting him against me so he can get their money."[68] Besides the connection to Israel, which can serve as a surrogate for Whiteness on its own, the flier alleged that Davis's had betrayed his race:

> Someone needs to tell Davis that his much acclaimed record as a federal prosecutor has about as much appeal in the black community as "Country boy Eddie" [a popular country music singer and morning radio variety show host in Alabama from 1958 to 1995]. . . . Asking blacks to vote for him is like asking a chicken to vote for Colonel Sanders—they can expect nothing short of misery and death. . . . He came out of oblivion, his only work experience was putting black folks in jail and now he tells us that Jews are our best friend. This man is very, very, very dangerous. . . . Lest we forget, it was Israel that stood with apartheid in South Africa. . . . If the current invasions, murder, and abuse within the Palestinian territory sound familiar, it's only because we've seen apartheid do exactly the same in the black villages of South Africa with Israel's support.[69]

When asked about the flier, Washington Booker, a Hilliard supporter and local Democratic operative, was quoted as saying, "It's a concern anytime anyone outside the black community tries to pick a representative for us. . . . That should be a red flag for our community. The Jews should pick leaders for their community, and we should pick leaders for our community." Booker added that federal prosecutors (Davis's previous job) were not trusted among African Americans: "'Federal prosecutor' is really a nasty word in Alabama. They're really reminiscent of the way the Ku Klux Klan used to ride at night."[70] Here, a Hilliard surrogate not only suggested that Davis related to Whites (i.e., Jewish Americans) or even that he was as good as White, but that he was bigoted against Blacks, comparing him with the notorious White racist terrorist group that is synonymous with animosity and violence toward African Americans. Davis responded quickly, telling a group of local party activists, "We as Democrats have no place for such racist views."[71]

The line is sometimes fine between being considered "racist," in Davis's words, and explicitly advocating support for one's community when that community historically has been disadvantaged by systemic racism. Hilliard told Mary Orndorff of the *Birmingham News* that his "number one priority . . . [was] to vote for the interests of the district"—a district that overwhelmingly was composed of African Americans.[72]

In contrast, Hilliard was quick to suggest that Davis did not have the best interests of African Americans in mind. An article about the contest published in the *Birmingham News* on May 23 quoted Hilliard as saying, "I don't go around saying everything is either black or white," though he rhetorically asked, "Which one of us has served the interests of the black community?" Orndorff, the journalist reporting on the story, wrote, "Republicans, not whites, are to blame for the extra scrutiny of his campaign finances over the years, especially after he made a controversial trip to Libya in 1997, he said."[73] Hilliard was quoted elsewhere as noting that his "'opponent was getting so much money' from supporters of Israel and Republicans."[74]

Hilliard's de-emphasizing of race as a factor was important, as was his emphasis on party differences. As we saw in his televised ad against Davis, he was able to use party as a surrogate for Whiteness when attacking Davis while maintaining a degree of plausible deniability with respect to "playing the race card." Such tactics are not new and historically have cut both ways, particularly in the Deep South. An Associated Press article dated June 2002 noted, "White candidates in years past [in Alabama] have aired commercials linking opponents with prominent black leaders, and black candidates have accused challengers of being linked to the white establishment."[75]

Several news stories during the contest reinforced Davis's claim that Hilliard was corrupt. There were numerous reports about Hilliard's ethics issues, including an official sanction in 2001 by Committee on Standards and Official Conduct of the U.S. House of Representatives stating that Hilliard had "engaged in serious misconduct that brought discredit to the House of Representatives" by using campaign funds for personal gain and failing to cooperate in the resulting investigation.[76] In March, the *Birmingham News* ran a story about allegations that a nonprofit organization called the National African American Center had operated out of his district office.[77] As noted above, these charges and similar, if unrelated, accusations surfaced in a number of Davis's television commercials, as well.

As should be clear at this point, not all of the racial discourse in this contest operated under the surface. Several journalists wrote openly about the importance of race in the election, and the candidates themselves, on a number of occasions, referred to how race was being used. For instance, the day before the Democratic primary, in a *New York Times* article about the election, David Halbfinger noted that Artur Davis "fear[ed] that Mr. Hilliard [would] 'play the race card' and try to smear him as an Uncle Tom." Halbfinger continued, "He could be right. Mr. Hilliard held a notepad in an interview Friday. On it someone had scrawled three talking points about his opponent. The third: 'Like Clarence Thomas.'"[78]

In the end, an editorial in the *Birmingham News* published on June 26 sided with Davis on the matter, claiming that "in a race in which both candidates were Black, Hilliard played the race card.... Yet voters saw through Hilliard's deceit and responded to Davis' relentless message that the 7th District had nothing to show for Hilliard's 10 years in Congress."[79]

CONCLUSION

These three case studies provide a closer look into how different electoral contexts (racial composition of the electorate, race of the candidates, and the intersection of race and party identification of the candidates) affect the way that race-based appeals operate. For Bob Corker, the ability (purposefully or otherwise) to tap into preexisting fears and resentments about people of color was effective because the vast majority of potential voters were White. Earl Hilliard had the opposite strategy: Rather than paint his opponent as "too Black" for the district, he argued that his opponent was not Black enough. Preexisting stereotypes were less effective for Betty Castor as she struggled to position herself as being as "American" as her Latino opponent in the context of an electorate that featured a disproportionate number of conservative-leaning minority voters, as well as Whites, who were compelled by Mel Martinez's heroic "escape" from communism and subsequent realization of the American dream.

While Harold Ford Jr. was largely seen as the embodiment of what is wrong with American public service, Mel Martinez was seen as everything that is right, protecting the nation against the evils of those who wish to do us harm. Artur Davis was finally (on his second try) able to erode Earl Hilliard's base of support by painting him as the candidate who more embodied the

(White) political establishment (via corruption and greed and the tendency to take advantage of his power). In that way, Davis showed that he was really "Blacker" than his opponent, turning the tables on Hilliard's key strategy.

More generally, the case studies in this chapter demonstrate the conclusions we came to in Chapter 4. The fact is that each of these election contests was novel in terms of the racial dynamics of the candidates involved, the voters, party alliances, and more. It is not hard to understand the media's compulsion to consistently report on the racial dynamics of such campaigns. It was, indeed, news. Yet as demonstrated especially in the case of the Tennessee Senate contest, it is evident that much of the media decided early on that race would be a significant frame within which to report on the election. That being the case, however, the consistency of such framing throughout the campaign was clearly tied to the highly racially charged rhetoric that flowed from the candidates, the party organizations, and outside interest groups. In these three cases in which race was a central feature of media reporting, we see that two of the candidates of color—Martinez and Hilliard—won. Ford lost, but only narrowly, outperforming among Whites, as many pundits expected early in the campaign. Thus, it remains an open question whether racialized media coverage of campaigns involving candidates of color is fundamentally negative or negatively affects the election hopes of candidates of color. We can see that this dynamic of racialized media coverage was also at work throughout the 2008 presidential campaign, the final case study to which we turn our attention.

7

Barack Obama, Race-Based Appeals, and the 2008 Presidential Election

WHEN WE BEGAN delving into the subject of racialized political communication in 2001, we never seriously imagined the possibility of a Black president. When we personally encountered Barack Obama for the first time in the Massachusetts State House chambers in 2004, among a giddy group of cheering teenagers (who by 2008 would be of voting age), we—like many Americans—got our first glimpse of a potentially serious run. Yet when we began assembling this book just before the announcement of Obama's candidacy in 2007, we thought little of his potential chances for presidential success.

The evidence and data in which we immersed ourselves (and that we reported in the previous chapters) led us to the same conclusion at which many Americans arrived by going on just a hunch. We were well aware of the paltry success rate Black candidates historically had running against White candidates. In fact, we knew that most politicians of color believed their chance for success in such situations was so slim that few even bothered to seriously attempt such an undertaking. By that point, we had seen hundreds of ads, and we knew that a Black candidate running for the presidency was likely to be more of a lightning rod for White candidates' and supporters' racist appeals than candidates for the U.S. House and Senate attracted over the past twenty years, especially since so much more was at stake. We were wary of how state and local, as well as national, news might treat him, being fully aware of the evidence of how the media covered both of Jesse Jackson's presidential campaigns; the momentum it provided for George H. W. Bush when the Willie Horton ad was revealed in 1988; and the studies showing how the media tended to hyperracialize Black candidates generally in House and Senate contests across the country. We knew the potential effect of these trends on a primarily White electorate that harbored negative preconceptions about Blacks and other people of color and Whites' historical unwillingness to support them for other political offices. Add to that the fact that only five African Americans had been elected as governors or U.S. Senators since Reconstruction (including Obama himself) and we came to the same conclusion that, we dare say, most people had before the Iowa caucuses early in 2008: Barack Obama had no chance to win the Democratic Party nomination, much less to win the plurality in enough states (all of which are majority-White) to secure 270 electoral votes.

What we did not anticipate was that over the course of an almost two-year campaign, Barack Obama and the circumstances of the 2008 election would not only validate most of the findings we report on in the first six chapters of this book, but that Obama would nonetheless become the president of the United States in the process. Given Obama's historic, unforeseen, even unimaginable election, we want to spend some time in this final chapter offering an account of how the research and conclusions we have presented played out in the racial drama of the 2008 primary and general election campaigns. Highlighting the role rhetoric, appeals, media coverage, and voters' choices played throughout the campaign, we also want to identify what happened. What changed among voters and the racial and political climate in the country that made Obama's election possible?

We begin our examination with the racial dynamics of the Democratic presidential primary, then move on to Obama's general election battle against Senator John McCain. Within these two general time periods, we closely investigate the forms of racist and racial appeals that dotted the electoral landscape, the sponsors of those appeals, and their potential effect on the voting public's perceptions of the candidates involved. We also look at the media's role in ratcheting up the competitive novelty of the contest and its key players and the part it played in perpetuating racial controversy to strengthen the racial drama it conveyed to the American people throughout the election. Finally, we offer an explanation for why the confluence of racial circumstances in this particular presidential contest led 53 percent of American voters to cast a ballot for Barack Obama as their choice for president of the United States.

OBAMA'S DREAM, CLINTON'S NIGHTMARE

Senators Barack Obama and Hillary Clinton began the Democratic presidential primary with similar challenges. Obama is half-Black (which in America historically has meant being, simply, Black). He had lost one congressional election against another Black candidate, who had garnered the lion's share of the district's majority-Black votes.[1] He had won a U.S. Senate seat in a contest in which he had to compete for White votes, becoming only the third Black senator elected in the United States since Reconstruction. He was well aware of his challenge: to walk that racial tightrope where he could, in a racially polarized country; convince enough Whites that he was one of them; and, at the same time, make sure that Blacks knew he was, is, and always would be one of them. He had to do this, moreover, against a frontrunning opponent who did not have to introduce herself, let alone racially sell herself, to White America and whose husband had already spent a political lifetime convincing Black Americans that he was the closest thing they had (and probably would ever have in the minds of many Blacks) to a Black president.[2]

What Clinton did not know, realize, or admit, however, was that she had any kind of racial challenge beyond drawing on her strong base of support in the Black community and, to a lesser degree, the Latino community. She apparently did not figure that she would have to think, strategize, or otherwise plan not only for the political, but also for the racial, challenges of running against a Black presidential candidate. Though given the history of American electoral politics and the relative obscurity of Obama until he declared his candidacy in 2007, why would she?

OBAMA'S RACIAL APPEAL

In Chapter 1, we described a variety of strategic purposes that motivate candidates of color to deploy racial appeals—that is, appeals that are racial in nature but do not rely on anti-minority sentiment for their persuasive power. If any candidate of color saw the import in mobilizing racial appeals in as many ways as possible, Obama did, knowing that he would need every advantage he could get in his uphill battle to win the Democratic nomination and, certainly, the presidency. Like many candidates of color who had come before him, Obama set out to convince White America that, despite the color of his skin, he more closely resembled them than he did the popular stereotypes many White Americans historically have embraced about Blacks.

However, Obama is biracial, with childhood ties in Kansas, Hawaii, and overseas, and attended Columbia and Harvard universities. None of these life circumstances made him a perfect fit with what many people stereotypically refer to as *the* Black community—that is, America's urban, Black middle and working class and the poor. But by every historical and contemporary adherence to the "one drop" rule (Bell 2008), Americans defined him as being Black. Obama certainly knew that a second, smaller, yet significant challenge would emerge: He would have to figure out a way to bridge the tripartite gulf among being seen as Black, as not Black enough, and as too Black. Obama clearly dealt with each of these challenges, with racial appeals replete in his political advertisements, as well as in other forms of public communication.

Mitigating Racial Difference: Inoculation

Depending on the poll one reads and when, anywhere from 85 percent to nearly 100 percent of eligible White voters throughout the campaign season reported that they would not hesitate to vote for a qualified Black candidate. A majority of Whites for some time have said that they would be comfortable electing a Black president. Seventy-two percent said so in 1972, and that percentage had climbed into the mid-80s by the end of the decade. The percentage dipped into the low 80s at times throughout the 1980s and then, beginning in the 1990s, climbed to a peak in 2008 at 94 percent.[3] This did not mean, however, that Black stereotypes did not persist in the minds of many White voters. In fact, a poll taken by Stanford University shortly before the general election found that 40 percent of White Americans held negative views about Blacks.[4] Despite the Obama campaign's frequent public statements that it had faith that the American people would look beyond race in the election, Obama's message strategy demonstrated otherwise.

In Chapter 1, we outlined several key content characteristics of the inoculation form of racial appeals deployed in political advertisements: first-person plural references; counter-stereotype references; and dominant White imagery. When we look at the varieties of collective group references in Table 7.1, we see that Obama went well beyond the typical first-person plural references such as "we," "us," "our," and the like. Although he used these terms often, he even more frequently used specific and more meaningful phrases that variously encouraged voters—primarily White—to view him through a prism of racial non-distinction.

Drawn from his popular Democratic Convention speech in 2004 (his ads frequently draw on sound bites and images from that speech), Obama frequently invoked the biblical admonition, "I am my brother's keeper," a way to ameliorate racial distinctions by highlighting what he often expressed in another phrase: "We each have a stake in each other." Elsewhere in his ads, Obama downplayed division and emphasized unity, using explicit terms. However, he also borrowed a phrase that, we found in our observations of many of the ads we analyzed in Chapter 1, is a mainstay in Black candidates' advertising rhetoric: describing themselves as individuals who can "bring people together." This phrase is interesting because it is one, we find, that is repeated over and over by Black candidates who run in contests in which they depend on White voters for electoral success. The racial meaning of the phrase is clear when one looks at Obama's ads especially and sees who most often used the phrase. Obama sometimes used this language to refer to himself, but more often than not, various surrogates and supporters used the phrase to talk about Obama—and in every case, those people were White.

TABLE 7.1 Collective and counter-stereotype references in Obama Democratic primary political ads

Collective/first-person references			
One people	Bring country together	I am my brother's keeper	End division
One voice	Brought people together	We have a stake in each other	Politics of division
One nation	Knows how to bring people together	Focus on what we have in common	Solutions, not divisions
Unity	Brings parties together	All of us	Unifying vision
Unite America		Represent all Americans	Will not let fear divide us
United States of America		Yes we can	
Not red–blue, White–Black America		We can make this happen	
		We have a choice	
		We have a chance	
		Our moment	
		Our time	

Counter-stereotype references			
Work	Tell the truth	Brilliant	Faith
Hard work	Scrupulously honest	Smart	Christian beliefs
Working	Speak honestly	Best qualified	Understands America
Working people	A president we can trust	Inspiring	Rooted in our values
Worked his way through	Honest answers	Successful	North Carolina values
Welfare to work	Trust us with the truth	Harvard Law School	South Dakota values
Dignity from work	Tell you the truth	Government alone won't solve problems	
		My own story	
		Ask more of ourselves	

In American culture, people of color are racialized. Whites are not; they are typical, normal, American—something we have pointed out several times throughout the book. The repetitive use of this phrase by Obama, and by other candidates of color before him, demonstrates that people of color in general, and candidates of color in particular, bear the burden of "bringing people together," of traversing the racial divide. When Obama invoked this phrase, he was saying that he recognized race and that he was aware of the racial divisions and barriers that keep people who do not look like him from voting for candidates who do. He was saying that he is able to mediate these differences. The bottom-line message here was that he understood both worlds, both groups, and both sides' racial attitudes and politics enough that he could bridge the gap. The deeper message was that he was able to translate his Blackness to the "mainstream" (read, "American," "White") in a way that is palatable to Whites' racial sensibilities.

This can be read in the image context in which each of these collective group words and phrases were used in Obama's ads. Only in three circumstances do Whites not make up the vast majority of people in Obama's political ads throughout the primaries: (1) when he was the only person in the ad; (2) when the ad pictured his family; and (3) when the ad was made specifically for the Puerto Rico primary or ran in the Spanish language in states with large Latino populations. Images in ads that featured Obama speaking to large crowds were diverse, although a careful examination reveals that the majority of people in those crowds were White. Ads that featured small groups of people, depicting Obama in a more personable, conversational posture, were overwhelmingly White, and many of them featured casts of all-White characters.

Countering Stereotypes

Obama's biography seemed to indicate that he was so unlike the popular Black stereotype that he was virtually White (and, of course, biologically, that is half-true). This has much to do with the discussion of racial authenticity discussed in previous chapters (and addressed in this context below). The variety and number of counter-stereotypical references in Obama's ads and campaign discourse illustrates the depth with which Obama must have feared that he could fall prey to the racial stereotypes that many White Americans have about Blacks. His approach was consistent with what we found in Chapter 1, as other candidates of color running against White opponents sought to inoculate themselves against racist predispositions.

Speaking to a group of predominantly Black supporters in Fort Worth, Texas, during the primaries, for example, Obama criticized Black adults for not being more attentive to their children. He argued that there were dangers in permitting Black youngsters to watch too much television, play too many video games, and eat too much junk food and admonished the adults to pay more attention to their children's homework. Obama invoked the "fried chicken" stereotype, as well, by asking whether Texas had outlets of the Southern-style fast-food franchise Popeyes: "Y'all have Popeyes out in Beaumont? I know some of y'all you got that cold Popeyes out for breakfast. I know. That's why y'all laughing.... You can't do that. Children have to have proper nutrition. That affects also how they study, how they learn in school."

While such comments may have been appropriate for, and effective with, his immediate audience—an audience that was in a position to weigh the criticism and the invocation of the stereotype—many in the wider audience were not in such a cognitive position. Priming racial schemata that contain Black stereotypes renders those stereotypes accessible during evaluation periods, which might not only serve to hurt Obama in the short run (the election), but might also perpetuate those stereotypes. That is, White voters' confirmation bias (Nickerson 1998) could result in a processing of the information that reinforces what they already (subconsciously) think about African Americans. The Obama campaign clearly expected that there would be a very different reaction to such language, that he would appear to be more palatable to Whites if he was seen criticizing Black folks. In other words, he spoke and acted in ways that ran counter to stereotypes to inoculate himself against negative predispositions that might otherwise inform evaluations of him.

Looking again at Table 7.1, we see that the counter-stereotype phrases Obama frequently invoked in his ads. Most can be grouped into four primary categories—hard work, self-reliance, trust, and American values. Similar to the collective group language, Obama did more than invoke the frequent catch-phrases and code words that point to these counter-stereotypical characteristics he possessed. He not only talked about hard work but spoke about the "dignity" of work—not just about how he had "worked his way through," but also about how that value extended to his fundamental ideological belief that "government alone won't solve problems." Then there were the "welfare" statements, made at a time when welfare had not been atop the national public agenda for more than a decade. There were values phrases, as well, all of which made the same underlying pitch: "I am one of you."

In Table 7.2, we see one of the Obama ads that typifies the characteristics found in the kind of racial inoculation appeals he deployed throughout the primary. It begins with language about unity—"one people," "us," and our common national allegiance. Obama's head and torso singularly appear in the frame, and the final frame, taken from his convention speech in 2004, provides a close-up of White people applauding and smiling to signal their approval. The following frame is a crucial one, because it provides a clear racial anchor for the overall message communicated throughout the remainder of the ad: It highlights "First Black" in a headline from the *New York Times* and refers to Harvard Law School while Obama is shown standing by a pillar of the institution. This signifies the counter-stereotypical characteristics of hard work, self-reliance, and intelligence and sets Obama apart as someone "different"—not different from Whites, but different from the stereotype of how Blacks are different from Whites. He is not different just because he went to college and earned a Harvard law degree; he is distinctive because he is a Black man who went to college, earned a law degree, and, while doing so, distinguished himself by becoming the first African American to head the prestigious institution's law review.

TABLE 7.2 Text of Barack Obama's racial inoculation ad, 2008

Ad image	Ad narration
Black-and-white still: Obama head shot, looking down	I'm Barack Obama and I approved this message.
Live, crowd at 2004 Democratic Convention fades to Obama speaking, fades to close-up of three White members in the crowd smiling	*Obama:* We are one people, all of us pledging allegiance to the Stars and Stripes.
Black-and-white still of Obama in front of Harvard Law School building, overlaid with image of *New York Times* headline: "First Black Elected to Head Harvard's Law Review"	*Narrator:* After college and law school, Barack Obama could have cashed in.
Black-and-white still of Obama as community organizer talking to two Black residents, fade to image of fence surrounding a defunct Chicago factory, with a sign that says, "Keep Out"	*Narrator:* Instead, he fought for change, working to rebuild an area torn apart by plant closings.
Live footage of Professor Lawrence Tribe of Harvard Law School in office, fade to three subsequent color images of Obama talking with White men	*Tribe:* It was inspiring, absolutely inspiring, to see someone as brilliant as Barack Obama take all of his talent and devote it to making people's lives better.
Black-and-white still of Obama seated in legislature, fade to black-and-white still of Obama talking to man and woman (text on screen says "Obama cut taxes for workers"), fade to color image of Obama in school classroom with children (text on screen says, "Barack Obama expanded health care")	*Narrator:* In Illinois, he brought Democrats and Republicans together, cutting taxes for workers and winning health care for children.
Live footage of White Republican Illinois state senator, fade to black-and-white still of Obama in office, writing	*Senator:* Senator Obama worked on some of the deepest issues we had, and he was successful in a bipartisan way.
Black-and-white still of Obama seated next to Republican Senator Dick Lugar (text on screen says, "Barack Obama: Arms Control"), fade to black-and-white still of Obama standing in front of U.S. Senate building (text on screen says, "Barack Obama: Ethics Reform")	*Narrator:* And in the U.S. Senate, he's led on issues such as arms control [and] landmark ethics reform.
Live footage of Senator Claire McCaskill, fade to live footage of Obama with partial images of people, fade back to McCaskill	*McCaskill:* It was hard to get that ethics bill passed. This is a man who knows how to get things done. He understands that we have to move forward, with a different kind of politics.
Live footage of Obama facing crowd at 2004 convention, fade to Obama with crowd of people behind him	*Obama:* There is not a liberal America or a conservative America. There is the United States of America.

The connotation inscribed in the imagery also defines the next frame, in which Laurence Tribe, Obama's former professor and a well-known constitutional law scholar, calls Obama's story "inspiring." But again, scores of people have gone from prestigious law schools to public service. What is particularly inspiring about Obama is that, for someone who so clearly broke the stereotypical mold of Black men in America, he chose not to pursue wealth but sought to help others—Black and White. The remaining frames in the ad speak to Obama's ability to get things done, particularly to "bring people together." While the phrase signals bipartisanship, one cannot ignore the fact that the remaining frames feature Whites who attest to Obama's ability to unify and the Black–White contrast in the images in which Obama is paired and engaged with one or more people—again, all White.

These kinds of racial inoculation appeals appeared throughout Obama's primary campaign ads and were repeated over and over throughout his other campaign communications, particularly in his public speeches. Sometimes he was less guarded about his language, invoking race explicitly rather than implicitly. For example, once he had mathematically secured the Democratic nomination in June, Obama told a group of supporters that he anticipated Republican attacks against him that involved race: "They're going to try to make you afraid of me: 'He's young and inexperienced and he's got a funny name. And did I mention he's Black?'" Several mainstream media outlets questioned whether Obama had "crossed the line" by mentioning this, although, as we have argued, such criticisms demonstrate either a lack of appreciation for the implicitly racial nature of much of the discourse that characterized the campaign to that point or a willful desire to resist labeling anything other than explicit racial communication as being racial.

Authenticity Appeals

Although Obama did not run against another Black candidate, with whom he might have had to compete over claims of racial authenticity, he nevertheless made cursory appeals to Black authenticity throughout his campaign. While such appeals came across more often in speeches and debates in which he addressed audiences significantly made up of Blacks, implicit appeals to authenticity did make their way into his political advertisements in at least two noticeable (and overlapping) ways that are consistent with our findings in Chapter 1 and with our Davis–Hilliard case study in Chapter 6. What is notable, however, is that the context is quite different. While our observation of appeals to authenticity in those other contests occurred in majority-Black districts, Obama was competing for electoral votes in fifty majority-White states and the District of Columbia.

One way that Obama deployed authenticity appeals is reflected in the language of his ads, primarily in ads that repeatedly referred to his life story. Here we see a constellation of terms that together promote a singular narrative. The terms include civil rights; civil rights attorney; the community; organizer; community organizer; poverty; streets of Chicago; neighborhoods devastated; those denied opportunity; the power of opportunity; opportunities; without barriers; and voter registration drive. Each of these terms help to situate Obama's years before beginning his political life within a community that was unlike any of those in which he had grown up or gone to college and law school.

Terms such as "the community" particularly signal the motivation behind the language deployed to solidify Obama's ties within and among Chicago's (and the broader) Black community and the kinds of socioeconomic problems faced by those who lived and worked each day in those circumstances. The language in Obama's ads provides another signal to substantiate his authentic Blackness, accomplished through his use of terms familiar to the Civil Rights Movement and Dr. Martin Luther King Jr. In his ads, Obama frequently used the term "dream," which, while referring to the more general American dream of economic freedom and opportunity, also appeals to Blacks more specifically and their association with King and the Civil Rights Movement.

Obama's ads and the language in his speeches also frequently included the admonition that the time for change (i.e., the time to elect Obama) was "now," using phrases such as "Our moment is now," "The time has come," and, in particular, "We cannot afford to wait." This last phrase is clearly intended to be associated with the title of one of King's books, *Why We Can't Wait*. Thus, between the language that articulated the pre-political days in Obama's biography and the Civil Rights–era terminology included in his quest to build an electoral movement, Obama conveyed a clear message to Black Americans: "Although I am unlike you in many ways, I am one of you." Extended further, the argument was that his authentic Blackness entitled him to Blacks' acceptance, support, and votes.

Parallel to the language, several images in Obama's advertisements also marked his claim to authentic Blackness. While an image signifying the time when Obama worked as a community organizer is included in the sixth frame of the ad in Table 7.2, another ad very similar to that one began with the same frames from the 2004 convention speech. When the ad narrative turned to Obama's life of public service after Harvard, a still image lasting for several seconds pictured the youthful Obama standing in a tattered room surrounded by Black people, after which an aerial shot of a large factory on Chicago's South Side appeared, followed by the same images in frames seven and eight in Table 7.2. The narrator's statement through this section of the new ad said: "After college, Barack Obama signed on as a community organizer for local churches, working to lift an area torn apart by plant closings." As did the language, the image of poor Blacks on the streets, in the churches, and outside the plants connected Obama with some sense of authentic Black experience that many claimed he did not have.[5]

In the end, it very well may have been the early endorsement of Oprah Winfrey that solidified Obama's Black authenticity, as well as his appeal to progressive women, who at that point may have been signaling that they did not feel they were betraying an obligation to continue women's long struggle to be treated equally in the United States by supporting the first female candidate who appeared to have a legitimate chance to be elected president. Winfrey's support was widely reported, and she hit the campaign trail, traveling to Iowa, New Hampshire, and South Carolina in the opening weeks of the primary contests. Winfrey had famously stayed away from politics throughout her career; her endorsement was powerful because it reinforced the notion that Obama was special and an accepted member of the Black community.

RACISM, DEMOCRATIC-STYLE

Toni Morrison's well-known characterization of President Bill Clinton as the "first Black president" gave Hillary Clinton a modicum of strategic comfort at the onset of the presidential campaign. Black and White Americans alike had become familiar with the practice of Black candidates' playing their presidential hands, usually folding just after the first round of bets were placed. Carol Moseley Braun, the Reverend Al Sharpton, and the Reverend Jesse Jackson had all taken the stage and used the bully pulpit they had purchased (metaphorically) by risking a presidential run. With their colorful language, they dared to remind America of its unfulfilled promise of racial equality, often enumerating the past and persistent sins perpetrated by White America on a victim class of Black Americans and other minorities. Everyone entertained their candor and at times even agreed with and cheered their assertions.

Many Black Americans supported them. Most White Americans did not. When the day came that these candidates gave up their presidential quests, neither Blacks nor Whites were surprised; it was back to presidential politics as usual. Black America hoped for a different outcome but accepted the likelihood that a White president who was empathetic to the concerns of the Black community was as close to a Black president as they could ever realistically expect. White Americans neither hoped for nor expected anything different. The Clinton campaign counted on both being true in 2008.

Threatened by a multiracial candidate whose growing appeal among White voters was predicated largely on erasing all but the veneer of race that Obama wore on his skin, Hillary Clinton was faced with the conundrum of how to respond. In the lowest moments of her bottomed-out campaign, the media and many other critics typically characterized her team's response as a set of isolated, knee-jerk reactions—what came to be repeated over and over in the media as her "kitchen sink" strategy. Nothing could be further from the truth. As chaotic as the campaign seemed, there was strategic forethought (which is to say, it was deliberate, not necessarily smart). Clinton's response was clear and simple and began long before the perceived end was near: She reminded White America that Barack Obama was Black and not like "us." It was not the typical racial strategy employed by conservatives with which we are familiar (e.g., Willie Horton or the attacks on Harold Ford Jr.). Among Democratic primary voters (many of whom were minorities, and many more of whom were supporters of racial progress), such an attempt would be risky. These appeals did not serve to remind Whites of all of the reasons they feared, mistrusted, and resented Black people. Instead, the strategy was simply to correct America's vision, to sharpen Obama's focus in a way that White America could see him—honorable as he might be—for what, arguably, he really was: a Black man who was wholly defined by race, not someone who transcended it. Clinton's message strategy to "Blacken" Obama would work if she could force a racial response, a response that would counter his notion of a colorblind, unified politics. The Clinton machine manufactured this message strategy using not only the candidate herself, but also a stable of White and Black surrogates, each of whose explicitly and implicitly racist remarks, racist innuendoes, and racial associations sought to accomplish this goal.

The Implicitly Racist Politics of "Hard Work"

In Chapters 1–3, especially, we emphasized several critical points that readers must always keep in mind as we discuss what we would argue was Senator Hillary Clinton's race strategy. We use the term "strategy" deliberately, in part to remind people of the dual-sided nature of racist appeals as they typically appear in contemporary electoral politics. On the one hand, we argue that Clinton deployed a planned message strategy that built up her own presidential appeal partly by appealing to long-held stereotypes about Blacks when she talked about or referred to her principal opponent, Barack Obama. That is, Clinton used a message strategy that deliberately mobilized particular linguistic tropes and imagery.

On the other hand, we point out that these tropes and imagery, though perhaps not chosen intentionally or specifically because of their racist potential, nevertheless possessed that potential. When we talk about Clinton's race strategy, we refer to a variety of messages communicated through campaign advertisements, candidate speeches, and the words of a host of campaign supporters and official campaign surrogates. The most prominent appeal in this category referred to the stereotypical relationship between Blacks and Whites and the issue of "work," which, interestingly enough, as we mentioned previously, perhaps has been the most frequent lens through which American political discourse about African Americans has been examined by scholars over the past two decades.

Obama's victory in Iowa took Clinton and her campaign team by surprise, to say the least. As Balz and Johnson (2009) tells the story, the Clinton campaign was outmaneuvered by a candidate whom it thought would be out of the contest after the Super Tuesday primaries and by a campaign staff that demonstrated it had a better command of the caucus process. Clinton countered by defeating Obama in New Hampshire, a contest the Obama camp thought it would win, riding the wave of the Iowa victory. The competition that resumed had the effect of Clinton sharpening not only her own message but, more important, her attacks on Obama. The first of these came through in a narrative about hard work in which Clinton repeatedly deployed the term to describe herself, in contrast to Obama. She often evoked the contrast as a difference between someone who works hard and someone who is all talk but no action.

The first clear sign of this came following Obama's victory in Iowa, when Clinton compared Obama to Martin Luther King Jr. in a peculiar way. Obama had mentioned King often in his remarks, reminding voters of a time when people had "the audacity to hope." Since the Iowa caucuses, he had given a number of stirring speeches, with a cadence and charisma reminiscent of King's. Clearly concerned about Obama's momentum (which is especially important given how contests for party nominations are structured), Clinton was quick to stay on message that Obama was little more than a pretty package with insufficient substance to get the job done. In doing so, she implicitly mobilized race by saying the following at a rally in New Hampshire: "Dr. King's dream began to be realized when President Lyndon Johnson passed the Civil Rights Act of 1964. It took a president to get it done." In effect, she rendered King (and by association, Obama) politically impotent by trivializing their oratorical skills.

Clinton continued her "hard work" versus "all talk" contrast with a thirty-second advertising spot that first aired on February 22, 2008, before the Texas primary. Titled "Deliver," the spot began with an image of several White ranch hands throwing bales of hay into the back of a pickup truck. The hot Texas sun is beating down on them in the middle of the day, and one can see the fatigue in their eyes. "Here in Texas, when there's work to be done, talk doesn't cut it," a male narrator with a deep voice says in an unmistakable Texas drawl. "You gotta roll up your sleeves, stand your ground, and deliver." The image fades from the ranchers to a silent moving image of Hillary Clinton speaking at a small gathering. The narrator continues talking over the imagery, which shifts from a group of children to an image of senior citizens to military veterans in rehabilitation to a large group of schoolchildren. "That's what Hillary Clinton does. She's fought for and delivered coverage for uninsured children, health care and dignity for our veterans, and better schools and better teachers." As the image fades back to the now setting sun on the wide-open Texas plains, the narrator concludes: "In Texas, it's better done than said, and when it's all said and done, Hillary delivers" (McIlwain 2009, 161).

Clinton hit the same theme in a speech she gave several days later to a mostly Black crowd gathered at one of South Carolina's historically Black colleges and universities. Speaking about one of her supporters, New York's Congressman Charles Rangel (who was sitting behind her on the stage), she told those gathered at the rally that she respected Rangel because he had worked hard to raise himself up from being a high-school dropout to become one of the most powerful members of Congress. Again, in an apparent contrast to Obama, Clinton said of Rangel: "He didn't get there by, you know, by leapfrogging. He got there by lots of hard work day in and day out."

This is implicitly racist on two levels and illuminates the racist appeal within Clinton's broader contrast narrative of hard work. First, like the comment made more than a year earlier by Senator Joe Biden, who referred to Obama as "articulate" and "clean" (a contrast to previous Black presidential candidates that was meant to be flattering to Obama), the hard work narrative relies on a tacit contrast between praise of a successful Black individual and the stereotypical African American Whites typically envision when they think about Blacks.[6] In other words, most of White America hears, "Unlike most Black folk, this man worked hard and earned what he's accomplished." Further, the comment about leapfrogging relies on another negative preconception many Whites harbor about Black Americans: that Blacks feel entitled to something they do not deserve, something they have not *earned*. Clinton thus was suggesting that, unlike Rangel, Obama (who was typical of most Blacks) wanted everything right away and was unwilling to work hard to get it. They would rather do something easy, such as talk their way into it.

In this way, the flip side of the hard work contrast (one who is all talk) resurrects another Black stereotype—that of the trickster, a theme that would be seized on even more prominently by Obama's opponents during the general election campaign. As McIlwain put it in an editorial at the time:

> The stereotype has a history, especially tied to black men who deal in the currency of words. The idea is that they dazzle the soft-minded with a persuasive prose, but leave them with nothing more than a feeling, at best. At worst, the charm in their speech leaves unwitting audiences with something quite different from what they were promised. In the blaxploitation films of the 1960s and '70s, the black slickster

was the pimp who charmed women into selling their bodies and remitting the proceeds. He was the drug dealer who seduced the poor and oppressed into a chemical high that left them poorer, physically damaged, in jail or dead. It was he whose inspirational orations were used to set a trap, to lure the innocent into the realm of the criminal. The slick trickster can't be trusted; his words are dishonest, serving only himself.[7]

In Clinton's narrative, the "hard work" trope signifies White Americans, while the talker, the speech giver, the smooth orator signifies the counter-image of the stereotypical African American out to get all he or she can, as quickly and as easily as he or she can. The contrast came through more clearly as the 2008 primary came to a close, Clinton fighting tooth and nail to somehow gain support for some argument that would—ironically—allow her to circumvent the primary rules in which the candidate with the most delegates at the end of the election won.

This argument came in a number of forms. For instance, Clinton argued vociferously for seating the delegates from Florida and Michigan, even though the state parties had ignored Democratic National Committee rules by having their selection contests too early in the process. The candidates agreed not to campaign in those states as a result of the violation (although Clinton held a fundraiser in Florida the weekend before the contest and had a rally on election night after the polls had closed), and it was widely assumed that the results would have no consequences in terms of actual delegates. Clinton won the plurality of delegates in both contests and claimed "victory." In June, she used racial rhetoric to argue for the delegates' seating:

> This work to extend the franchise to all of our citizens is a core mission of the modern Democratic Party. From signing the Voting Rights Act and fighting racial discrimination at the ballot box to lowering the voting age so those old enough to fight and die in war would have the right to choose their commander-in-chief, to fighting for multilingual ballots so you can make your voice heard no matter what language you speak.[8]

Such language reflects insensitivity to the complex dynamics of American racism that lends credence to concerns about the possibility of meaningful representation of people of color by Whites—even Whites who have previously demonstrated interest in and support for and by communities of color.

Then, in making her argument that Democratic Party super-delegates should nullify the primary election results because she was more electable in the general election, Clinton invoked race implicitly when she stated, "I have a much broader base to build a winning coalition on." Clinton continued that a recent poll had "found how Senator Obama's support among working, hardworking Americans, white Americans, is weakening again, and how whites in both states who had not completed college were supporting me. . . . There's a pattern emerging here."[9] The comment was roundly criticized, not simply because Clinton had invoked race, but because her language was perceived as reflecting her belief that (real) Americans are hardworking (working-class) Whites, precisely the voters Obama was having the most difficult time courting.

In May, Terry McAuliffe, Clinton's campaign chair, appeared on *Meet the Press* to defend Clinton's statement and actually contributed to the perception of the campaign's racial insensitivity, saying:

> Literally nobody has worked harder, as you know, than President Clinton. . . . [B]oth Clintons have worked their whole life on civil rights issues; Hillary, her entire life, has been working on issues, on education, on health care. They both have been out there fighting hard. This is the end of a long campaign.[10]

In fact, while Clinton's remarks were made in reference to an Associated Press story, she was not quoting it. Rather, in her interpretation of the story's content, she revealed (or, at least, conveyed) that she implicitly associated "hardworking" with Whites. But McAuliffe was not finished. When pushed by Tim Russert, the host of *Meet the Press,* with critical words from delegates to the Democratic National Convention, McAuliffe replied, "And you know what? I can put up 30, 40 more super-delegates who will say, you know, talk about what the Clintons have done on the race issue. First of all, I hate that . . . race is even in the—we should not have it. We shouldn't have race, we shouldn't have gender."[11] Far from simply trying to defend Clinton's racist remark, McAuliffe attempted to render the claims of racism insignificant by declaring that as many, if not more, folks disagreed, and he dismissed race as a serious issue in voters' decision-making processes by noting that he and the White candidate for whom he was speaking wished that race were not involved in the campaign.

Surrogates

As we demonstrated in the discussion of other campaigns, a considerable portion of race-based appeals comes from surrogates rather from the candidates themselves. Because many Black leaders lined up behind Hillary Clinton early in the primary season, their voices lent additional support to the notion that Obama was not authentically Black, or even the best choice to represent interests of the Black community. In December 2007, for example, the Civil Rights icon Andrew Young stated that he thought Obama was too

young to be president now but that he did want him to be president some-
day.[12] Bob Johnson, the billionaire founder of Black Entertainment Television,
attacked Obama at a Clinton rally, suggesting that he had been doing drugs
while the Clintons were fighting for racial justice, a suggestion he tried unsuccessfully to deny later in the day.[13]

In March 2008, Geraldine Ferraro, a campaign figurehead for Clinton and
former Democratic candidate for vice president, claimed that Obama had
done as well as he had in the contests to that point only because he was
Black.[14] When the comment was challenged as racist, Ferraro simply argued
that because she had fought for the rights of racial minorities, being called
"racist" was out of bounds. In the end, Ferraro reluctantly resigned her symbolic post on the Clinton campaign.

Although not a surrogate for Clinton's campaign (as he was a candidate
for president himself), Ralph Nader joined in the racist attacks against Obama
in the summer of 2008, telling the *Rocky Mountain News* that Obama was
"talking White" and playing into "White guilt":

> There's only one thing different about Barack Obama when it comes to
> being a Democratic presidential candidate. He's half African-American.
> Whether that will make any difference, I don't know. I haven't heard
> him have a strong crackdown on economic exploitation in the ghet-
> tos. Payday loans, predatory lending, asbestos, lead. What's keeping
> him from doing that? Is it because he wants to talk white? He doesn't
> want to appear like Jesse Jackson? We'll see all that play out in the
> next few months and if he gets elected afterwards. . . . I mean, first of
> all, the number one thing that a black American politician aspiring to
> the presidency should be is to candidly describe the plight of the poor,
> especially in the inner cities and the rural areas, and have a very
> detailed platform about how the poor [are] going to be defended by
> the law, [are] going to be protected by the law, and [are] going to be
> liberated by the law. Haven't heard a thing. . . . He wants to show that
> he is not a threatening . . . another politically threatening African-
> American politician. He wants to appeal to white guilt. You appeal to
> white guilt not by coming on as black is beautiful, black is powerful.
> Basically he's coming on as someone who is not going to threaten the
> white power structure, whether it's corporate or whether it's simply
> oligarchic. And they love it. Whites just eat it up.[15]

Nader criticized Obama for things that prominent Black leaders had not criticized him for publicly, implying that they were all being fooled and that he
knew better than they did what was best for the Black community.[16] He was
not, however, alone in his concern, as the Reverend Jesse Jackson demon-

strated in late July when he was caught on an open microphone saying that he would like to castrate Obama because of his racially inoculating campaign rhetoric.[17]

Perhaps the most noteworthy (and powerful) racist attacks came from former President Bill Clinton. The day before the primary contest in New Hampshire in January—the same day that Hillary Clinton made the unflattering comparisons to Martin Luther King who needed a (White) president to "get it done"—Bill Clinton referred to Barack Obama's record of opposing the war in Iraq as a "fairy tale." Ordinarily, this would not trigger any concern about racial messages, but the phrase perfectly echoed Biden's remarks about Obama being "clean" and "articulate."

More notable, however, is the remark Bill Clinton made in South Carolina the day after Obama won the primary there. Asked about the importance of the contest, Clinton compared Obama with Jesse Jackson, noting that Jackson, too, had won the primary in South Carolina (which has the largest proportion of Black voters) twice. The message was that Black support is not nearly sufficient to secure a nomination and win in a general election contest against a Republican, but the comments also suggested that Black voters would vote for any Black candidate—that Obama was not special (or different from other politically impotent Black leader who could not "get it done").

These types of racist appeals (and repudiations of Hillary Clinton's own racist appeals) by surrogates contribute to racial frames that Obama wished to avoid. Even when she distanced herself from the remarks (such as when Geraldine Ferraro resigned from the campaign), the reality is that plausible deniability and claims of no racist intent are part and parcel of post–Civil Rights–era American political campaigns in which race has been a factor. Clinton benefited from the attacks the same way that an objectionable remark by a trial attorney can resonate with a jury even if it is withdrawn or struck from the record. One cannot unring the proverbial bell, as it were.

The Wright Stuff

The most racially relevant attacks on Barack Obama during his presidential run—both in the nomination contests and during the general election—may very well have been those that involved his former pastor, the Reverend Jeremiah Wright. Attempts to link Obama to the controversial ideas of Wright, a Black Liberation theologian, began during the primaries and continued throughout the campaign, although Obama effectively deflected the thrust of the damage by giving a speech that he had never intended to give on March 18, 2008.

The controversy began in February, when Obama was asked a question during a Democratic candidate debate in Cleveland about whether he would accept the endorsement of the Reverend Louis Farrakhan, the former leader of the Nation of Islam. Obama stated that he had rejected Farrakhan's anti-Semitic remarks over the years and eventually said that he renounced Farra-khan's endorsement. Russert, one of the reporters on the debate panel, was not discouraged by Obama's distancing, though, and took another approach. Noting that Wright (Obama's Christian minister) had once spoken kindly of Farrakhan, Russert set in motion the politics of association that would plague Obama throughout the campaign.[18]

If that two-degree separation had been the only aspect of Obama's associ-ation with Wright to surface, we would not have to devote an entire section to the controversial preacher. What followed, however, was unprecedented. Edited clips of Wright's sermons began to appear on the Internet and quickly made their way to radio talk shows, and then to the mainstream media. Wright's apparent "anti-America" rhetoric became a focal point of discussion for a number of weeks, with Obama forced to answer questions about whether he had been in attendance during those sermons, whether he agreed with the sentiments, and how closely he was associated with Wright.

It is impossible to disentangle the Wright controversy from race, despite the valiant attempts of those who continued to invoke Wright for political gain. The fact is that Wright's comments, though taken out of context, were rooted in his understanding of the Christian Bible and the tradition in many predominantly Black churches of being openly critical about systems that continue to oppress America's poor and of-color communities. For Obama's critics, Wright became a visible and convenient surrogate for Obama in a rhe-torical strategy that rested on the assumption that a member of a Black church was an uncritical sponge, absorbing and internalizing any and all mes-sages that emanated from the pulpit.

As a result, Obama had to deliver the speech that he had hoped not to give. He was forced to speak openly and directly about race, thereby acknowl-edging his own race and endangering his carefully crafted "post-racial" frame. On March 18, 2008, Obama gave his "A More Perfect Union" speech in Phila-delphia. In his remarks, Obama took great risks, talking frankly about the realities of race in America. Speaking like a college professor, Obama acknowl-edged the racial tensions throughout American history, tracing the roots of the conflict back to the founding and noting that the Constitution provided a foundation on which an unequal society would be built. Obama said that it took a war and civil disobedience "to narrow the gap between the promise of our ideals and the reality of their time," and continually stated that we (still) need to move toward "a more perfect union," echoing the language of the Constitution's preamble.

He then spoke of his personal journey, arguing that "in no other country on earth is my story even possible." Addressing to the Wright situation, he claimed that the preacher had used "incendiary language" that served to "denigrate the greatness and the goodness of our nation." Obama distanced himself from Wright's remarks, if not from Wright himself, by claiming that Wright had "expressed a profoundly distorted view of this country." Obama said that the comments were both wrong and divisive at a time when we need to come together.

At this point, Obama might have moved on to talk about the policy issues that he was seeking to address, play into broad notions of patriotism, and otherwise push past "race" as an issue. Instead, however, he went on to say that "race is an issue that . . . this nation cannot afford to ignore right now." He warned against distorting reality by amplifying stereotypes, saying, "We've never really worked through these issues." Finally, Obama explained that Reverend Wright had been socialized during a time when segregation was legal and prejudice was much more blatant and hostile than it is now. This, Obama argued, informed Wright's ideas and passions.

Obama had to be careful to not alienate his progressive minority and far-left White supporters by completely dismissing Wright's ideas while convincing others that he did not share such sentiments, even if he understood and appreciated their origins. He argued that it was improper to dismiss anger or resentment among Blacks as anecdotal and irrelevant and that to do so would only widen the chasm between the races. He said that the legacy of discrimination is real and that it is not just in the minds of Black people.

Clearly referring to the "White resentment" academic literature, Obama noted that a similar anger exists within segments of White America. He claimed that opportunity too often is seen as a zero-sum game, with Whites (especially the descendants of immigrants) competing with people of color. As a consequence, resentment builds over time. Such White resentments—like Black anger—are not always expressed in polite company, but they have helped to shape the political landscape. In sum, Obama offered that, just as Black anger has proved counterproductive, White resentment has distracted attention from the "middle-class squeeze."

The political importance of his speech was that he at once handled the "Wright problem" and reinforced themes that were already in place in his campaign. He noted several times that people would have to work together; that Blacks' struggles should be linked with wider struggles; and that the problem with Wright's comments was that he spoke as if the nation was static, failing to recognize the progress that had been made and to believe in the progress that could be made. "America can change," Obama said. "That is the true genius of this nation."

From a rhetorical standpoint, the speech was impeccable.[19] Obama invoked the Aristotelian elements of "ethos" (by situating himself—at once Black and White—as having unique insight into the issue), "logos" (by carefully but concisely connecting America's racist history with its contemporary problems) and "pathos" (by appealing to affective components of the human experience—most notably, when he spoke about his White grandmother's bigotry and when he told a story about a White girl and an elderly Black man who were working together on his campaign). From a framing perspective, the speech permitted him at once to "transcend race" (as he clearly had attempted to do from the start) while acknowledging the racial problems that exist in America. Finally, he put forth a vision of racial progress, sending a signal that if he were elected, he would be attentive to our collective desire to move past these tensions.

By the end of April, Obama had distanced himself from Wright, formally left his church, and hoped to put the issue behind him. Having fanned the flames of racial controversy throughout the primary season, the mainstream press effectively ignored Wright during the general election campaign. However, Wright's image, words, and ideas could be found throughout the communications of the Republican candidate John McCain's supporters, if not from the McCain campaign directly.[20]

RACIST APPEALS FROM CONSERVATIVES AND REPUBLICANS

Racist appeals were at least as prevalent from conservatives and Republicans during the general election contest as they were from Democratic opponents and their surrogates during the primaries. Those attacks can be categorized into two main (and interrelated) themes that are consistent with racist attacks in other campaigns, as we have demonstrated to this point: otherness and untrustworthiness.

Otherness: "He Is Not One of Us"

As we have seen in other electoral contexts and with respect to the immigration issue, the otherness narrative can operate as an overarching category that encompasses the sentiments inherent in both types of racist appeals. That is, because Whites are perceived to be the norm in American culture, people of color are inherently "other," a fact that can be highlighted for effect if doing so does not activate voters' conscious racial sensibilities. In other words, referring to a minority candidate as "untrustworthy" (i.e., trying to pass oneself off as something or someone one is not) also casts the candidate as different from the ideal of the "ordinary" American. Still, there are specific and discrete messages that play most directly into this "not like us theme," and many of them emerged after Labor Day.

Obama as Elitist

As happens so often, some of the messages seized on in the general election were those that had surfaced in the heat of the primaries. One such message that meets this criterion in the current case was the image of Obama as an "elitist." In April, he was recorded making disparaging comments about "Middle America." As he answered a question at a function in San Francisco about why he was having trouble winning support among working-class Whites, he said, "They get bitter; they cling to guns or religion or antipathy to people who aren't like them or anti-immigrant sentiment or anti-trade sentiment as a way to explain their frustrations." Hillary Clinton pounced on the comment, labeling it "elitist and out of touch," which is a refrain that seemed to have had limited effect in the context of the primaries but set the stage for a barrage of similar claims later in the year.

Representative Lynn Westmoreland, a Republican from Georgia, was comparing the vice-presidential nominee Sarah Palin and Obama's wife, Michelle, when he said: "Just from what little I've seen of her and Mr. Obama, Sen. Obama, they're a member of an elitist-class individual that thinks that they're uppity."[21] The term "uppity" has clear and deep racial implications. Painting Obama as "elitist" is effective largely because of the deep-seated presumption among Whites that African Americans should "know their place." "Uppity" historically has almost always been followed by the "N word," or, in more polite circles through the Jim Crow era, by "Negro." Westmoreland claimed ignorance of any racial connotation of the term.[22]

Several speakers at the Republican National Convention in Minneapolis made comments that reflected each of the themes we have identified. The "otherness" frame came in a number of forms from a number of speakers. Rudy Giuliani, former mayor of New York City and a Republican presidential hopeful in 2008, noted in his speech that Obama had been a "community organizer," and the audience laughed. Although the line did not appear to be planned as a joke in and of itself, the audience then held up "ZE-RO" signs, as if to indicate that such work is of no importance or value. Giuliani went on to say that "[Obama] never had to lead people in crisis," which indicated a lack of understanding, a lack of empathy, or a purposeful and perhaps strategic discounting of the crisis poor folks have faced, particularly (in this context) in urban communities such as those in which Obama had worked. Sarah Palin picked up this theme, as well, saying that "a small town mayor is like a community organizer, except that you have actual responsibilities." Later, referring to the presidency, Palin said, "It's not just a community, and it doesn't need an organizer." This comment (1) trivializes the notion of community by placing "just" in front of it; and (2) devalues the work that is done in inner cities by leaders—many of whom (like Obama) eschew personal wealth and fame to pursue such paths. This form of "otherness" suggests that there is something wrong with Obama for not having taken full advantage of his Harvard education and making something of himself by seeking financial success. Where "real Americans" work, people like Obama "organize." To an immediate audience that was approximately 99 percent White (and a wider audience of potential voters that was also disproportionately White), the racist implications of this line of rhetoric are easy to identify.

Obama as Muslim/Arab/Terrorist

In an online ad released in late summer titled, "The One," John McCain's campaign used language and imagery that, *Time* magazine said, might suggest to Christians that Barack Obama was the antichrist.[23] Religion, as the Jeremiah Wright controversy demonstrated, was a pervasive issue in the campaign, with many conservatives arguing that Obama was secretly a Muslim. We discuss the secrecy aspect in the following section, but the accusation that he is a Muslim taps directly into the "other" frame, particularly for White fundamentalist Christians, a usually reliable voting constituency for the Republican Party that most analysts acknowledged would need to be mobilized to vote to counteract the new voters expected to go to the polls to support Obama in his historic run.

One favorite quip of McCain–Palin supporters at rallies was the easy juxtaposition of "Obama" with "Osama" (i.e., Al-Qaeda's leader Osama bin Laden). A real estate office in Hendersonville, North Carolina, was explicit about the "other" frame on its marquee: "Osama–Obama; Not American; Not Welcome." A billboard in southwestern Missouri, featuring a cartoonish image of Obama in a head wrap with the text "Barack 'Hussein' Obama Equals More Abortions, Same-Sex Marriages, Taxes, Gun Regulations," invoked Obama's middle name to suggest that he was Muslim. A mailer distributed by the Virginia Republican Party seems to have been a photograph of Obama altered in a way that makes him look like Bin Laden. The image appears behind text that reads, "American Must Look Evil in the Eye and Never Flinch."

At a rally in Denver, an Obama supporter had his or her (the supporter is not on camera) patriotism questioned and was told that "Satan is on [his or her] side," while the words "terrorist," "socialist," and "communist" were repeatedly applied to "Hussein" Obama (who at some points is referred to as "Osama"). One woman suggested that if Obama were elected, we would get "free turbans." A man called Obama a "Muslim communist" in addition to the offensive (but not particularly racist) "bum" and "piece of crap."

Obama as Un-American

A number of third-party groups ran advertisements that fit this aspect of the "other" frame. Here, the argument was that Obama was not patriotic—in fact, in many instances the ads suggested that he was actively working to subvert American values and, possibly, national security. The National Republican Trust Political Action Committee ran a series of spots arguing that Obama had tolerance for terrorists, criticizing Obama's opposition to denying driver's licenses to undocumented workers, and linking his "redistributive" economic plan to support for "illegals" and terrorists. The Pennsylvania Republican Party released an ad titled "Bitter" that put forth a group of White folks (and one Black man with his child) who were supposedly the target of Obama's "elitist" comment about his inability to win over rural White Democrats during the primaries. Another ad used altered photographs of U.S. leaders meeting with leaders of rogue nations to suggest that Obama's belief in diplomacy with enemies of the U.S. was naïve. The spot included an image of Obama shaking hands with Iranian President Mahmoud Ahmadinejad.

Images and conversation circulated on the Internet relating to Obama's not always wearing an American flag pin on his lapel and not putting his hand on his heart during the national anthem. An email purporting to be an official transcript from *Meet the Press* circulated about the latter issue, ostensibly fooling many into believing that it was authentic. Rife with typographical errors, the transcript appeared to relay a conversation between Obama and a retired Air Force general in which Obama was quoted as saying:

> As I've said about the flag pin, [I] don't want to be perceived as taking sides. There are a lot of people in the world to whom the American flag is a symbol of oppression. And the anthem itself conveys a war-like message. You know, the bombs bursting in air and all. It should be swapped for something less parochial and less bellicose. I like the song "I'd Like to Teach the World to Sing." If that were our anthem, then I might salute it. We should consider to reinvent our National Anthem as well as to redesign our Flag to better offer our enemies hope and love. It's my intention, if elected, to disarm America to the level of acceptance to our Middle East Brethren. If we as a Nation of warring people, should conduct ourselves as the nations of Islam, whereas peace prevails. Perhaps a state or period of mutual concord between our governments. When I become President, I will seek a pact or agreement to end hostilities between those who have been at war or in a state of enmity, and a freedom from disquieting oppressive thoughts. We as a Nation have placed upon the nations of Islam an unfair injustice. My

wife disrespects the Flag for many personal reasons. Together she and I have attended several flag burning ceremonies in the past, many years ago. She has her views and I have mine. Of course now, I have found myself about to become the President of the United States and I have put aside my hatred. I will use my power to bring CHANGE to this Nation, and offer the people a new path of hope. My wife and I look forward to becoming our Country's First Family. Indeed, CHANGE is about to overwhelm the United States of America.

The email concludes, "Yes, ladies and gentlemen, you heard it right. This could possibly be our next President." The reason to seriously consider a dirty campaign trick from a non-official source is that the opportunity to convince folks that a candidate for president would subscribe to (let alone, state) such ridiculous ideas is heightened when deeply held subconscious predispositions make such an argument more acceptable. Because many Whites consider African Americans as not appreciating or revering America the way they do, it is easier to convince them that a Black candidate would subscribe to such beliefs.

A third-party group called Wake Up USA similarly posted fantastic lies on the Internet, accusing Obama of using "hypnosis" in his speeches. The group produced a video entitled *The Rise of the United Socialist States of America* that listed all of "Barack Hussein Obama's" radical friends and predicted what would happen if Obama were elected, including "increased company shakedowns by Jesse Jackson, Al Sharpton and their ilk, if your company is not color-coded to their requirements. Black Reparations on the horizon?"

Of course, the most significant disagreements between McCain and Obama (and between most McCain's supporters and Obama) were based on differences in ideology and on policy issues. However, even those contrasts have different types and degrees of potential effect in the evaluation of candidates when one's opponent is a person of color.

Obama as Liberal

From Jesse Helms's attacks against Harvey Gantt ("dangerously liberal") in the 1990s to Republicans' attacks against Harold Ford Jr. ("the most liberal member of Tennessee's congressional delegation") in 2006, we have seen the "liberal" label employed often against candidates of color. At the Republican National Convention, former U.S. Senator (and presidential hopeful) Fred Thompson of Tennessee referred to Obama as making a "teleprompter speech designed to appeal to America's critics abroad." He used language that turned Obama's historic run on its side by noting that it was history-making because Obama was "the most liberal, most inexperienced nominee ever to run for president."

Finally, Thompson said that the United States needed a president who felt no need to apologize for the United States, referring, presumably, to Obama's foreign policy positions and opposition to the war in Iraq. Similarly, former Arkansas Governor Mike Huckabee (also a Republican presidential nominee in 2008) expressed concern about the "European ideas" that Obama had brought back from his trip overseas, meaning that such values are not American ideas. Also at the convention, former Massachusetts Governor Mitt Romney (yet another presidential hopeful) said, to raucous applause, "There has never been a day when I was not proud to be an American," referring to Michelle Obama's statement that for the first time in her adult life, she was really proud of her country.

Obama as Child

In one of the debates, John McCain referred to Obama as "that one," pointing his finger toward him in a playful gesture. Rather than being intentionally racist, he was dismissing Obama as not ready to be president. On its own, that is a legitimate campaign strategy. But referring to an African American opponent in a way that puts him in the position of a child or grandchild is consistent with centuries of Whites' treating African Americans as children. Ever since Obama had become the presumptive Democratic nominee, the McCain campaign had attempted to portray him as not having enough experience to be president. After McCain chose the relatively inexperienced Sarah Palin as his running mate, however, that argument lost any potential for effectiveness. The "other" frame served as a surrogate for that theme.

In short, people who were looking for a reason to justify not voting for Obama, apart from his race, could find psychological comfort in the idea that he simply was "not like us." For some, he was too unsophisticated (a "thug"), and for others, he was too sophisticated ("elitist" or "uppity"). For some, he was identified with radical Black theology, and for others, he was (secretly) a Muslim. For some, he gave aid and comfort to America's enemies, and for others, he sought to undermine the revered free-enterprise economic system on which the nation was built. As we noted above, many of these claims gained additional power as a result of implications that Obama not only embodied these negative characteristics, but that he was lying about who he really was to fool the voters—things that made him both "dangerous" and "liberal."

Untrustworthy

The stereotype that African Americans are untrustworthy comprises three interrelated components: (1) predispositions linking Blacks with criminality; (2) the belief that Blacks are "shifty" and skillful at running cons; and (3) an assumption that Blacks feel entitled to receive that which they do not deserve (i.e., laziness and entitlement). In much of the campaign discourse, Obama was painted as a skillful orator, with no substance; as a political opportunist; and as an elitist who was out of touch with "normal" Americans. While this is an effective strategy in general, these ideas also fit neatly with stereotypes that African Americans are shifty, slick, always scamming, and looking to help themselves to that which they do not deserve. Black athletes and celebrities (Giuliani called Obama a "celebrity senator," suggesting that he is all flash and no substance or hard work) are stereotyped as self-promoting and arrogant. In short, the various images of the black man in the American imagination were combined and ascribed to Barack Obama. As we saw in the primary season, these themes were consistently invoked from various angles. After Obama secured the nomination, the narrative was employed in similar ways by conservatives and Republicans.

At the Republican National Convention, Fred Thompson centered his remarks on vivid descriptions of John McCain's torture in Vietnam, contrasting McCain's action and experience with Obama's "talk." Playing on Obama's "A change you can believe in" theme, Thompson said that McCain had "character you can believe in," suggesting that Obama's character was in question. Thompson went on to say that Washington had had its share of "smooth talkers and big talkers," adding, "Obviously, it still has." The stereotype of African Americans—particularly African American men—as shifty, fast-talking, and untrustworthy was primed by suggestions that Obama talked a good game but was really trying to fool everyone for his own benefit. He, unlike McCain, it was suggested, would not put the country first. Senator Joe Lieberman of Connecticut said that Obama was "gifted and eloquent" but that "eloquence is no substitute for a record."

Other comments from the Republican National Convention that support this theme included the statement by Michael Steele, former U.S. Senate candidate from Maryland and soon-to-be chairman of the Republican National Committee, that "mere words about change are not enough to transform this nation"; Rudy Giuliani's statement that Obama "broke his promise" (referring to Obama's pledge to accept public financing and feeding into stereotypes about lack of trustworthiness and willingness to say anything to get what one wants), and his joke that Obama did not think Sarah Palin's hometown was "cosmopolitan enough" or "flashy enough" (playing into the stereotype of the slick-talking and arrogant black man, an attack used against Harold Ford Jr. in his senatorial bid in Tennessee in 2006);[24] and Alaska Governor Sarah Palin's many statements, such as that there was "a time to campaign and a time to put our country first" (playing into the stereotype that Blacks put themselves and their needs above all else), that Obama was two-faced when it came to working people, that being a leader was "not just mingl[ing] with the right people," that Obama made "dramatic speeches before devoted followers" and that he never used the word "victory" unless he was talking about his own campaign, that "there are some candidates who use change to promote their careers, and then there are other candidates, like John McCain, who use their careers to promote change," that America needed leaders who were "good for more than talk," and that "for a season, a gifted speaker can inspire with his words, but for a lifetime, John McCain has inspired through his deeds." Some of Palin's speech, in fact, was quite acerbic. She mocked Obama on a number of occasions, at one point predicting what change he would make "after he's done turning back the waters and healing the planet."

The conservative group Freedom's Defense Fund ran an ad for one week in Michigan that was strikingly reminiscent of the Willie Horton spot. In the ad, a direct link was made between the Detroit's shamed Mayor Kwame Kilpatrick and Barack Obama. The implication was that "they" (African Americans) were all the same (criminal, untrustworthy). The ad explicitly noted that a candidate's "friends" matter. Implicit in this particular appeal to the "untrustworthy" stereotype was the assumption that, unlike Whites (who are colorblind and therefore willing and able to look out for all types of people), people of color "stick together" and look out only for one another.

When former Congressman Tom DeLay was on *Hardball*, he employed the "untrustworthy" frame by suggesting that people called Obama's philosophy "what it is" (e.g., socialist, communist, anti-American, terrorist-supporting) and noting that "the real Obama" was surfacing. He went on to differentiate Obama from a "legitimate liberal" such as Congressman Barney Frank, for whom DeLay said he had "great respect." In contrast to Frank, according to DeLay, Obama wanted to "shred the Constitution."

Mike Goldfarb, the national spokesperson for McCain's campaign, suggested that Obama had "shady" connections with people who were anti-Semitic, anti-Israel, and anti-American. As we noted above, the "Middle East wedge" is not an unfamiliar tactic in contests involving Black candidates, whether they are running against White or Black opponents. Since U.S. support for Israel has been unconditional, any suggestion that a candidate or public official is empathetic or sympathetic to the Palestinian perspective is equivalent to an accusation of being un-American or tolerant of terrorism.

Related to this argument is one particular high-profile incident at a town hall meeting that was widely reported as an important moment in the campaign for McCain. After a woman informed him that she believed Obama was an Arab, McCain famously corrected her. McCain was widely praised for (finally) standing up to the ignorance and hate that surfaced among supporters at his events, but others noted that his admonition of the woman came by way of saying that Obama was "a good man," contrasting that characterization with "Arab." Perhaps, however, McCain was arguing that Obama was "a good man" because he was not being dishonest about his religion.

EXPLICIT DISCUSSION ABOUT RACE

As was the case during the nominating season, much of the language from the campaigns, from surrogates, and from the press during the general election campaign was composed of implicit racial and racist messages. As we saw in the primary contests, however, there were also a number of times when race was explicitly addressed.

Explicitly Racist Appeals

Videos of McCain-Palin supporters at rallies, particularly in Pennsylvania and Ohio, circulated on the Internet. In addition to the countless rally goers who can be seen and heard shouting such "othering" phrases as "socialist" and "terrorist," some were overtly explicit about their racial animosity. One supporter gleefully boasted a monkey doll identified as Obama, and vendors at a conservative convention sold "Obama Waffles" in which Obama was depicted in an Aunt Jemima–like manner, with racially offensive phrases and images scattered around the box. McCain-Palin supporters felt very comfortable violating American cultural norms of equality in public and in front of cameras as they emotionally—with anger (reflected in passionate screams) or fear (reflected in tears)—stated their opposition to Obama in overtly racist terms. A supporter at one rally said, "I'm afraid if he wins, the Blacks will take over." Another argued that Obama was not qualified to be president by saying, "When you've got a Negra runnin' for president, you need a first-stringer." Still another said, "He is friends with the terrorists of this country." This final claim resonates on a number of levels. Besides the Obama–Osama coupling, much attention was given to the relationship between Obama and the former Weather Underground member and community activist Bill Ayers.[25]

Less than a week before the general election, the explicitly racist messages at McCain-Palin rallies showed no signs of waning. At a rally in Denver, a little girl repeatedly created monkey sounds and mannerisms while her family chanted, "Nobama." She then called Obama "a monkey president," while her little sister (we assume) was heard to say, "a monkey from Tarzan" (twice). In Pottsville, Pennsylvania, a McCain supporter chanted "bomb Obama" and clearly indicated that he knew about plans to assassinate Obama if he was elected, indicating a gun with his fingers. Another man, with a sign that read, "Democrat for McCain," admitted that he would "never vote for a Black man." Our favorite from this rally was a man who stated clearly that he did not "want to sound racist" when he stated that he did "not want a Black man running [his] country."

Public officials were somewhat less crass in their explicit appeals to race, but the appeals came nonetheless. In most instances, McCain's supporters sought to defuse the historical component of Obama's run. Michael Steele, perhaps the best-known Black Republican on the landscape at the time, gave a stirring speech at the Republican National Convention that greatly energized the crowd. He addressed race directly by saying that "the ideal of a colorblind society is worth fighting for, because each man, woman and child is an individual, not a member of some hyphenated . . . group." Similarly, Mike Huckabee addressed race when he spoke, personalizing his intolerance of racism: "I witnessed firsthand the shameful evil of racism." He said that he had respect for Obama's securing of the nomination: "We celebrate this milestone because it elevates our country, but the presidency is not a symbolic job." With this point, we recall Geraldine Ferraro's claim that Obama's nomination was akin to an affirmative action hire. Huckabee was essentially arguing that we need more than the mere symbolism that a Black president can offer.

Tom DeLay was less sophisticated in his approach. When he appeared on MSNBC's *Hardball* with Chris Matthews, DeLay called Obama a "radical" and a "Marxist" and referred to his relationship with Jeremiah Wright and Bill Ayers as evidence of those claims. Playing explicitly on White racial resentment, DeLay noted that the problem with Jeremiah Wright was not his "outrageous" sermons but that he was "a Black liberation theology preacher," suggesting that such a perspective is, in and of itself, contrary to American values. With the clear association of Obama with Wright, the "other" frame is clearly established.

Some of the most explicit appeals to race surprised us because of the utter lack of awareness or concern about being perceived as bigoted. For example, a newsletter sent out by the Chaffey County Republican Women's Club in California included an illustration of a dollar bill that featured an image in the center in which Obama is dressed like a donkey (the symbol of the Democratic Party). The words "United States Food Stamps" is written across the top, and pictures of stereotypically Black food—a bucket of Kentucky Fried Chicken, a slab of ribs, Kool-Aid, and watermelon—are scattered about. The group's president, Diane Fedele, said that she simply wanted to deride a comment Obama had made over the summer about how as an African American he "doesn't look like all those other presidents on the dollar bills." Said Fedele, "It was strictly an attempt to point out the outrageousness of his statement. I really don't want to go into it any further. I absolutely apologize to anyone who was offended. That clearly wasn't my attempt." Fedele said she concocted the image because she was offended that Obama would draw attention to his own race.

Adding that she did not think in racist terms, Fedele noted that she had once supported the Republican Alan Keyes, who is Black, for president. "I didn't see it the way that it's being taken. I never connected," she said. "It was just food to me. It didn't mean anything else." She said she also was not trying to make a statement linking Obama and food stamps, although her introductory text to the illustration connects the two: "Obama talks about all those presidents that got their names on bills. If elected, what bill would he be on????? Food Stamps, what else!"

Rejecting the "Race Card"

When the conservative political action committee produced the "Willie Horton" ad in 1988, the Reverend Jesse Jackson issued a statement highlighting the racist message that it implicitly contained. Similarly, some Black leaders were vocal about the implicit racism and overt bigotry that permeated the 2008 presidential campaign. In the most notable incident, Congressman John Lewis, a veteran of the Civil Rights Movement of the 1950s and 1960s, issued a statement criticizing the McCain–Palin campaign for not speaking out against the bigotry among their supporters and for engaging in rhetoric that encouraged it:

> As one who was a victim of violence and hate during the height of the Civil Rights Movement, I am deeply disturbed by the negative tone of the McCain–Palin campaign. What I am seeing reminds me too much of another destructive period in American history. Senator McCain and Governor Palin are sowing the seeds of hatred and division, and there is no need for this hostility in our political discourse.

Lewis also noted that George Wallace, the segregationist former governor of Alabama and onetime presidential candidate, had "never thr[own] a bomb. He never fired a gun, but he created the climate and the conditions that encouraged vicious attacks against innocent Americans who were simply trying to exercise their constitutional rights. Because of this atmosphere of hate, four little girls were killed on Sunday morning when a church was bombed in Birmingham, Alabama."

The McCain campaign was very animated in its response to the criticism, and the Obama campaign came to McCain's defense, arguing that McCain and Palin were not intentionally racist (which, of course, was not at all what Lewis was arguing). But Obama's response allowed him to appear to be "sensible" with respect to racial issues, while Lewis could be the foil, the radical, who could stand as a convenient contrast to Obama for White Americans.

U.S. Senator Lindsey Graham, one of McCain's supporters, claimed on *Face the Nation* that Lewis's comments were "an absolute offense to people like [him]." He went on to say, "We're not going to be intimidated by this playing the race card simply because Senator Obama's record has been attacked in a very fair way." Of course, Lewis was not reacting to attacks on Obama's record; he was reacting to "pallin' around with terrorist" comments, Obama monkeys, and "Osama–Obama" signs. The reality, however, is that the rampant bigotry exposed at those rallies quickly spiraled out of the control of either McCain or Palin. When McCain chastised a man for saying that he was afraid of Obama, he was booed by the crowd.

The response to Lewis's claims, however, highlights the reason that there is danger in minority candidates' pointing out the racism that is used against them in campaigns. They cannot do it themselves for fear of confirming the stereotype that minorities are always hypersensitive about race, using it in place of "legitimate" issues to get what they want (but do not deserve). Such was the response to Obama's comment in the summer when he predicted that Republicans would use race in the campaign against him. Even when surrogates attempt to call out racist attacks on behalf of a candidate, though, the counter-response is almost always the same: It is they (the minorities) who are "playing the race card." Such a Catch-22 situation is characteristic of the power of hegemonic structures.

OBAMA WINS

Obama did not simply win the election. He won convincingly. A margin of 7.2 percent of the popular vote may not sound like a lot, but that represents more than 9.5 million voters and is the largest margin of victory for a president since 1988. Further, when one considers only five Black candidates have won high-profile statewide office (U.S. senator or governor) since Reconstruction, Obama's ability to win the plurality of the vote in enough states to secure 365 electoral votes is impressive. He won 43 percent of the White vote nationwide, as well as 67 percent of the Hispanic vote and 95 percent of the Black vote.[26] Further, in many of the states that he ultimately lost, he was competitive until the end.

Both Democrats and Republicans, whether they intended to or not, invoked language and images that were more effective because they were used against an African American candidate, and Obama used racial language consistent with what we found in our comprehensive analysis of other federal election campaigns that involved racial minority candidates. Obama was portrayed as "other" in a number of ways (elitist, un-American, Muslim, liberal) and was accused, both implicitly and explicitly, of being a liar, a con artist, and a phony. Both of these strategies—"othering" and accusations of dishonesty— are potentially more effective against a candidate of color because of preexisting negative associations that Americans (not only White Americans) have about people of color and, in this case, African Americans in particular.

Those whose definition of "racist" is narrowly construed to include only overt bigotry (including bigotry against Whites) have signaled Obama's election as proof of the lack of anti-Black racism in America, often to argue that those who advocate for racial justice should "get over it" because Obama's presence in the White House means that Blacks now have "the power" in America. What we have demonstrated, however, is that Obama won the election in spite of America's racism—a feat that certainly would not have been possible even a few years ago, let alone a generation ago, but one that does not singularly mark the end of four hundred years of systemic racism. As we discuss in the Epilogue, there is great cause for racial progressives to celebrate the accomplishment of Obama's election, but a tremendous amount of progress is yet to be made.

Racialized Campaigns

What Have We Learned, and Where Do We Go from Here?

A S IT IS with any kind of complex phenomena, developing substantive claims about, evidence of, and enduring explanations for how race and electoral politics intersect in America's recent history and present day is difficult. Some things stay relatively the same, as we find in our studies here. Racial prejudices and stereotypes persist in America's racial imagination; the types of race-based advertising appeals and individuals' statements we have analyzed here bear witness to this fact.

Candidates often use any and every kind of tool available to them to persuade voters to elect them—sometimes even appealing to the most deplorable human attitudes to accomplish their electoral goals. This has not changed since the time that Blacks were first seen—in principle—as citizens and became more or less viable members of the American electorate. The news media, whether we see them as elite opinion leaders, watchdogs of democracy, agenda setters, gossipmongers, or muckrakers, always seem to gravitate to that which is new, controversial, sensational, and sometimes even interesting. Racial matters seem to have always fit that bill.

These relative mainstays of America's social, racial, and political landscape make our efforts easier because they situate our present electoral situation within a historically grounded context that provides a firm base for many of the arguments and conclusions we offer throughout the book. Thus, when we talk about racial stereotypes, prejudice, and political communications that make use of them, we have history to help illuminate our contemporary assessment. When we say, for example, that a candidate's claim that his Black opponent gets paid but does not work might resonate with White voters, it should not seem too far-fetched to most Americans because we know that just twenty years ago more than half of all Whites believed that Blacks were more lazy than they were hardworking.[1] When we point out, for example, that it is perfectly reasonable to expect that the media will be interested in the racial dynamics and controversies of someone like Deval Patrick running for governor in Massachusetts, our claim should not sound so inconceivable because no African American had ever run and had a chance to win in the state, and at the time only one other Black man had ever been elected governor of any state—and that was just fifteen years before. So America's racial history does provide a convenient backdrop for the interpretations, claims, and conclusions we have made throughout the book.

But so much about race, politics, and American elections has changed—in the past year, in the past two, in the past decade. Only a complete cynic would look at the complexion of the man currently sitting in the Oval Office and not believe that we have not made considerable racial progress, especially given the fact that until Obama's election, Americans had only three times elected an African American to represent a state's majority White citizenry as governor or U.S. senator. The (literal) complexion of the country has change, and continues to rapidly change, becoming darker, given the influx of immigrants from Latin America in particular. This is so much the case that that the label "minority" we use sometimes throughout the book is arguably outdated as a descriptor. Despite the numerical realities, however, Whites have a power majority in the United States and are likely to retain it for some time.

But that is not all. People's racial sensibilities have changed. Perhaps it is because for so long we have been unable to talk about racial issues in the public sphere—constrained by "political correctness," social prohibitions, fear of our lack of civility, or simply our sheer inability to broach the subject with even our children.[2] But it seems that more and more Whites vociferously object to even the thought of being labeled "racist." Many express resentment because they have diverse friendship circles, yet still people describe them with phrases such as "White privilege" and references to White supremacy. Simply put, America's demographics are drastically shifting, as are people's thinking and feelings about race. We refer to this as "racism fatigue." It is this kind of shift, however—from a posture of racial optimism and progress, on the one hand, to racism fatigue, on the other—that complicates the claims and conclusions we make in this book. Simply put, it is sometimes hard to put our finger on exactly what is happening.

These complexities notwithstanding, having made and substantiated our conclusions throughout the book and especially in the last three chapters, there are a couple of items we return to—a final set of thoughts that might focus readers' attention on some aspects of America's racial politics that we think are crucially important and others that we as scholars must continue to pursue.

We hope that we have been clear about what we see as one of the most significant barriers to racial equality over the past forty years: the conflation of intent with effect. Particularly in the most contemporary era of "gotcha" politics (and "gotcha" journalism), there is a tendency to see racism at work whenever someone who is not White talks about race or whenever a person of color says something unkind about a White person. This was made abundantly clear early on in Barack Obama's presidency, when he convened a so-called White House Beer Summit to publicly instigate a conversation between Professor Henry Louis Gates of Harvard University, who is Black, and James Crowley, the White police sergeant in Cambridge, Massachusetts, who allegedly profiled and wrongfully arrested Gates.

First, Obama was criticized for the statement he made in response to the incident shortly after it was made public. Among other things, Obama pointed out, "What I think we know separate and apart from this incident is that there's a long history in this country of African-Americans and Latinos being stopped by law enforcement disproportionately. That's just a fact."[3] When Obama later convened the conversation between the two men—a public display of how America could and should view this racial conflict as a teachable moment about race, an exercise in the value of racial dialogue—political leaders and members of the American public similarly castigated him.

In one poll, almost half of the respondents said that they disapproved of the way that Obama handled the Gates issue—his initial comments, as well as the public forum he provided for Gates and Crowley to "dialogue." Further, people translated their disapproval of Obama's handling the Gates issue into disapproval of his presidential job performance overall.[4] Public outcry seemed to be aimed less at the issue of racial profiling in general or the circumstances of the Gates controversy in particular as it was at Obama personally. People objected to the fact that the president was taking the opportunity to talk about race at all, and even worse, that he encouraged others to do the same. As the results of our experiments in Chapter 2 and Chapter 3 seem to indicate, in today's political and racial climate, people appear to be extremely reticent to even countenance the subject of race, and they view those who do with considerable disdain. So while it may be a step in the right direction that potential voters may not react categorically in a negative manner when exposed to race-based appeals, this more general eschewing of racial talk is, in our view, extremely problematic.

The American public's tendency to conflate intent and effect is reflected in the inclination to view public discourse about race in general as repugnant. Perhaps more important, though, is that it also expresses itself in the occasions that prompt such discussion and the direction conversations about race typically take in today's political context. For instance, over the course of less than a week in January 2010, three nationally recognized Democrats were "caught" having made racially insensitive remarks about President Barack Obama. Former President Clinton is reported to have said to Senator Edward Kennedy, while seeking an endorsement for the Democratic primary nomination for Senator Hillary Clinton in 2008, that "a few years ago, this guy would have been getting us coffee."[5] U.S. Senate Majority Leader Harry Reid was reported to have remarked (also during the campaign) that Obama was "light-skinned" and that he spoke with "no Negro dialect, unless he wanted to have one." The author of the book in which this quote was reported went on to say that Reid was convinced that Obama's race would hurt him more than help him.[6] Finally, the ousted Illinois Governor Rod Blagojevich told *Esquire* magazine that he was "blacker than Barack Obama" and complained that the president was doing more to help "Wall Street more than Main Street."[7] While each of these comments is insensitive, concerns race, and involves Democrats who are becoming noted for such statements, they are not all equally "racist," as many would argue.

If we contrast Reid's and Clinton's comments, for instance, there was clearly vastly differing intent behind each (Reid was praising; Clinton seems to have been insulting). What matters to us, however, is the extent to which the comments reveal an understanding by these leaders of how race works in America. For Clinton, Obama (and other African Americans) had not come far enough to be prepared to run for president successfully against a Republican opponent. Reid's comment reflects his understanding that if America were to embrace any African American candidate for president, one who appeared to be "less Black" would be preferable.

Both comments are offensive and reflect a tremendous lack of tact (why Reid used the antiquated term "Negro," for instance, is anyone's guess), but there is a discernible difference between these comments and those made by U.S. Senator Trent Lott, who was forced to resign a leadership position after he told the former segregationist presidential candidate Strom Thurmond at a birthday party in 2002 that the nation "wouldn't have had all these problems" if Thurmond had been elected president in 1948. The difference, however, is not intent. None of these speakers intended to be offensive by his remarks. Rather, we ought to focus on the underlying systemic issues that are revealed in such comments. While Lott's remarks reflect a sentiment that America was a better place during Jim Crow, Reid's and Clinton's reflect that America still has a lot of work to do if there is to be true equality among Blacks and Whites. Similarly, Blagojevich's comment reflects the notion that poverty is still disproportionately of color in America, so that poor Whites have much in common with Blacks.

As long as racial discourse in America remains stalled in "gotcha" mode, no further meaningful progress is likely to be made. All references to race by Whites does not constitute racism, and all success by Blacks and Latinos is not, in and of itself, a symbol that racism is over and need not be considered further. Quite to the contrary, in fact, as we demonstrate throughout this book: Considerable racial animosity and resentment is manifested in myriad ways throughout the political system. As researchers who focus on latent racial attitudes (e.g., implicit associations) have demonstrated, the explicit norm of racial equality has not erased subconscious predispositions about people of color. Instead, it has masked the underlying attitudinal constructs that interfere with meaningful progress such that the barriers to be overcome remain largely invisible.

The problem, of course, is that it is difficult for Americans in particular to (1) accept that they are not in total control of their own minds; and (2) believe that they harbor any racial resentment or prejudice at all. The subconscious is still a mystery to researchers and the public alike, but accepting the general premises that constitute nearly a century's worth of research in psychology and related fields is an important first step toward relieving the cognitive dissonance that occurs from having such biases surface. In other words, if we can just accept that racism is part of the way we have been socialized to operate, we can deal more effectively with the effects of that aspect of our social and political culture. Instead, we have spent most of our time denying our own inherent racism, trying to find people who are *really* racist by catching them talking about race so we can label them "racists." In this way, we are able to excuse our own dangerous and harmful predispositions as benign compared with those of others who have been "caught" making insensitive statements: "I am not racist. Look at him! That's a racist!"[8]

Research tools have advanced to the point where we can start to learn more about reflexive (as opposed to reflective), pre-conscious responses to race-related stimuli. What parts of the brain, for instance, are activated when a person of color is exposed to a racist message in a newspaper story or by a candidate in a political campaign? What in particular about the racial message are they responding to? How do Whites respond to each compared with people of color? What other physiological responses can be detected?

To get past the race filters that humans possess, we need to drill deeper (metaphorically, of course) into the human brain to tap into responses that cannot be controlled or altered by research participants. While current methods do not provide a perfect picture of such psycho-physiological dimensions to the questions we consider here, they certainly move us forward and allow us to explore the issues in a way that addresses some of the nagging concerns with which researchers of racial attitudes have had to contend. By revealing answers to some of those mysteries, we can convince Americans to eschew defensiveness about racist biases and work meaningfully to address the systemic roots of racial injustice.

Notes

INTRODUCTION

1. This norm has been variously referred to in the extant literature, underlying a variety of theories that attempt to explain the shifting racial landscape in the post–Civil Rights era, including new racism, aversive racism, symbolic racism, and color-blind racism: see Bobo, Kluegel, and Smith 1997; Bonilla-Silva 2006; Kinder and Sears 1981; McConahay and Hough 1976.

2. Maggie Haberman, "'Osama' Mud Flying at Obama," *New York Post,* January 20, 2007, 4.

3. America's PAC is a conservative political action committee that aims to increase the ranks of African Americans in the Republican Party. Its website is at http://www .americaspac.com.

4. "Campaign Ads and Attitudes," *USA Today,* October 27, 2006, A19.

5. Michael Sokolove, "Why Is Michael Steele a Republican Candidate?" *New York Times Magazine,* March 26, 2006, 32; Monica Haynes, "Black Leaders Say Swann's Opinions on Issues Vital to Minorities," *Pittsburgh Post-Gazette,* March 26, 2006, B1; Sam Fullwood III, "Blackwell Not a Friend to Blacks," *Cleveland Plain Dealer,* May 11, 2006, B1.

6. Toby Harnden, "Dream Coming True for Gifted Black Politician: Times Are Changing in the Deep South," *Daily Telegraph* (London), June 25, 2002, 13.

7. Diane Cardwell, "In Shirley Chisholm's Brooklyn, Rancor over White Candidacy," *New York Times,* June 25, 2006, 1.

8. See Bositis 2002b. For a full discussion on the distinctions between Civil Rights–era and post–Civil Rights–era Black candidates, see Gillespie 2009.

9. See the website of the National Association of Latino Elected Officials, at http:// www.naleo.org.

CHAPTER 1

1. Mike Glover, "Obama Says Republicans Trying to Scare Voters," Associated Press, July 31, 2008, available at http://www.breitbart.com/article.php?id=D928S7080&show_article=1.

2. White's study should be distinguished from the others in that it was not conducted within the scope of a political campaign contest. It focused more on responses to racial cues in news media stories. We should also point out that, in addition to the welfare-based appeal, White tested racial cues related to stories about the Iraq War.

3. Relying on the archive gave us the most systematic way to conduct our analysis of advertising spots and the best way to document the ads we analyzed so they can be reviewed easily by scholars who want to replicate the study. We acknowledge that relying on ads from the archives produces some limitations. The archive does not give us access to every political ad from contests involving minority candidates who ran for the U.S. House and Senate. In addition, all we know about the ads in the archive is that they were produced by the sponsoring candidate. The archive does not provide information about whether or when any individual ad actually aired. These limitations notwithstanding, the archive provided us with the greatest number of ads for review in the most systematic medium possible.

4. The ads in our analysis we independently coded by the authors. The consistency and inter-coder reliability of our coding was accomplished and measured in several ways. First, a pilot study was conducted in which the authors coded, discussed, and developed a framework for codifying all non-objective variables—this primarily included all variables except ad identification variables and demographic variables. Inter-coder reliability on each of these measures in the pilot study was sufficiently high. The sample coded in the data reported in this book was initially conducted independently by the two authors. Subsequent to the coding, we extracted a 10 percent random sample of ads that was coded by each of the authors. Inter-coder reliability measures were then performed, assessing two-way agreement between both authors on the sample and three-way agreement between the authors and the coding of the sample when they were coded in the original sample. Reliability was calculated using ReCal (1.0 and 2.0), an online reliability assessment tool for both two and multiple coders (available at http://dfreelon.org/utils/recalfront/recal2/#doc). Variables were excluded based on considerations of both Krippendorff's alpha and percent agreement. Krippendorff's alpha coefficients below .74 were excluded if percent agreement was below 90 percent but retained if above. Similarly, variables with percent-agreement scores below 90 percent were retained if their alpha coefficients were .74 or above. This led us to exclude two variables.

5. We want to be explicit that we recognize that, as with any form of content analysis, our interpretations of certain content follow from our own knowledge, background, and expertise in looking at, in our case, racial components of political ads. Any attempt to interpret the racialized nature of political content is in every case a subjective endeavor, whether done by us or by any other scholar. We aim here to try to impose some logic to what is an otherwise purely subjective interpretation. First, we do not attempt to make clear-cut decisions about what constitutes a race-based appeal. Second, the best we can hope to do is be clear about the assumptions on which our interpretations are based. Third, we frame the decisions we do make as varying degrees

of evidence we believe appears in any given ad that might lead to a range of potential interpretations. This, we believe, grounds our interpretations in the most analytical way possible.

6. In fact, part of the reason America is somewhat in a stalled position with respect to racial progress is that most discussions of "racism" have come to revolve around accusations of one person or another being "a racist." Since such intent can almost never be proved over another's objection, there is no space for progress.

7. Throughout this work, we use the term "Latino" or "Latina" to refer broadly to people who identify culturally with parts of the world inhabited by Spanish-speaking peoples or Central and South America. We recognize that this is problematic on a number of levels, not the least of which is that it propagates a heuristic that tends to categorize a diverse group as monolithic. Further, even if we were to ignore the confla-tion of heritage, there is thoughtful discussion about whether "Latino" is a race or an ethnicity. For example, the 2010 U.S. Census form allows for multiple indications of race, but "Latino" is available only as an ethnicity. In these instances, researchers must make decisions and trust that the transparency is sufficient to alert readers to the potential pitfalls of such choices. We decided to treat "Latino" as a racial classification in the context of U.S. politics because the rhetoric most closely parallels that of Afri-can Americans and Asians, even if their collective historical situation does not. For instance, three prominent congressional caucuses center on race/ethnicity: the Con-gressional Black Caucus, the Congressional Hispanic Caucus, and the Congressional Asian Pacific American Caucus. Further, a healthy body of scholarly literature focuses on the degree of cooperation and conflict between Latinos and African Americans with respect to political representation, particularly in urban centers, that treats the groups as parallel descriptive entities. We follow that tradition, although we readily acknowledge that the reality of lived experiences is significantly more complicated than this categorization reflects.

8. As we demonstrate later, stereotypes can be invoked without words, using "videostyle." For a particularly rigorous examination of the ways in which gender and racial/ethnic stereotypes "collide" and the effects such collisions can have on voter evaluation, see Gordon and Miller 2005.

9. Gerald Carlson versus William D. Ford, Fifteenth Congressional District, Michi-gan, 1984, Political Communication Center (PCC) ad code 31874, "Racist."

10. The numerical discrepancy between the stereotype/counter-stereotype is a result of one of the stereotype variables being excluded because of low inter-coder reli-ability and because "liberal" is included in the group of stereotypes in the formula, though we discuss it under the subject heading of racialized language.

11. While we carefully considered analyzing a sample of contests between two White candidates as a basis for comparison, we ultimately determined that doing so would not provide enough substantive additional data to elaborate some of our results and conclusions about how race-based appeals are constructed. However, we do not simply disregard the importance such a comparison might have in the abstract. We essentially grant what some might see as the "worst case scenario"—that a sample of ads from White versus White contests would show no significant difference from those in our sample. That is, we grant that ads by White candidates running against White opponents would show similar patterns of negativity, address the same policy

issues, focus more on image than issues, and so on. Our primary point of contention is that the game changes significantly when the opposing candidate is not White. That is, ads are likely to be interpreted differently when the opposing face in the ad is a racial minority.

12. Peter Fitzgerald versus Carol Moseley Braun, U.S. Senate, Illinois, 1998, PCC ad code 78479, "Twisted."

13. Toby Moffett versus Gary Franks, U.S. Senate, Connecticut, 1990, PCC ad code 49098, "Rent."

14. Several examples highlight exceptions to the general content and underlying strategies of both racist and racial appeals. For instance, it is important to note that on rare occasions, one finds a candidate of color making a potentially racist appeal. That is, despite the candidate's racial background, his or her ad relies on some form of anti-minority stereotype for its efficacy. An example would be a candidate named Vernon Robinson, an African American man who ran as a Republican for a congressional seat in North Carolina in 2004 and 2006. His ad referred to themes related to Blacks and out-of-wedlock fathers, freeloading Mexican illegal aliens, and Blacks' reliance on racial quotas. Similarly, White candidates feature ads that make racial appeals. Again, an example from North Carolina illustrates this point. In his Senate run against Harvey Gantt in 1990, Jesse Helms, who had a notorious reputation for being a bigot, produced an ad designed—perhaps—to try to mitigate that aspect of his reputation, with the possible hope of blunting Blacks' mobilization against him. The ad featured Helms at a home for children with developmental disabilities. The final frame of the ad, which lingers for several seconds, pictures Helms shaking hands with a little Black boy, as if to say, "See, I like Black people." Again, however, racist appeals by candidates of color are rare, and few candidates have the kind of reputation that Helms had.

15. Alan Wheat versus John Ashcroft, U.S. Senate, Missouri, 1994, PCC ad code 59858, "Dream."

16. While we do consider the presence of a racial stereotype as a kind of "attack," stereotypes and the valence of the ads are coded and considered independently. Saying that this percentage of ads with racist potential are attack ads, then, does not reflect the presence of the racial stereotype already incorporated into the IRP.

CHAPTER 2

1. According to the U.S. Census Bureau's "American Community Survey, 2006–2008," 71 of 435 (16%) congressional districts (including Hawaii's two seats) and one state (Hawaii) contained a population of which the majority was not White. In the 111th Congress, 63 of those 73 seats (85%) were occupied by a member of a racial minority group. There were 17 people of color in the 111th Congress who represented districts (or, in the case of Illinois, a state) in which the majority of citizens were White. Put another way, 63 of the 80 (79%) people of color in the 111th Congress were elected in districts or states where the majority of the population was not White.

2. Several experimental studies have found consistency with these theories. Manipulating news stories about crime as stimuli, for instance, Gilliam and Iyengar (2000) found modest effects of the inclusion of a suspect's race (Black) as a visual cue such that negative attitudes about Blacks were heightened among White respondents, but not among Black respondents.

3. Although there are certainly important and identifiable limitations of experimental work, it provides the most useful methodology to study the processes of decision-making and attitude formation. While external validity is compromised, internal validity is greatly heightened. As Gilliam and Iyengar (2000, 563) note, "Experiments have the well-known advantage of greater precision in estimating causal effects." While there is limited ability to generalize from the results, there is much that can be understood about the perception of minority candidates and the processing of racial messages within these constraints.

4. In an attempt to provide control (see Shadish, Cook, and Campbell 2002) we hold gender constant. We chose to use male candidates primarily because there are (and have been) far more male members of Congress than female members of Congress. Although we find that unacceptable at a normative level, we are concerned that using female candidates (or one female and one male candidate) would introduce confounding factors to the design.

5. After production, the advertisements were further vetted using a focus group of graduate students who are familiar with the literature on implicit and explicit race-based appeals and reviewed by several anonymous reviewers who evaluated the spots for the funding organization that supported the experiments.

6. The TESS studies in this chapter and Chapter 3 were funded by NSF Grant 0647660, Diana C. Mutz and Matthew Davis, principal investigators and NSF Grants 0819271 and 0818839, Jeremy Freese and Penny Visser, principal investigators. More information about TESS, including sampling methodology, is available at http://tess .experimentcentral.org/index.html.

7. The scale is the most recent of several versions of the scale (see Kinder and Sears 1981; Sears, van Laar, Carillo, and Kosterman 1997).

8. These measures are from Dawson (2001) and are used to assess various aspects of respondents' racial-group linkage and loyalty that may be primed when exposed to racialized advertising messages.

9. Necessary sample size was determined prior to deploying each of the two experiments. According to Cohen (1992), the required number of participants was calculated to be fifty-nine per group (small effect size). This number was exceeded in each experiment.

10. It is important to note that the question about voting choice and the feeling-thermometer items were asked first, as they were designed to be the dependent variables. We expect that if we had asked about appeals to race before asking about vote choice or feeling thermometer ratings that there would have been a priming effect such that those who thought that a candidate invoked race would be less likely to support him.

11. In each of these models, however, some of the control variables reached conventional levels of statistical significance. Income was positive and significant at $p < .05$, indicating that wealthier respondents preferred Herbert. Two of the dichotomous indicators for geographical region (Northeast, $p < .10$; Midwest, $p < .05$) were also positive, indicating that participants in those regions preferred Herbert, as well.

12. Also intuitive is the relationship between reported media attentiveness and anticipated mobilization ($r = .339$; $p < .01$).

13. Gallup Organization, "Phi Delta Kappa/Gallup Poll," June 5–29, 2000, available at http://www.gallup.com.

14. This dynamic was at work during Barack Obama's candidacy for president, for example. In August 2008, after Obama made a statement that Republicans were trying to make Americans afraid of him, in part because he was Black, a spokesperson for the McCain campaign (and later McCain himself) said that Obama was "playing the race card . . . from the bottom of the deck" (Meade 2008).

CHAPTER 3

1. The summary of a March 2008 poll by the Pew Center for the People and the Press noted that "the balance of party identification among African American voters has remained relatively stable in recent years; the Democrats now hold a 72% to 4% advantage, virtually unchanged from 2004": Pew Center for the People and the Press, "Few Voters Identify as Republicans: Democrats Now Have the Advantage in 'Swing States,'" 2008, available at http://pewresearch.org/pubs/773/fewer-voters-identify-as-republicans. Further, exit polls reported by CNN after the 2008 elections indicate that 95 percent of African Americans voted for Barack Obama and 93 percent of African Americans voted for selected Democratic candidates for the U.S. House of representatives (CNN 2008).

2. It was clear as early as October 2009 that a significant number of African American candidates would be running for Congress and statewide offices on the Republican Party ticket in 2010. An article in the *Washington Independent* mentioned the Texas railroad commissioner Michael Williams, who was seeking a U.S. Senate seat, as well as the candidates Ryan Frazier (U.S. Senate from Colorado), Allen West (U.S. House of Representatives from Florida), and Lou Huddleston (U.S. House of Representatives from North Carolina): see Weigel 2009.

3. Toby Herndon, "Dream Coming True for Gifted Black Politician: Times Are Changing in the Deep South." *London Telegraph,* June 25, 2002, 13.

4. We want to be clear that our principal point of interest is in Blacks' preferences and voting behavior rather than the particular structural dynamic of how these may operate specifically within majority-minority districts. We mention it only because in contemporary contexts, appeals to authenticity by Black candidates are generally used when both candidates, as well as the plurality of voters, are Black. As we discuss below, there may be electoral risks for Black candidates who appeal to authenticity in a contest in which a significant number of potential voters are White.

5. With authenticity appeals, our conception of intent differs in several notable respects from White candidates' deploying potentially racist appeals. While Black candidates may certainly unwittingly construct ads that voters might interpret as appealing to authenticity, we presume that candidates deploy authenticity appeals more or less intentionally. That is, by its very nature, an authenticity appeal aims to make race and racial group consciousness salient, especially given the historical normative function of authenticity rhetoric within Black communities. While Black candidates may not deconstruct the depths of the concept the way we do here, they make authenticity appeals knowing not only that such appeals are likely to find fertile ground within the Black electorate, but also that such appeals traditionally have been acceptable—at least in the practice of deploying them. That is, unlike racist appeals, there has been no similar prohibition against making claims to racial authenticity within Black communities.

6. The persistence of this norm can be seen in the continued existence and relevance of the Congressional Black Caucus in the U.S. Congress and in scores of such legislative organizations in state and local governments throughout the country.

7. As in Chapter 2, these participants were recruited and the data were collected by Time-sharing Experiments for the Social Sciences (TESS), funded by National Science Foundation (NSF) grant 0647660, Diana C. Mutz and Matthew Davis, principal investigators, and NSF grants 0819271 and 0818839, Jeremy Freese and Penny Visser, principal investigators. More information about TESS, including sampling methodology, is available at http://tess.experimentcentral.org/index.html.

8. In the test group, where we intended for Herbert to invoke race, 19 percent of participants believed that he had invoked race but Jackson had not; 7 percent actually perceived the reverse. In the control group, 15 percent believed that Herbert had invoked race while Jackson had not, while 11 percent perceived the reverse.

CHAPTER 4

1. Multiple coders were trained in the coding procedures for the study, after which each coded a random sample of ten stories in a practice session. Following this, we discussed the coding of each story and variable with the coders, clarifying criteria and resolving discrepancies. Each coder then coded the same set of thirty randomly selected stories, from which we assessed inter-coder reliability. Each coder's data were compared with those of the others and with the same stories coded by the researchers. We used percentage agreement and Cronbach's alpha to make our assessment. This yielded two separate classes of variables. The first included a set of primarily objective data coded for, all of which were above 95 percent (percentage agreement) and .95 (Cronbach's alpha). The other set of variables include a number of "tone" questions, such as the tone of the headline with respect to each candidate or the racial tone of the story. Each of these received mixed reliability results. Ultimately, we decided to drop all of the tone variables from our analysis.

2. Given the lack of difference throughout our analysis, news stories and editorials are included with no practical distinction.

3. An additional reference is included if a racial reference was found in the headline of the story, thus adding more weight in the scale to this item.

4. We do not go into more depth in analyzing photographs because the Lexis-Nexis database provides potentially unreliable indications of photographs across different publications. Neither does it provide us with actual images to reliably distinguish various features of the photographs.

CHAPTER 5

1. Media Matters for America, "Report: Dobbs' Immigration Obsession Out of Step with CNN's News Coverage," July 27, 2009, available at http://mediamatters.org/reports/200907270039.

2. Mary Rae Bragg, "Border-Protection Bill on Tap," *Dubuque Telegraph Herald,* December 27, 2005, A3.

3. We generated our sample from candidates' ads accessible in 2006 on YouTube, because their placement on the video site made them much more likely to be viewed

by people outside the districts or states that the ads' sponsors represented. Ads were included in the pool if they were produced during the 2006 election cycle and the majority of their content (measured by length) focused substantively on the issue of immigration. We do not contend that the ads are representative of all ads that ran during the 2006 election. Rather, we assert that, for our demonstration, the ads in our sample represent a range that was typical regarding the focus on the issue of immigration and provided enough reliable evidence about how such ads might produce a racialized narrative about immigration policy.

4. For an in-depth investigation of this relationship, see "Militarized Zones: Gender, Race, Immigration, Environment," special issue, *Political Environments* 10 (2003): esp. 17–22.

5. This was the framing of most scholarship on race and welfare policy: see, e.g., Katz 1990.

6. While the term "code word" is seldom found in academic literature, it generally belongs to the category of speech referred to as "euphemisms"—indirect terms used to blunt the offensiveness or harshness of more direct language. For an illuminating consideration of the purposes and power of euphemistic coded language, see Allan and Burridge 1991.

7. The U.S. State Department describes the terrain of the Canadian border as "mostly plains with mountains in the west and lowlands in the southeast" and its climate as temperate to arctic. It describes the southern border region with Mexico, by contrast, as "coastal lowlands, central high plateaus, and mountains," with a climate that is "tropical to desert": U.S. Department of State, "Background Note: Canada," February 18, 2010, available at http://www.state.gov/r/pa/ei/bgn/2089.htm; idem, "Background Note: Mexico," May 14, 2010, available at http://www.state.gov/r/pa/ei/bgn/35749.htm.

8. Scholars discussing the idea of "Whiteness" express this sense of White racial invisibility in America that is generally treated not as racial or ethnic but as the normative standard of Americanness: see Jensen 2005.

CHAPTER 6

1. Two other African Americans have served in these positions. David Paterson assumed the governorship of New York State after a resignation, and Roland Burris was appointed to fill the remainder of Barack Obama's U.S. Senate term in 2009, after Obama vacated it to become president.

2. According to estimates in the U.S. Census Bureau's "American Community Survey, 2006–2008," Tennessee was 79.3 percent White in 2006.

3. "A Corker–Ford Senate Race," *Chattanooga Times Free Press*, August 5, 2006, B6.

4. Jackson Baker, "Pushing On: State Senator Rosalind Kurita Challenges the Odds and the Opposition in Her Bid for a U.S. Senate Seat," *Memphis Flyer*, March 10, 2006, available at http://www.memphisflyer.com/memphis/pushing-on/Content?oid =1124793.

5. For example, when White conservative protesters at "tea party" rallies and town hall meetings in the summer of 2009 declared, "We want our country back!" critics alleged that there was a racial component—intended or otherwise, conscious or otherwise—to such declarations, as the protests were aimed at the first African American president.

6. "Conservative Bob versus a Liberal," *Chattanooga Times Free Press,* September 10, 2006, F5.

7. Andy Sher, "Representative Ford's Voting Record under Attack by Corker," *Chattanooga Times Free Press,* September 13, 2006, A1.

8. Idem, "Ford Attacks Corker on Illegal Workers," *Chattanooga Times Free Press,* September 22, 2006, A1.

9. Edward Lee Pitts, "Bulk of Ford's Cash Flows from Out of State," *Chattanooga Times Free Press,* August 25, 2006, A1.

10. Andy Sher, "Corker Says Ford Family Not an Issue in Senate Race," *Chattanooga Times Free Press,* August 16, 2006, A1.

11. Idem, "Corker Critical of Ford Family," *Chattanooga Times Free Press,* October 7, 2006, A1.

12. Angie C. Marek, "Tennessee Senate: Corker Goes after Ford's Family," *U.S. News and World Report,* October 23, 2006, available at http://www.usnews.com/usnews/news/articles/061023/23tennessee.htm.

13. Former State Senator John Ford of Tennessee was subsequently found guilty on federal corruption charges and sentenced to fourteen years in jail in addition to a sixty-six-month sentence on bribery charges handed down in 2007: U.S. Attorney's Office, Department of Justice, "Former Tennessee State Senator John Ford Sentenced to Fourteen Years Imprisonment for Wire Fraud and Concealment of Material Facts in Connection with His Undisclosed 'Consulting' for Tenncare Contractors," press release, 2008, available at http://memphis.fbi.gov/dojpressrel/pressrel08/me092908.htm

14. Andy Sher, "Corker, Ford Heat Up Memphis," *Chattanooga Times Free Press,* October 8, 2006, A1.

15. "A Corker-Ford Senate Race."

16. "A Senate Race in Play," *Chattanooga Times Free Press,* October 3, 2006, B6; "First Debate: Style versus Substance," *Chattanooga Times Free Press,* October 9, 2006, A1; "Something Voters Should Know," *Chattanooga Times Free Press,* October 13, 2006, B7.

17. Michael Davis, Herman Wang, and Ian Berry, "Wamp Says Ford Changes Tune for Audience," *Chattanooga Times Free Press,* September 29, 2006, B7.

18. Michael Davis, "Ford Returns Contributions from Playboy, Others," *Chattanooga Times Free Press,* August 16, 2006, A1.

19. John Files, "A Playboy Party at the Super Bowl: A Wink and an Invitation," *New York Times,* October 26, 2006, available at http://www.nytimes.com/2006/10/26/us/26adbox.html.

20. Andy Sher, "Corker Calls for RNC to Pull Ad," *Chattanooga Times Free Press,* October 21, 2006, B1.

21. "Republicans Still Run Dirty Ad," *Chattanooga Times Free Press,* October 28, 2006, B6.

22. "Mehlman: Controversial Ford Attack Ad Is 'Fair.'" MSNBC.com., October 24, 2006, available at http://www.msnbc.msn.com/id/15404235.

23. This claim, put forth most prominently by Mendelberg (2001), is, as we noted earlier, the primary point of contention between Mendelberg and Huber and Lapinski (2006), whose work finds that implicit messages are more likely to be recognized as racial and thus not to have the same degree of effectiveness as Mendelberg and others have found in their work. For a detailed exchange on this point, see Huber and Lapinski 2008; Mendelberg 2008a, 2008b.

24. Michael Davis, "Ford Wonders If Race Now in Race," *Chattanooga Times Free Press,* October 4, 2006, A1.

25. Kauffman, Elisabeth. 2006. "Campaign '06: The G.O.P. Gets Nervous in Tennessee." *Time,* October 20, available at http://www.time.com/time/nation/article/0,8599,1548892,00.html.

26. Ibid.

27. Andy Sher, "Independent Ad Broaches Ethnicity in Senate Race," *Chattanooga Times Free Press,* October 14, 2006, B1.

28. Idem, "Race Could Be a Factor in Corker–Ford Contest." *Chattanooga Times Free Press,* October 22, A1.

29. "Race Will Matter in U.S. Senate Contest," *Chattanooga Times Free Press,* October 25, 2006, B2.

30. "Editorial: Brainstorming the Vote," *Memphis Flyer,* November 25, 2006, available at http://www.memphisflyer.com/memphis/editorial-brainstorming-the-vote/Content?oid=1131604.

31. In January 2006, Robert Menendez of New Jersey was appointed to the U.S. Senate by Governor Jon Corzine after Corzine vacated the seat to become governor. Menendez was subsequently elected to a full term later that year. Salazar resigned his Senate seat to become secretary of the interior in 2009, and Mel Martinez resigned his seat in the fall of 2009, leaving Menendez as the only sitting Latino in the U.S. Senate.

32. Florida is the fourth-largest state in the United States, with ten media markets. A combined $24 million in hard money was spent on this race (Common Cause 2004), and millions more poured into the state from the national committees (Campaign Finance Institute 2004) and interest groups.

33. Larry Lipman and Brian E. Crowley, "Senate Hopefuls Wrap up Statewide Push on Wing," *Palm Beach Post,* November 2, 2004, 8A.

34. Steve Bousquet and Anita Kumar, "Looking beyond a Divisive Campaign," *St. Petersburg Times,* November 1, 2004, 1B.

35. Andrea Stone, "Hispanic Vote Crucial in Florida Senate Battle," *USA Today,* October 12, 2004, 15A.

36. Brian DeBose, "Younger Cubans in Florida Less Inclined to Back GOP," *Washington Times,* November 2, 2004, A7.

37. Adam Becker, "Senate Hopefuls Put Al-Arian Aside in Final Debate before Election," *University Wire,* October 26, 2004, available at http://www.highbeam.com/doc/1P1-101760967.html.

38. For a review of this literature, see Kaufmann 2003.

39. Steve Bousquet and Anita Kumar, "Senate Hopefuls Quilt Minority Support," *St. Petersburg Times,* October 11, 2004, 1B.

40. Idem, "New Volleys Fired in Bitter Senate Contest," *St. Petersburg Times,* October 28, 2004, 5B.

41. Anita Kumar, "New Castor TV Ad Takes Fight to Martinez," *St. Petersburg Times,* October 5, 2004, 3B.

42. Brian E. Crowley and Larry Lipman, "Senate Candidates Spare No Efforts in Final Days," *Palm Beach Post,* October 31, 2004, 21 A1.

43. Larry Lipman and Brian E. Crowley, "Castor Presses Attack on Martinez's HUD Integrity; Martinez Camp Dismisses Allegations as 'Fabrications,'" *Palm Beach Post,* October 29, 2004, 16A.

44. Steve Bousquet and Anita Kumar, "Martinez, Castor Stump along I-4 Corridor," *St. Petersburg Times*, October 31, 2004, 5B.

45. Idem, "One More Push: Castor, Martinez Focus Last Hours on Strengths," *St. Petersburg Times*, November 2, 2004, 1B.

46. Martinez's family did, in fact, send him to the United States as a child in the early 1960s, where he was placed in foster care for a number of years until his parents were able to join him.

47. Although it is beyond the scope of this study, we wish to point out that the repeated claims of "strength" by Martinez, while also standard fare in American politics, may work disproportionately to advantage male candidates against female candidates because of stereotypes about women being "the weaker sex."

48. Larry Lipman and Brian E. Crowley, "Castor Challenges Martinez to Drop Negative Ads," *Palm Beach Pilot*, October 21, 2004, 1A.

49. Joe Follick and Lloyd Dunkelberger, "Castor Vows to End Attack Ads," *Ledger*, October 21, 2004, 1B.

50. Larry Lipman and Brian E. Crowley, "Ad Shows Martinez's Moms; His Rival Zeros in on Wages," *Palm Beach Pilot*, October 22, 2004, 14A.

51. Paul Pinkham and Charlie Patton, "Senate Foes Jab in Duval," *Florida Times-Union*, October 27, 2004, available at http://jacksonville.com/tu-online/stories/102704/met_17024753.shtml.

52. Al-Arian was acquitted of some charges in 2005 and entered into a plea agreement on others, resulting in a five-year prison sentence and eventually more charges of contempt when he refused to cooperate with investigators on another investigation: "Al-Arian Released after Five Years to Await Second Trial," *USA Today*. September 2, 2008, available at http://www.usatoday.com/news/nation/2008-09-02-al-arian_N.htm.

53. Steve Bousquet, "Stain of Al-Arian on Martinez, New Castor Ad Claims," *St. Petersburg Times*, October 12, 2004, 3B.

54. Anita Kumar and Steve Bousquet, "Castor, Martinez Trade More Jabs," *St. Petersburg Times*, October 30, 2004, 1B.

55. Larry Lipman, "Castor Ads Seek to Attract Central Florida Moderates," *Palm Beach Pilot*, September 14, 2004, 4A.

56. Pinkham and Patton, "Senate Foes Jab in Duval."

57. It is worth noting, as well, that this spot was a clear attempt to mitigate a perceived advantage for Castor with women, as Martinez talked about his foster families and his biological mother, noting that his "three moms in their seventies and eighties" were "independent, strong women who still give me advice."

58. There needs to be more rigorous scientific testing of this proposition. Although we tested ideology in our experiments in Chapter 2 and Chapter 3, we did not directly measure the effect of party identification. However, controlled experiments involving minority candidates need to be done in which partisanship can be isolated to test for effects.

59. Mary Orndorff, "Hilliard Says, 'I Vote for the Working People,'" *Birmingham News*, May 23, 2002, 1A.

60. Hilliard's son Earl Hilliard Jr. is involved in the Democratic field of candidates to replace Davis in 2010.

61. In that campaign, for instance, an e-mail by Elizabeth Wilson, a spokesperson for Majette, surfaced that read, "We can't allow McK [*sic*] to paint Denise as the White

candidate." It went on to advise that the campaign "work the streets in a posse, in T-shirts, probably no White folks if it is a Black neighborhood." A news story revealed that McKinney and members of her staff were critical of the e-mail, saying that using Blacks to work Black neighborhoods was "wrong" and an example of "racial profiling." McKinney's campaign manager, Bill Banks, was quoted as saying, "I can't believe that Majette's campaign looks at the color of your skin the minute you walk in her door. . . . That's disgraceful, and that's not what Georgia is about." According to the report, "Some McKinney supporters have called Majette 'Tomette,' a play on the pejorative term 'Uncle Tom.' A McKinney ad states Majette 'sold us out.'" In response, Majette addressed a crowd by saying, "I know what's going on. . . . I know what it's like to be a Black woman in America, having a Black husband in America, having teenage sons in America": Bill Torpy and Rhonda Cook, "McKinney Says Majette Guilty of Racial Profiling," *Atlanta Journal-Constitution,* August 15, 2002, D3.

62. Seth Mnookin, "A Star's Setback," Salon.com, May 15, 2002, available at http://www.salon.com/news/politics/feature/2002/05/15/booker.

63. Jeff Zeleny, "Jesse Jackson Apologizes for Remarks on Obama," *New York Times,* July 10, 2008, A18.

64. Mary Orndorff, "Davis Sees Donation Surge: His Contributions Triple over Hilliard's in Forty-Five Days," *Birmingham News,* May 25, 2002, A1.

65. Idem, "Ad Watch," *Birmingham News,* June 1, 2002, n.p.

66. David M. Halbfinger, "Generational Battle Turns Nasty in Alabama Primary," *New York Times,* June 3, 2002, A10.

67. The flier was listed as being from "friends to re-elect Earl Hillard for Congress in the Seven Congressional District." The misspelling of Hilliard's name and improper form of the word "Seventh," along with Hilliard's persistent denials of its authenticity, lead one to suspect that it did not come from Hilliard's campaign. Jay Reeves, "House Race Takes Twist," *Gadsden Times*/Associated Press, June 1, 2002, C1.

68. Ibid.

69. John Mercurio, "Racially Charged: Middle East Politics Heat up Alabama House Contest," *Roll Call,* May 2, 2002, n.p.

70. Ibid.

71. Anne Rush, "Davis Blasts Flier as Smear Politics," *Birmingham News,* May 4, 2002, n.p.

72. Orndorff, "Hilliard Says, 'I Vote for the Working People,'" 1A.

73. Ibid.

74. Idem, "Davis Sees Donation Surge," 1A.

75. Jay Reeves, "Anti-Semitic Leaflet Surfaces in Alabama House Race," Associated Press, June 1, 2002.

76. Orndorff, "Hilliard Says, 'I Vote for the Working People,'" 1A.

77. Idem, "Hilliard Denies Nonprofit Center Used Office," *Birmingham News,* March 14, 2002, 1C.

78. Halbfinger, "Generational Battle Turns Nasty in Alabama Primary," *New York Times,* June 3, A10.

79. "A Great Trade: Voters in Seventh District Choose Potential All-Star in Davis," *Birmingham News,* June 26, 2002, n.p.

CHAPTER 7

1. Obama, then a state senator in Illinois, challenged Congressman Bobby Rush for the Democratic nomination in 2000. Rush won with 61 percent of the vote to Obama's 31 percent in a four-way race.

2. Hillary Clinton's gender was also a significant barrier to her election. While the dynamics that characterize that disadvantage are worthy of exploration, they are well beyond our scope here. We would add, however, that Clinton's ability to convince voters that she was a closer match to the "ideal" presidential figure was enhanced by her most prominent opponent's also not looking like other presidents. This fact in no way eliminates the effect of sexism on her efforts, but we believe it is a mitigating factor that warrants our consideration of race separately from an equally rigorous consideration of gender.

3. "General Social Survey, 1972–2008," cumulative data file, National Opinion Research Center, University of Chicago.

4. "Poll: Racial Views Steer Some away from Obama," Associated Press, September 20, 2008, available at http://www.msnbc.msn.com/id/26803840.

5. This, of course, was the essential claim made by the journalist Debra Dickerson (2005) that helped to touch off the debate surrounding Obama's authenticity. It should be noted that much of the content of the book received harsh criticism for its analytical simplicity.

6. In fact, Biden added that such a combination was so rare as to be fictitious, calling it "a fairy tale."

7. Charlton D. McIlwain, "Clinton Veering Close to Stereotypes," *Newsday,* February 25, 2008, A27.

8. "Transcript of Clinton's Remarks in Boca Raton Florida," *Time,* 2008, available at http://thepage.time.com/transcript-of-clintons-remarks-in-boca-raton-florida.

9. Kate Phillips, "Clinton Touts White Support," *New York Times,* May 8, 2008, available at http://thecaucus.blogs.nytimes.com/2008/05/08/clinton-touts-white-support.

10. Video for this segment of the May 11, 2008, episode of *Meet the Press* is available at http://www.msnbc.msn.com/id/21134540/vp/24566231#24566231.

11. A natural question emerged during the primary battle between Clinton and Obama: What systemic pressure is stronger—racism or sexism? We might infer from the ultimate result that patriarchy is the more persistent or powerful of the two, but a number of factors should be considered when entertaining the question. First, anecdotal evidence of one historical election, however notable, is not sufficient to settle such a complicated debate. Second, it is important to note that while Obama won the Iowa caucuses, he lost the New Hampshire primaries that took place the next week. The differences between the very public displays of support required at caucuses and the private indications of support provided during primaries may not be insignificant in this regard. In the former context, concerns (conscious or subconscious) about Black men's ability to be trusted, willingness to play by the rules, laziness, or lack of intellect are free to surface in ways that they may not in a caucus or even in an public opinion poll in which an answer has to be spoken to another person. However, it is important to acknowledge that, much like racism, sexism operates largely at the subconscious level. Although it is beyond the scope of our exploration in this volume, the degree to which

gender stereotypes were invoked (and subsequently relied on) by voters in the Democratic primaries must be explored fully, with consideration of how each campaign's communication activated sexist stereotypes that might have disadvantaged Clinton.

12. Paige Bowers, "A Civil Rights Divide over Obama," *Time,* January 31, 2008, available at http://www.time.com/time/politics/article/0,8599,1708862,00.html.

13. "Clinton Backer Appears to Raise Obama's Drug Use," CNN, January 14, 2008, available at http://politicalticker.blogs.cnn.com/2008/01/14/clinton-backer-raises -obamas-drug-use.

14. "Clinton-backer Ferraro: Obama Where He Is Because He's Black," ABC News, March 11, 2008, available at http://blogs.abcnews.com/politicalpunch/2008/03/clinton -backer.html. Obama addressed the comment skillfully when he appeared on *Good Morning America,* noting that the best way to become president was clearly not to be Black and have a name like his.

15. "Nader: Obama Trying to 'Talk White,' Appeal to 'White Guilt,'" ABC News, June 25, 2008, available at http://blogs.abcnews.com/politicalpunch/2008/06/nader -obama-try.html.

16. After Obama won the election, Nader told a radio station in Houston that the choice for the new president would be "whether . . . to be Uncle Sam for the people of this country or Uncle Tom for the giant corporations": ibid.

17. Jake Tapper and Jennifer Parker, "Jesse Jackson Apologizes for Open Mic Slight against Obama," ABC News, July 10, 2008, available at http://abcnews.go.com/GMA/ Vote2008/story?id=5346657&page=1.

18. In addition to the central importance of Wright to the race-related campaign and media discourse, there is a tangential but perhaps equally important racial element in the association of Wright, Farrakhan, and Obama. As we described in Chapter 6 in relation to the Hilliard–Davis contest in Alabama, the relationship between African Americans and Jewish Americans has often served as a surrogate for Black authenticity. In the debate, both Hillary Clinton and Tim Russert suggested that association with anti-Semitic remarks from a supporter could signal a lack of support for Israel as an ally. There are potential electoral consequences in the primaries and the general election if such a claim takes hold, because such beliefs confirms preexisting ideas that Black Americans are less committed to the Israeli state and Israeli interests than are White Americans.

19. For a comprehensive analysis of the "A More Perfect Union" speech by scholars and journalists, see Sharpley-Whiting 2009.

20. In fact, McCain promised not to invoke Wright, a promise that he kept. However, third-party groups that supported McCain unleashed a flurry of advertisements the Sunday and Monday prior to the election in November.

21. BET News, "Westmoreland Calls Obama 'Uppity,'" September 8, 2008, available at http://www.bet.com/WebApplications/betRoot/Templates/Extended/Posting _ArticleExtended.aspx?NRORIGINALURL=%2FNR%2Fexeres%2F53882E1F-5695 -4982-A850-49CCA638E060.htm&FRAMELESS=false&NRNODEGUID={53882E1F -5695-4982-A850-49CCA638E060}&NRCACHEHINT=Guest.

22. "Westmoreland Defends Calling Obama 'Uppity,'" *Atlanta Journal Constitution,* September 5, 2008, C3.

23. Amy Sullivan, "An Antichrist Obama in McCain Ad?" *Time,* August 8, 2008, available at http://www.time.com/time/politics/article/0,8599,1830590,00.html.

24. This also plays into the "other" frame, as it suggests that Obama is an "out-of-touch elitist."

25. Sarah Palin spent the better part of a week using the term "pals around with terrorists" to refer to Obama's relationship with Ayers.

26. "Election Results 2008: Exit Polls," *New York Times,* November 5, 2008, available at http://elections.nytimes.com/2008/results/president/exit-polls.html.

EPILOGUE

1. "General Social Survey, 1972–2008," cumulative data file, National Opinion Research Center, University of Chicago.

2. See Po Bronson and Ashley Merryman, "Is Your Baby Racist?" *Newsweek,* September 6, 2009, available at http://blog.newsweek.com/blogs/nurtureshock/archive/2009/09/06/nurtureshock-cover-story-for-newsweek-is-your-baby-racist.aspx.

3. "Obama Criticizes Cambridge Police in Gates Case." *Boston Globe,* July 23, 2009, available at http://www.boston.com/news/local/breaking_news/2009/07/obama_critiiciz.html.

4. Pew Research Center for the People and the Press, "Obama's Ratings Slide across the Board: The Economy, Healthcare Reform, and Gates Grease the Skids," July 30, 2009, available at http://people-press.org/report/532/obamas-ratings-slide.

5. Carl M. Cannon, "New Campaign Book: Bill Clinton's Remark about Obama Angered Teddy Kennedy," *Politics Daily,* January 9, 2010, available at http://www.politicsdaily.com/2010/01/09/bill-clinton-to-teddy-kennedy-in-new-campaign-book-obama-should.

6. Marc Ambinder, "The Juiciest Revelations in *Game Change,*" *Atlantic,* January 8, 2010, available at http://www.nytimes.com/aponline/2010/01/11/us/AP-US-Blagojevich-Esquire.html?_r=2.

7. "Blagojevich: 'Blacker' than Obama Comment 'Stupid.'" *New York Times,* January 11, 2010, available at http://www.nytimes.com/aponline/2010/01/11/us/AP-US-Blagojevich-Esquire.html?_r=2.

8. While space does not permit, it is sometimes helpful to conceptualize systemic racism and individual prejudice as distinct by using the former as an adjective (e.g., "I am racist") and the latter as a noun ("She is a racist"). We see very little value in the use of "racist" as a noun, as it becomes a political hot potato and deflects from the meaningful socialization of racism (and sexism and heterosexism and classism) that constitutes the whole of hegemonic power. "Racist" describes part of what we all are; it does not define us (or some of us). Thus, the label (the noun) is not only inaccurate in its narrowness; it is counterproductive.

References

Abrajano, Marisa A., Jonathan Nagler, and R. Michael Alvarez. 2003. "Race-Based versus Issue Voting: A Natural Experiment: The 2001 City of Los Angeles Elections." Paper presented at the Midwest Political Science Association Conference, Chicago, April 3–6.

Akbar, Na'im. 1984. "Afrocentric Social Sciences for Human Liberation." *Journal of Black Studies* 14:395–414.

Allan, Keith, and Kate Burridge. 1991. *Euphemism and Dysphemism: Language Used as Shield and Weapon.* New York: Oxford University Press.

Allen, Richard L., Michael C. Dawson, and Ronald E. Brown. 1989. "A Schema-Based Approach to Modeling an African American Racial Belief System." *American Political Science Review* 83:421–441.

Allport, Gordon. 1979. *The Nature of Prejudice.* New York: Basic Books.

Austin, J. L. 1963. *How to Do Things with Words.* New York: Oxford University Press.

Balz, Daniel, and Haynes Johnson. 2009. *The Battle for America 2008.* New York: Viking.

Banaji, Mahzarin R., Curtis Hardin, and Alexander J. Rothman 1993. "Implicit Stereotyping in Person Judgment." *Journal of Personality and Social Psychology* 65:272–281.

Barber, John T., and Oscar H. Gandy Jr. 1990. "Press Portrayal of African American and White United States Representatives." *Howard Journal of Communications* 2:213–225.

Baron, Andrew Scott, and Mahzarin R. Banaji. 2006. "The Development of Implicit Attitudes: Evidence of Race Evaluations from Ages 6 and 10 and Adulthood." *Psychological Science* 17:53–58.

Barthes, Roland. 1978. *Image, Music, Text.* New York: Hill and Wang.

Basil, Michael, Caroline Schooler, and Byron Reeves. 1991. "Positive and Negative Political Advertising: Effectiveness of Ads and Perceptions of Candidates." In *Television and Political Advertising, Volume 1: Psychological Processes,* ed. Frank Biocca, 245–262. Hillsdale, N.J.: Lawrence Erlbaum Associates.

Bell, Derrick. 2008. *Race, Racism, and American Law.* Aspen, Colo.: Aspen Publishers.

Bledsoe, Timothy, Susan Welch, Lee Sigelman, and Michael Comb. 1995. "Residential Context and Racial Solidarity among African Americans." *American Journal of Political Science* 39:434–458.

Bobo, Lawrence, James R. Kluegel, and Ryan A. Smith. 1997. "Laissez-faire Racism: The Crystallization of a Kinder, Gentler, Antiblack Ideology." In *Racial Attitudes in the 1990s: Continuity and Change,* ed. Steven A. Tuch and Jack K. Martin, 15–41. Westport, Conn.: Praeger.

Bonilla-Silva, Eduardo. 2006. *Racism without Racists: Colorblind Racism and the Persistence of Inequality in the United States.* Lanham, Md.: Rowman and Littlefield.

Bositis, David. 2002a. "Party, Redistricting, and Minority Representation: The Southern States, 1992–2002." Paper presented at the Redistricting 1992–2002: Voting Rights and Minority Representation Conference, Washington, D.C., May 22, available at http://www.jointcenter.org/ whatsnew/conference_on_redistricting.htm.

———. 2002b. *2002 National Opinion Poll: Politics.* Washington, D.C.: Joint Center for Political and Economic Studies.

Brians, Craig Leonard, and Martin P. Wattenberg. 1996. "Campaign Issue Knowledge and Salience: Comparing Reception from TV Commercials, TV News, and Newspapers." *American Journal of Political Science* 40:172–193.

Butler, Judith. 1997. *Excitable Speech: A Politics of the Performative.* New York: Routledge.

Caliendo, Stephen M., and Charlton D. McIlwain. 2006. "Minority Candidates, Media Framing, and Racial Cues in the 2004 Election." *Harvard International Journal of Press/Politics* 11:1–25.

Caliendo, Stephen M., Charlton D. McIlwain, and Aleisha Karjala. 2003. "Reading Race: An Experimental Study of the Effect of Political Advertisements' Racial Tone on Candidate Perception and Vote Choice." Paper presented at the annual meeting of the Midwest Political Science Association, Chicago, April 3–6.

Campaign Finance Institute. 2004. "Party Independent Spending Soars." Available at http://cfinst.org/pr/prRelease.aspx?ReleaseID=55.

Caruso, Eugene M., Nicole L. Mead, and Emily Balcetis. 2009. "Political Partisanship Influences Perception of Biracial Candidates' Skin Tone." *Proceedings of the National Academy of Sciences of the United States of America,* November 23, 2009, available at http://www.pnas.org/content/early/2009/11/20/0905362106.

Chaudhary, Anju G. 1980. "Press Portrayal of Black Officials." *Journalism Quarterly* 57: 636–641.

Clawson, Rosalee A. 2002. "Poor People, Black Faces: The Portrayal of Poverty in Economics Textbooks." *Journal of Black Studies* 32:352–361.

Clawson, Rosalee A., and Rakuka Trice. 2000. "Poverty as We Know It: Media Portrayals of the Poor." *Public Opinion Quarterly* 64:53–64.

Clay, William L. 1993. *Just Permanent Interests: Black Americans in Congress, 1870–1991.* New York: Amistad Press.

CNN. 2004. "Election results: U.S. Senate Florida Exit Poll." Available at http://cnn.com/ ELECTION/2004/pages/results/states/FL/S/01/epolls.0.html.

———. 2008. "Election Center 2008: Exit Polls." Available at http://www.cnn.com/ ELECTION/2008/results/polls.

Cohen, Cathy J., and Michael C. Dawson. 1993. "Neighborhood Politics and African American Politics." *American Political Science Review* 87:286–302.

Cohen, Jacob. 1992. "A Power Primer." *Psychological Bulletin* 112:155–159.

Coleman, Robin M. 2000. *African American Viewers and the Black Situation Comedy: Situating Racial Humor.* New York: Routledge.

Conyers, James E., and Walter L. Wallace. 1976. *Black Elected Officials: A Study of Black Americans Holding Governmental Office.* New York: Russell Sage Foundation.

Common Cause. 2004. "2004 Race: Florida Senate." Available at http://www.opensecrets.org/races/summary.php?cycle=2004&id=FLS2.

Copeland, Gary, and Karen Johnson-Cartee. 1991. *Negative Political Advertising: Coming of Age.* Hillsdale, N.J.: Lawrence Erlbaum Associates.

Cottle, Simon, ed. 2000. *Ethnic Minorities and the Media: Changing Boundaries.* Philadelphia: Open University Press.

Cross, William E., Jr. 1991. *Shades of Black: Diversity in African American Identity.* Philadelphia: Temple University Press.

Davis, Darren W., and Brian Silver. 2003. "Stereotype Threat and Race of Interviewer Effects in a Survey on Political Knowledge." *American Journal of Political Science* 47:33–45.

Dawson, Michael C. 2001. *Black Visions: The Roots of Contemporary African-American Political Ideologies.* Chicago: University of Chicago Press.

Delgado, Richard, and Jean Stefancic. 1999. *Critical Race Theory: The Cutting Edge,* 2nd ed. Philadelphia: Temple University Press.

Dickerson, Debra. 2005. *The End of Blackness: Returning the Souls of Black Folk to Their Rightful Owners.* New York: Anchor.

Domke, David. 2001. "Racial Cues and Political Ideology: An Examination of Associative Priming." *Communication Research* 28:772–801.

Drago, Edmund L. 1992. *Black Politicians and Reconstruction in Georgia: A Splendid Failure,* 2nd ed. Athens: University of Georgia Press.

Entman, Robert M., and Andrew Rojecki. 2001. *The Black Image in the White Mind.* Chicago: University of Chicago Press.

Feldman, Stanley, and Leonie Huddy. 2005. "Racial Resentment and White Opposition to Race-Conscious Programs: Principles or Prejudice?" *American Journal of Political Science* 49:168–183.

Fiske, Susan T. 1998. "Stereotyping, Prejudice, and Discrimination." In *Handbook of Social Psychology,* 4th ed, ed. Daniel T. Gilbert, Susan T. Fiske, and Gardner Lindzey, 357–414. Boston: McGraw-Hill.

Foucault, Michel. 2005. *Discipline and Punish: The Birth of the Prison.* New York: Vintage.

Frederickson, George M. 1971. *The Black Image in the White Mind: The Debate on Afro-American Character and Destiny, 1817–1914.* Middletown, Conn.: Wesleyan University Press.

Gandy, Oscar H., Jr. 2001. "Racial Identity, Media Use, and the Social Construction of Risk among African Americans." *Journal of Black Studies* 31:600–618.

Garramone, Gina M. 1985. "Effects of Negative Political Advertising: The Role of Sponsor and Rebuttal." *Journal of Broadcasting and Electronic Media* 29:147–159.

Garramone, Gina M., Charles K. Atkin, Bruce E. Pinkleton, and Richard T. Cole. 1990. "Effects of Negative Political Advertising on the Political Process." *Journalism, Broadcasting and Electronic Media* 34:299–311.

Gebser, Jean. 1985. *The Ever-Present Origin.* Athens: Ohio University Press.

Geertz, Clifford. 1977. *The Interpretation of Cultures*. New York: Basic Books.

Gerber, Alan. 1996. "African Americans' Congressional Careers and the Democratic House Delegation." *Journal of Politics* 58:831–845.

Gibbons, Arnold. 1993. *Race, Politics, and the White Media: The Jesse Jackson Campaigns*. New York: Lanham.

Gilens, Martin. 1996. "'Race-Coding' and White Opposition to Welfare." *American Political Science Review* 90:593–604.

———. 1998. "Racial Attitudes and Race-Neutral Social Policy: White Opposition to Welfare and the Politics of Racial Inequality." In *Perception and Prejudice: Race and Politics in the United States*, ed. Jon Hurwitz and Mark Peffley, 171–201. New Haven, Conn.: Yale University Press.

———. 1999. *Why Americans Hate Welfare: Race, Media, and the Politics of Anti-Poverty Policy*. Chicago: University of Chicago Press.

———. 2000. "The Black Poor and the 'Liberal Press.'" *Civil Rights Journal* 5:18–26.

Gillespie, Andra, ed. 2009. *Whose Black Politics? Cases in Post-Racial Black Leadership*. New York: Routledge.

Gilliam, Frank D., Jr., and Shanto Iyengar. 2000. "Prime Suspects: The Influence of Local Television News on the Viewing Public." *American Journal of Political Science* 44:560–573.

Glaser, James M. 1995. "Black and White Perceptions of Party Differences." *Political Behavior* 17:155–177.

Gordon, Ann, and Jerry L. Miller. 2005. *When Stereotypes Collide: Race/Ethnicity, Gender, and Videostyle in Congressional Campaigns*. New York: Peter Lang.

Grainey, Timothy F., Dennis R. Pollack, and Lori A. Kusmierek. 1984. "How Three Chicago Newspapers Covered the Washington-Epton Campaign." *Journalism Quarterly* 61:352–363.

Grossman, Beth, Robert Wirt, and Anthony Davids. 1985. "Self-Esteem, Ethnic Identity, and Behavioral Adjustment among Anglo and Chicano Adolescents in West Texas." *Journal of Adolescence* 8:57–68.

Guinier, Lani. 1995. "The Representation of Minority Interests." In *Classifying by Race*, ed. Paul E. Peterson, 21–49. Princeton, N.J.: Princeton University Press.

Hall, Stuart, ed. 1997. *Representation: Cultural Representations and Signifying Practices*. Thousand Oaks, Calif.: Sage.

Hall, William S., William E. Cross Jr., and Roy Freedle. 1972. "Stages in the Development of Black Awareness." American College Testing Program Research Report, no. 50:1–21.

Hajnal, Zoltan L. 2007. *Changing White Attitudes toward Black Political Leadership*. New York: Cambridge University Press.

Hancock, Angie Marie. 2004. *The Politics of Disgust: The Public Identity of the Welfare Queen*. New York: New York University Press.

Harris-Lacewell, Melissa V. 2006. *Barbershops, Bibles, and BET: Everyday Talk and Black Political Thought*. Princeton, N.J.: Princeton University Press.

Heatherington, Mark J. 2006. *Why Trust Matters: Declining Political Trust and the Demise of Political Liberalism*. Princeton, N.J.: Princeton University Press.

Henderson, George, and Thompson Olasiji. 1995. *Migrants, Immigrants and Slaves*. Washington, D.C.: University Press of America.

Henry, P. J., and David O. Sears. 2002. "The Symbolic Racism 2000 Scale." *Political Psychology* 23:253–283.

Hero, Rodney E., and Caroline J. Tolbert. 1995. "Latinos and Substantive Representation in the U.S. House of Representatives: Direct, Indirect, or Non-existent?" *American Journal of Political Science* 40:851–871.

Herring, Mary, Thomas B. Jankowski, and Ronald E. Brown. 1999. "Pro-Black Doesn't Mean Anti-White: The Structure of African-American Group Identity." *Journal of Politics* 61:336–386.

Holmes, Malcolm D., Brad W. Smith, Ed A. Munoz, and Adrienne B. Freng. 2008. "Minority Threat, Crime Control, and Police Resource Allocation in the Southwestern United States." *Crime and Delinquency* 54:128–152.

Hovland, Carl I. 1957. *The Order of Presentation in Persuasion*. New Haven, Conn.: Yale University Press.

Howell, Susan E., and William P. McLean. 2001. "Performance and Race in Evaluating Black Mayors." *Public Opinion Quarterly* 65:321–343.

Huber, Gregory A., and John S. Lapinski. 2006. "The 'Race Card' Revisited: Assessing Racial Priming in Policy Contests." *American Journal of Political Science* 50:421–440.

———. 2008. "Testing the Implicit–Explicit Model of Racialized Political Communication." *Perspectives on Politics* 6:125–134.

Ifill, Gwen. 2009. *The Breakthrough: Politics and Race in the Age of Obama*. New York: Doubleday.

Iyengar, Shanto, Mark D. Peters, and Donald R. Kinder. 1982. "Experimental Demonstrations of the 'Not-so-Minimal' Consequences of Television News Programs." *American Political Science Review* 76:848–858.

Jackson, Ronald. L., II, and Susan M. Heckman. 2002. "Perceptions of White Identity and White Liability: An Analysis of White Student Responses to a College Campus Racial Hate Crime." *Journal of Communication* 52:434–450.

Jamieson, Kathleen Hall. 1992. *Dirty Politics: Deception, Distraction, and Democracy*. New York: Oxford University Press.

Jamieson, Kathleen Hall, Paul Waldman, and Susan Sherr. 2000. "Eliminate the Negative? Categories of Analysis for Political Advertisements." In *Crowded Airwaves: Campaign Advertising in Elections,* ed. James A. Thurber, Candace J. Nelson, and David A. Dulio, 44–64. Washington, D.C.: Brookings Institution.

Jensen, Robert. 2005. *The Heart of Whiteness: Confronting Race, Racism, and White Privilege*. New York: City Lights.

Joint Center for Political and Economic Studies. 2009. "African Americans in Statewide Elective Office: Recent Trends, 2002–2007." Available at http://www.joint center.org/index.php/current_research_and_policy_activities/political_participation/ black_elected_officials_roster_introduction_and_overview/african_americans_in _statewide_elective_office.

Jordan, Winthrop D. 1974. *The White Man's Burden: Historical Origins of Racism in the United States*. New York: Oxford University Press.

Kahn, Kim Fridkin, and Patrick J. Kenney. 1999. "Do Negative Campaigns Mobilize or Suppress Turnout? Clarifying the Relationship between Negativity and Participation." *American Political Science Review* 93:877–889.

Kaid, Lynda Lee, and Anne Johnston. 1991. "Negative versus Positive Television Advertising in U.S. Presidential Campaigns, 1960-1988." *Journal of Communication* 41:53-64.

Kapano, Baruti N. 2002. "Rap Music as an Extension of the Black Rhetorical Tradition: 'Keepin' It Real.'" *Western Journal of Black Studies* 26:204-214.

Kamalipour, Yahya R., and Theresa Carilli, eds. 1998. *Cultural Diversity and the U.S. Media.* Albany: State University of New York Press.

Katz, Elihu, and Paul Lazarsfeld. 1955. *Personal Influence: The Part Played by People in the Flow of Mass Communications.* New York: Free Press.

Katz, Michael. 1990. *The Undeserving Poor: From the War on Poverty to the War on Welfare.* New York: Pantheon.

Kaufmann, Karen M. 2003. "Black and Latino Voters in Denver: Responses to Each Other's Political Leadership." *Political Science Quarterly* 118:107-125.

Kern, Montague. 1989. *Thirty-Second Politics: Political Advertising in the Eighties.* Westport, Conn.: Praeger.

Kinder, Donald R., and Lynn M. Sanders. 1996. *Divided by Color: Racial Politics and Democratic Ideals.* Chicago: University of Chicago Press.

Kinder, Donald R., and David O. Sears. 1981. "Prejudice and Politics: Symbolic Racism versus Racial Threats to the Good Life." *Journal of Personality and Social Psychology* 40:414-431.

Kinder, Donald R., and Nicholas Winter. 2001. "Exploring the Racial Divide: Blacks, Whites, and Opinion on National Policy." *American Journal of Political Science* 45:439-453.

Lai, James S. 1999. "Racially Polarized Voting and Its Effects on the Formation of a viable Latino-Asian Pacific Coalition." In *1998-1999 National Asian Pacific American Political Almanac,* ed. Don T. Nakanishi and James S. Lai, 156-185. Los Angeles: University of California Press.

Larson, Stephanie G. 2005. *Media and Minorities: The Politics of Race in News and Entertainment.* Lanham, Md.: Rowman and Littlefield.

Lippmann, Walter. 1922. *Public Opinion.* New York: Harcourt, Brace.

Liu, Eric, and Nick Hanauer. 2008. *The True Patriot.* Seattle: Sasquatch Books.

Lublin, David. 1999. "Racial Redistricting and African-American Representation: A Critique of 'Do Majority-Minority Districts Maximize Substantive Black Representation in Congress?'" *American Political Science Review* 93:183-186.

McCombs, Maxwell. 2004. *Setting the Agenda: The Mass Media and Public Opinion.* New York: Polity Press.

McCombs, Maxwell E., and Donald L. Shaw. 1972. "The Agenda Setting Function of Mass Media." *Public Opinion Quarterly* 36:176-187.

McConahay, John B. 1986. "Modern Racism, Ambivalence, and the Modern Racism Scale." In *Prejudice, Discrimination, and Racism,* ed. John F. Dovidio and Samuel L. Gaertner, 91-125. Orlando: Harcourt Brace Jovanovich.

McConahay, John B., and Joseph C. Hough Jr. 1976. "Symbolic Racism." *Journal of Social Issues* 32:23-45.

McCormick, Joseph, and Sekou Franklin. 2000. "Expressions of Racial Consciousness in the African American Community: Data from the Million Man March." In *Multiracial Politics in America,* ed. Yvette Alex-Assensoh and Lawrence J. Hanks, 315-336. New York: New York University Press.

McCormick, Joseph, II, and Charles E. Jones. 1993. "The Conceptualization of Deracialization: Thinking through the Dilemma." In *Dilemmas of Black Politics: Issues of Leadership and Strategy*, ed. Georgia A. Persons, 66–84. New York: HarperCollins College Publishers.

McIlwain, Charlton D. 2009. "Leadership, Legitimacy, and Public Perceptions of Barack Obama." In *Whose Black Politics? Cases in Post-Racial Black Leadership*, ed. Andra Gillespie, 155–172. New York: Routledge.

McIlwain, Charlton D., and Stephen M. Caliendo. 2009. "Black Messages, White Messages: The Differential Use of Racial Appeals by Black and White Candidates." *Journal of Black Studies* 39:732–743.

McIlwain, Charlton D., and Lonnie Johnson Jr. 2003. "Headache and Heartbreak: Negotiating Model Minority Status among African Americans." In *The Emerging Monoculture: Model Minorities and Benevolent Assimilationism*, ed. Eric Mark Kramer, 110–123. Westport, Conn.: Praeger.

McIntosh, Peggy. 1992. "White Privilege and Male Privilege: A Personal Account of Coming to See Correspondences through Work in Women's Studies." In *Race, Class, and Gender: An Anthology*, ed. Margaret L. Anderson and Patricia Hill Collins, 70–81. Belmont, Calif.: Wadsworth.

McLaren, Peter. 1994. "White Terror and Oppositional Agency: Towards a Critical Multiculturalism." In *Multiculturalism: A Critical Reader*, ed. David. T. Goldberg, 45–74. Cambridge, Mass.: Blackwell.

McLeod, Kembrew. 1999. "Authenticity within Hip-Hop and Other Cultures Threatened with Assimilation." *Journal of Communication* 49:134–150.

Matsuda, Mari. 1993. *Words that Wound: Critical Race Theory, Assaultive Speech, and the First Amendment*. Boulder, Colo.: Westview.

Meade, Robin. 2008. "Did McCain or Obama Play the Race Card?" CNN.com, August 1. Available at http://mxp.blogs.cnn.com/2008/08/01/did-mccain-or-obama-play -the-race-card.

Mendelberg, Tali. 1999. "Executing Hortons." *Public Opinion Quarterly* 61:134–157.

———. 2001. *The Race Card: Campaign Strategy, Implicit Messages, and the Norm of Equality*. Princeton, N.J.: Princeton University Press.

———. 2008a. "Racial Priming Revived." *Perspectives on Politics* 6:109–123.

———. 2008b. "Racial Priming: Issues in Research Design and Interpretation." *Perspectives on Politics* 6:135–140.

Merrit, Sharyne. 1984. "Negative Political Advertising: Some Empirical Findings." *Journal of Advertising* 13:27–38.

Morris, John D., Marilyn S. Roberts, and Gail F. Baker. 2001. "Emotional Responses of African American Voters to Ad Messages." In *The Electronic Election: Perspectives on the 1996 Campaign Communication*, ed. Lynda Lee Kaid and Dianne G. Bystrom, 257–274. Mahwah, N.J.: Lawrence Erlbaum Associates.

Ngai, Mae M. 2005. *Impossible Subjects: Illegal Aliens and the Making of Modern America*. Princeton, N.J.: Princeton University.

Nickerson, Raymond S. 1998. "Confirmation Bias: A Ubiquitous Phenomenon in Many Guises." *Review of General Psychology* 2:175–220.

Niemann, Yolanda Flores. 2001. "Stereotypes about Chicanas and Chicanos." *Counseling Psychologist* 29:55–90.

Peffley, Mark, and Jon Hurwitz. 2002. "The Racial Components of 'Race-Neutral' Crime Policy Attitudes." *Political Psychology* 23:59–75.

Peffley, Mark, Jon Hurwitz, and Paul M. Sniderman. 1997. "Racial Stereotypes and Whites' Political Views of Blacks in the Context of Welfare and Crime." *American Journal of Political Science* 41:30–60.

Perry, Huey L., ed. 1996. *Race, Politics, and Governance*. Gainesville: University of Florida Press.

Persons, Georgia, ed. 1993. *Dilemmas of Black Politics: Issues of Leadership and Strategy*. New York: HarperCollins College Publishers.

———. 2009. *Beyond the Boundaries: A New Structure of Ambition in African American Politics*. New Brunswick, N.J.: Transaction.

Phinney, Jean S. 1990. "Ethnic Identity in Adolescents and Adults: Review of Research." *Psychological Bulletin* 108:499–514.

Reeves, Keith. 1997. *Voting Hopes or Fears? White Voters, Black Candidates, and Racial Politics in America*. New York: Oxford University Press.

Roddy, Brian L., and Gina M. Garramone. 1988. "Appeals and Strategies of Negative Political Advertising." *Journal of Broadcasting and Electronic Media* 32:415–428.

Schmermund, Anke, Robert Sellers, Brigit Mueller, and Faye Crosby. 2001. "Attitudes toward Affirmative Action as a Function of Racial Identity among African American College Students." *Political Psychology* 22:759–773.

Sears, David O., Collette van Laar, Mary Carillo, and Rick Kosterman. 1997. "Is It Really Racism? The Origins of White Americans' Opposition to Race-Targeted Policies." *Public Opinion Quarterly* 61:16–53.

Shadish, William R., Thomas D. Cook, and Donald T. Campbell. 2002. *Experimental and Quasi-experimental Designs for Generalized Causal Inference*. Boston: Houghton Mifflin.

Shapiro, Michael J. 1995. "Every Move You Make: Borders, Surveillance, and Media." *Social Text* 23:21–34.

Sharpley-Whiting, T. Denean. 2009. *The Speech: Race and Barack Obama's "A More Perfect Union."* London: Bloomsbury.

Shelby, Tommie. 2002. "Foundations of Black Solidarity: Collective Identity or Common Oppression?" *Ethics* 112:231–266.

Sigelman, Carol K., Lee Sigelman, Barbara J. Walkosz, and Michael Nitz. 1995. "Black Candidates, White Voters: Understanding Racial Bias in Political Perceptions." *American Journal of Political Science* 39:243–265.

Smith, Charles E., Jr., Robert D. Brown, John M. Bruce, and L. Marvin Overby. 1999. "Party Balancing and Voting for Congress in the 1996 Elections." *American Journal of Political Science* 93:877–889.

Smith, Robert C. 1990. "Recent Elections and Black Politics: The Maturation or Death of Black Politics?" *PS: Political Science and Politics* 23:160–162.

Sniderman, Paul M., and Thomas Piazza. 2004. *Black Pride, Black Prejudice*. Princeton, N.J.: Princeton University Press.

Stanley, Harold W., and Richard G. Niemi. 1995. "The Demise of the New Deal Coalition: Partisanship and Group Support, 1952–92." In *Democracy's Feast: Elections in America*, ed. Herbert F. Weisberg, 220–240. Chatham, N.J.: Chatham House.

Sullivan, John L., Amy Fried, and Mary G. Dietz. 1992. "Patriotism, Politics, and the Presidential Election of 1988." *American Journal of Political Science* 36:200–234.

Tate, Katherine. 1995. "Structural Dependence or Group Loyalty? The Black Vote in 1992." In *Democracy's Feast: Elections in America,* ed. Herbert F. Weisberg, 179–194. Chatham, N.J.: Chatham House.

Taylor, Charles. 1994. "The Politics of Recognition." In *Multiculturalism: A Critical Reader,* ed. David. T. Goldberg, 75–106. Cambridge, Mass.: Blackwell.

Terkildsen, Nayda. 1993. "When White Voters Evaluate Black Candidates: The Processing Implications of Candidate Skin Color, Prejudice, and Self-Monitoring." *American Journal of Political Science* 37:1032–1053.

Terkildsen, Nayda, and David F. Damore. 1999. "The Dynamics of Racialized Media Coverage in Congressional Elections." *Journal of Politics* 61:680–699.

Thompson, Vetta L. Sanders. 1999. "Variables Affecting Racial-Identity Salience among African Americans." *Journal of Social Psychology* 139:748–761.

———. 2001. "The Complexity of African American Racial Identification." *Journal of Black Studies* 32:155–165.

Valentino, Nicholas A., Vincent L. Hutchings, and Ismail K. White. 2002. "Cues that Matter: How Political Ads Prime Racial Attitudes during Campaigns." *American Political Science Review* 96:75–90.

Valentino, Nicholas A., Michael W. Traugott, and Vincent L. Hutchings. 2002. "Group Cues and Ideological Constraint: A Replication of Political Advertising Effects Studies in the Lab and in the Field." *Political Communication* 19:29–48.

West, Cornel. 1993. *Race Matters.* New York: Vintage Books.

West, Cornel, and Michael Lerner. 1996. *Jews and Blacks: A Dialogue on Race, Religion, and Culture in America.* New York: Plume.

White, Ismail K. 2007. "When Race Matters and When It Doesn't: Racial Group Differences in Response to Racial Cues." *American Political Science Review* 101:339–354.

White, Joseph. 1991. "Toward a Black Psychology." In *Black Psychology,* 3rd ed., ed. Reginald Lanier Jones, 5–13. Berkeley, Calif.: Cobb and Henry.

Weigel, David. 2009. "Black GOP Candidates Mount Serious 2010 Bids Nationwide." *Washington Independent,* October 6, available at http://washingtonindependent.com/62304/black-gop-candidates-mount-serious-2010-bids-nationwide.

Wielhouwer, Peter W. 2000. "Releasing the Fetters: Parties and the Mobilization of the African-American Electorate." *Journal of Politics* 62:206–222.

Williams, Linda F. 1990. "White/Black Perceptions of the Electability of Black Political Candidates." *National Political Science Review* 2:45–64.

Zatz, Marjorie S. 1987. "Chicano Youth Gangs and Crime: The Creation of a Moral Panic." *Crime, Law and Social Change* 11:129–158.

Zilber, Jeremy, and David Niven. 2000. "Stereotypes in the News: Media Coverage of African Americans in Congress." *Harvard International Journal of Press/Politics* 5:32–49.

Zucchino, David. 1999. *The Myth of the Welfare Queen.* New York: Scribner.

Zuckerman, Marvin. 1990. "Some Dubious Premises in Research and Theory on Racial Differences." *American Psychologist* 45:1297–1303.

Index

Page numbers followed by the letter "*f*" refer to figures, those followed by "*t*" refer to tables, and those followed by "n" refer to endnotes.

CHARLTON D. McILWAIN is Associate Professor of Media, Culture and Communication at New York University. He is the author of *When Death Goes Pop: Death, Media and the Remaking of Community* and *Death in Black and White: Death, Ritual and Family Ecology.* He is coeditor of *The Routledge Companion to Race and Ethnicity.*

STEPHEN MAYNARD CALIENDO is Professor of Political Science at North Central College in Naperville, Illinois. He is the author of *Inequality in America: Race, Poverty and Fulfilling Democracy's Promise* and *Teachers Matter: The Trouble with Leaving Political Education to the Coaches.* He is coeditor of *The Routledge Companion to Race and Ethnicity.*